THE ANNALS

OF

100 SQUADRON

Being a Record of War Activities of the Pioneer Night
Bombing Squadron in France during the period March 1917
to November 11th 1918, including its operations against German
Towns whilst serving in the Independent Force of the R.A.F.

By Major C. Gordon Burge, o.b.e.

With a Foreword by

Air-Marshall Sir Hugh Trenchard, k.c.b., d.s.o.

The Naval & Military Press Ltd

in association with

The Imperial War Museum
Department of Printed Books

Published jointly by

The Naval & Military Press Ltd

Unit 10 Ridgewood Industrial Park,

Uckfield, East Sussex,

TN22 5QE England

Tel: +44 (0) 1825 749494

Fax: +44 (0) 1825 765701

www.naval–military-press.com

and

The Imperial War Museum, London

Department of Printed Books

www.iwm.org.uk

AIR MARSHAL SIR HUGH TRENCHARD, K.C.B., D.S.O.

The ANNALS
of 100
SQUADRON

Being a Record of the War activities of the Pioneer Night
Bombing Squadron in France during the period March 1917
to November 11th 1918, including its operations against German
Towns whilst serving in the Independent Force of the R.A.F.

By Major C. Gordon Burge, O.B.E.

With a Foreword by
Air-Marshal Sir Hugh Trenchard,
K.C.B., D.S.O.

Illustrated

PUBLISHED BY HERBERT REIACH, LIMITED
9 KING STREET, COVENT GARDEN
W.C. 2

CONTENTS

FOREWORD

Army and Navy Club,
Pall Mall,
London, S.W.1.
13th December, 1918.

Dear Burge,

I would like to let you know what I think of No. 100 Squadron, the first complete night flying squadron that was sent to the Western Front.

It arrived, as you know, in March, 1917, and was under my command for practically the whole of its time in France.

It started with a splendid name and within a few weeks I was counting on it as one of my best weapons for hitting the enemy.

It was of the utmost value during all the heavy fighting in 1917, and it never spared itself in all the work it had to do.

Ite remained on the Western Front until October, 1917, when it proceeded to the Nancy Area in order to begin bombing Germany. There it went through one of the hardest winters we have had, but it kept up its great reputation and increased it. The pilots and observers were always cheery and ready to carry out any work asked of them, and in the worst weather they showed the utmost determination to get to the targets they had been ordered to bomb, very often in thunderstorms or thick fog and mist. Many times they attempted the work when it was impossible to see the ground from above 100 feet, owing to mist.

The rank and file were noted amongst squadrons for being exceptionally good at keeping their engines and machines in serviceable order; this was not easy and the men very often worked all day and all night.

In 1918 it still kept up its great name and was one of the quickest squadrons I have ever had under my command at learning new type machines when it was re-equipped with Handley-Pages.

I can only say that it was one of " the great squadrons " of the war, and I was very proud to have had the honour of commanding such an efficient squadron.

I wish all the members of the squadron the best of luck in their future careers.

Yours very sincerely,

H. Trenchard

Maj Gen

INTRODUCTION

*I*N compiling this work on the annals of No. 100 Squadron, I
have endeavoured to make it as interesting as I possibly can,
avoiding the inclusion of substance which would not be of general
interest to the majority of its readers; but at the same time making
it a complete record of the Squadron's work in the Great War,
now brought to a victorious end. I sincerely trust that the objects
aimed at in compiling this book will achieve the desired results, and
should the book merely give to but a few of those who have served
with the Squadron some pleasant recollections, I shall feel satisfied
with my labours.

The book is intended to give to all ranks a complete record of
the Squadron's work, which work throughout the whole of its
Active Service career has been magnificent, and on which we can
rightly look back with great pride; the record speaks for itself,
and when in after years we read but a few of the old Squadron's
achievements, I feel sure that there will be many a heart which will
beat with pride in looking back at those grand old days when
100 Squadron was helping to make history, and fighting for the
existence of the British Empire and for civilization. I should like
to add here that the book is also intended as a War Memorial Book
for those who gave their lives for their country and civilization
whilst serving with the Squadron. It will serve as a lasting
testimony to their patriotism and sacrifice. To the relatives of
those fallen we offer once again our sincere and heartfelt
sympathies, and we trust that they will accept this book as a token of
our sincere regret in their great loss.

I have included in the book the names of all ranks who served
with the Squadron, with their addresses, with the idea of individuals
being able to keep in touch with one another and so renew
acquaintances. It is hoped that the same spirit of comradeship,
which has existed in the Squadron throughout its war services, will

so continue as to strengthen the traditions, now our pride, which have been built up. I trust that the book will be of great help in achieving this end. I will endeavour here to express upon all members that we do not want to see a decline in the comradeship which exists now most strongly, but hope when we are once again home and in our different spheres of occupation we shall not forget the old Squadron, but renew acquaintances as frequently as is possible.

All members, I am sure, will heartily agree with me when I say that it is to be hoped that 100 Squadron will not be disbanded after the War, but that it will be given its place in the list of Regular Squadrons comprising the Royal Air Force. Those members of the Squadron who remain in the Royal Air Force after the War will take with them our highest traditions, which we hope to see permanently established.

I am indebted to those officers, N.C.O.'s and men who have most kindly contributed or given me suggestions in the compiling of this book and to my Office Staff for the many laborious hours spent in overtime in compiling the records. In particular I would like to thank Lieut-Colonel Ewart, O.B.E., for the great help he has afforded me, and Air Mechanic Hardwick for devoting very much of his time each evening to the typewriter.

C. G. BURGE.

France, 13th December, 1918.

LIEUT.-COL. M. G. CHRISTIE, C.M.G., D.S.O., M.C.,

WHO FORMED AND COMMANDED THE SQUADRON FROM FEBRUARY 23RD TO DECEMBER 10TH, 1917.

1OO SQUADRON

CHAPTER 1

" Oh! East is East and West is West,
But ' out there' the twain do meet,
And ' Erbert Smiff ' greets 'ere de Vere
On the same old Mess Room seat.
Here there is neither East nor West
Money nor breed nor birth,
For you've all got to grin, when your luck's not in,
And you've all got to prove your worth."

THE Squadron was formed in England from Squadrons in the Home Defence Wing, for the purpose of night bombing, and was the first night bombing unit to proceed to France. The mobilization was actually carried out at Farnborough in February, 1917, and was taken over by the Administrative Staff, consisting of the Commanding Officer, Major Christie, the Recording Officer, Capt. Waddington, the Equipment Officer, Lieut. Petch, and the Flight Commanders, Capt. Sowerby, Capt. McLaughrey, and Capt. De Brandon. The last named Officer was unable to leave with the Squadron finally owing to an accident while flying from Yorkshire to Farnborough.

On the 18th of March the Transport Section, consisting of 15 LEYLAND HEAVY TENDERS, 5 WORKSHOP LORRIES, 8 LIGHT TENDERS, and 8 MOTOR CYCLES, left for their Port of Embarkation, Portsmouth, under Capt. Sowerby and Lieut. Petch, where they embarked for Rouen, arriving without mishap on the 20th of March.

The personnel of the Squadron left Farnborough under Major Christie on the 21st of March, for Southampton, where it embarked for Le Havre *en route* for Rouen.

All embarked on the G.E. Steamship ARCHANGEL, and tried to make themselves as comfortable as the crowded state of the ship would allow.

The crossing to Le Havre was accomplished without mishap, and was a very fair one, as fair as could be expected across the English Channel at this time of the year, a number falling victims to the well-known complaint of " *mal de mer.*" The boat arrived

AN F.E.2B. MACHINE READY FOR A RAID.

about 2 a.m., but disembarkation did not commence until 6 o'clock.

After parading on the Quay the Squadron marched up to the Rest Camp, where it remained until the afternoon of the 23rd. Here the usual medical inspection was held, and all were embarked for Rouen, which place was reached on the morning of the 24th.

A march to the Rest Camp, and a Parade for kit inspection followed this, and here the Squadron were supplied with their first equipment for modern warfare, the Gas Mask.

The Personnel now joined forces with the Transport, and 100 Squadron was complete in ground equipment for the first time on French soil.

On the 26th of March the Convoy left Rouen en route for G.H.Q., passing the night at NEUFCHATEL, where the troops were billeted, and reached St. André early in the afternoon of the 27th, taking up its position on the Aerodrome to await the arrival of the machines.

On the 28th the machines appeared, consisting of twelve F.E.2B.'s, all of which arrived quite safely, and were here equipped with their luminous instruments, comprising Compasses, Rev. Counters, Aneroids, Air Speed Indicators, and Watches. Here

2

also the machines were fitted with bomb dropping gear to carry 25 lb. and 112 lb. bombs.

On the 1st of April the Squadron left for IZEL LE HAMEAU, where it arrived the same day.

The N.C.O.'s and men were billeted in the village, and the Officers were accommodated in the Nissen Huts adjoining the Aerodrome. Here four B.E.2E.'s arrived and were fitted up in the same way as the F.E.2B.'s.

The first operation was carried out by the Squadron on the night of 5/6-4-17, when DOUAI AERODROME was attacked. On this night also the first casualty occurred, when Lieut. Rickard and A.M. Barnes failed to return from the second show. Full particulars of this raid will be found in the section of this work dealing solely with Squadron operations.

The Squadron now proceeded to metaphorically "dig itself in" and throw all its energies into the work for which it was formed.

The Squadron remained at IZEL LE HAMEAU Aerodrome up to the 16th of May, together with No. 11 Squadron, who were day flying on F.E.'s, and, except for the usual routine work, nothing of interest occurred.

Orders were now received for the removal of the Squadron to TREXENNES Aerodrome near AIRE, and it was at this aerodrome that the concert pitch of the Squadron's work was

A B.E.2.E MACHINE TAKING OFF ON A RAID.

reached. On this aerodrome the machines were installed in permanent hangars, with plenty of space and workshop accommodation.

Squadron No. 43 was on this Aerodrome when we arrived, but moved soon afterwards, giving us a free run of the place until we left in October. Here 100 Squadron was first brought into contact with Enemy Aircraft. Situated near the Aerodrome at a distance of about $1\frac{1}{2}$ miles was the large steel factory of ISEBERGES, the most important in the district, and turning out the heaviest weight of metal in this part of France. Enemy Aircraft were very active on fine nights, and the barrage put up from this factory by anti-aircraft and machine guns, together with the seachlights was a very impressive sight, but although the German machines obtained hits on the factory and surrounding villages, no bombs were actually dropped on the Aerodrome. The enemy seemed to be well aware of the Squadron's position, and its work was certainly causing him a great deal of inconvenience. This was apparently proved, much to the Squadron's discomfort, when he commenced shelling the Aerodrome with a large calibre gun. On Sunday morning, the 22nd of July, the weather was exceptionally clear and fine, and at about 7.30 a.m., a series of explosions caused everyone to be on the qui-vive. The origin of these explosions was not clearly determined until a machine was discovered overhead, and it became apparent that it was spotting for some long range gun. Near the Aerodrome, about half a mile away, was a large ammunition dump, which together with the steel factory on the other side, made the position of the Aerodrome a very precarious one. The first shell dropped directly in front of an unoccupied hangar, previously used by No. 43 Squadron, but did no damage apart from blowing a hole in the ground sufficiently large to put a machine into.

Just previous to this shell arriving, orders were given for all ranks to take to the sandpit situated on the other side of the main road, and away from the Aerodrome, but while this order was being carried out the second shell dropped right in front of another hangar in which were two F.E.2B. machines. Unfortunately men were working on machines in this hangar, and large pieces of shell tore

AN F.E.2.B. MACHINE FITTED WITH POM-POM GUN.

their way through the sides, killing Air Mechanics Evans and Sowerby.   By this time a scene of considerable excitement was being enacted in the Officers' quarters, and from all tents, pyjama-clad individuals were seen to issue forth, and take to their heels across country.   No further shells were sent on to the Aerodrome, and soon order was restored and stock of the damage was taken. This proved to be singularly light, the casualties being two killed, and four injured, one hangar rendered practically useless, and three machines damaged beyond repair. The walls of some of the offices were riddled with pieces of shell, but were easily reparable.

Repairs were immediately started, machines replaced, and the Squadron resumed its work of irritating the Hun with greater zeal than ever, and determined to hit him back with extras.

After this episode it was thought by many that this was only the forerunner of a series of enemy raids, but happily they proved false prophets. A fair number of bombs were dropped on the surrounding districts, but happily none fell on the Aerodrome itself. At this time a scheme was introduced to outwit the Hun, and protect the Aerodrome from aerial bombardment. This took the form of a dummy Aerodrome, which was situated on a waste piece of land about two miles away. A lighting set, installed to supply electricity to flares set out on the Aerodrome, with two air mechanics in attendance, succeeded in drawing off a large amount of the enemy's fire. It will be of interest to the Squadron to remember the names of Air Mechanics Templeton and Fisher, who must have passed some exciting nights together, judging from the number of bombs which were dropped on this field.

Soon after the episode of the shelling, rumour had it that an enemy had been found stating that TREZENNES Aerodrome was to be wiped out at all costs. This started a period of great ground activity, and all ranks under officers were working like galley slaves making dug-outs, all with the fixed idea of evading a direct hit. Some of these got finished, others did not, but those that were finished proved to be very useful as a protection against the falling shrapnel from the anti-aircraft guns.

- The weather throughout July, August and September was extremely favourable for night operations, and raids were carried out on all nights possible. Our number of casualties were extremely light, most of them being (a pilot's worst enemy at night) " forced landings."

One operation of note that was carried out with considerable success, was the bombing of a gun which had the habit of shelling DUNKIRK. This operation was carried out from BRAY DUNES Aerodrome.

7

A short description of TREZENNES Aerodrome will possibly be of interest, as this period of the Squadron's existence will probably remain in the minds of its members as one, if not the most pleasant resting place that the Squadron has known.   Situated near AIRE, and within easy distance of ST. OMER, outings for the troops could easily be arranged, and a well stocked Canteen could be kept up. The billets were fairly comfortable, and a Recreation Room fitted up with a stage enabled the Concert Party organized by Sgt. Major May to entertain the troops on wet evenings.   The Officers' quarters were situated well away from the Aerodrome, and consisted of bell tents, and a comfortable mess and ante-room, in which many a merry night was held.   Nissen huts were being erected towards the end of October, but owing to the removal of the Squadron were not inhabited by them.   Good accommodation for transport and workshops was available, and a proper system of camp drainage was well under way.

Another institution which had its beginning in the Squadron, the Operations Room, was a place of interest, especially before a raid, when all pilots and observers went to get the last details before going to their machines.   In this were all the maps, charts, photographs of targets, and details of the number of raids carried out by individual pilots and observers, as well as congratulatory telegrams received by the Squadron from Headquarters.   The start of a Night Flying Squadron on a raid is a most impressive sight, especially from the ground, and a short description is given here by an eye-witness.

" Just before dark the machines would be got out of their hangars, and loaded up with bombs in accordance with the armament laid down in the daily operation orders.   Then they would be got into line of flights, and ready to be taxied out to the flare path. Flares were out and ready for lighting at the appointed time. Pilots and observers would arrive, climb into their machines, and await the order to start.   Presently an orderly is seen doubling down to the flight ordered to start first.   Directly afterwards the roar of an engine was heard, and machine number one was on its way to the flare path.   A hurried shout to the Flares Officer, conveying to him the names of the pilot and observer, together with the number of the machine and time away, and in less than a minute machine number one was on the flare path, engine all out, and fast disappearing in the failing light, until its navigation lights fast dwindling into twin stars were all that could be seen.   Hardly had this machine left the ground, when the second was after it, soaring into the night, its twin lights following the first, and so on until all the machines were in the air, which seemed full of the drone of engines, getting fainter and fainter until the silence of a summer's evening once more reigned supreme.   The mechanics who had been engaged in the despatch of the machines are seen strolling back to pass the time in what manner they cared until the return of the machines.   The average time taken on a raid was about two hours, according to the distance away of the targets.   Quickly the time slips by, and all are beginning to cast their eyes around the sky to try and pick up the lights of a returning machine.   Soon the exclamation ''There's one,'' as a pair of rapidly moving lights could just be made out, getting nearer and nearer.   Soon the drone of an engine could be heard, the pilot could be seen blinking his lights, intimating that he was going to land, and required the flares on to give him his position. These were put on and sometimes a searchlight beam was displayed on the ground.   One last turn to get into the wind, and the machine is gliding towards the flare path, the roar of the engine gradually lessens, and dies away, and in a few moments the slight shock of the machine landing is heard.   Immediately the engine roars out again, and the pilot taxis the machine towards the hangars. He shouts his name to the Flare Officer who notes the time of arrival of the machine, and then hands his machine over to his mechanics, who either overhaul it, and load it up for another raid, or put it away in its hangar.   The pilot then makes his way to the C.O.'s office to hand in his report, and retires to the mess for a little well earned refreshment.

It is feared that the above is a very crude description of the work on a Night Flying Aerodrome, as seen from the ground, but the sight once seen must remain in the mind of the observer as one of the most impressive he has ever witnessed.''

Of the Squadron's work at TREZENNES there is nothing further to note, except the usual routine up to the evening of the 2nd of October, when orders were received to pack up all necessary materials for an immediate move. This work continued all through the night, and at 10.30 a.m. on the 3rd, the convoy moved off to entrain at ST. OMER for BARISEY-LA-COTE, a small station in the East of France, N.E. of NEUFCHATEAU. Here the Squadron arrived at 6.30 a.m. on the 5th. An advance party at once left for the Aerodrome at OCHEY, some seven miles away. The arrival at this Aerodrome was not impressive, as it was pouring with rain, and everyone was a little fed up after two nights in a French train, but in the afternoon it brightened up a little, and the arrival of a Staff Officer with some definite information made life look much brighter. Here this Officer made hurried arrangements with the French for the supply of rations as much on the English scale as possible, much to the annoyance of the A.S.C. authorities, who had to make local calculations for all supplies wanted, the English and French details being very different. The Aerodrome at OCHEY was formerly used by the French Aviation as a training ground, and was a large one with permanent hangars, conveniently situated near the road, with the hutting on the other side. This appeared to be a very admirable arrangement, and so it was for peace time requirements, but subsequent events proved the opposite.

Machines which were coming by air from TREZENNES had not yet turned up, and later information was received that they were hung up at FISMES, owing to bad weather. Eventually they arrived safely, Major Christie being the first to land on the new Aerodrome, and one might say that he was the first pilot to land in the new Independent Force area. Situated as it is, this Aerodrome was handy for arranging outings in bad weather for the officers and men to TOUL, about 9 miles to the North, and NANCY about fourteen miles North East, both towns being well stocked with shops and restaurants.

The first raid by the Squadron was on MARLENBACH JUNCTION (see section of this work devoted to operations) in which six machines took part, all returning safely. The Huns had now intimation of the Squadron's occupation of OCHEY Aerodrome, and soon began to make matters pretty hot, for one evening soon after dinner everyone was startled by a terrific bang in the vicinity of the camp. This was followed by another explosion, and then the anti-aircraft defences of the Aerodrome, which consisted of two French "Archies," opened fire, causing a great deal of commotion. An incinerator close to the camp was going all out, and the Hun must have made a line on this, one bomb injuring an officer, and killing a

HANGAR ON FIRE   (NOT DUE TO ENEMY ACTION).

mechanic belonging to 216 R.N.A.S. Squadron, which had recently arrived at this Aerodrome. Things began to get rather uncomfortable, and soon through enemy raids the Squadron had a number of machines put out of action, while transport suffered likewise. It was clearly seen that something would have to be done, although extra anti-aircraft guns had been installed by the French, who also were running a night bombing squadron from the same Aerodrome, suffering rather badly on more than one occasion, one hangar being entirely destroyed together with three machines by two direct hits.

Orders were now received to take out all M.T. vehicles to a position a mile from the Aerodrome on all evenings when a raid was possible, keeping them as much screened as possible by the trees.

The hangars had also to be emptied of all valuable equipment every evening and all taken to the other side of the Aerodrome. This entailed a great amount of labour, as well as making the working day very short, for the work had to be started early in the afternoon. It was when operating from this side of the Aerodrome that an accident happened causing the death of Capt. Scudamore, Flt. Sergt. Green, and three other ranks. This loss was deeply felt by the Squadron, as Capt. Scudamore was a great favourite and Flt. Sgt. Green had been with the Squadron since its formation. On this Aerodrome occurred the only serious fire the Squadron had, when one of the large sleeping huts, occupied by eighteen officers, took fire, and was burnt to the ground in spite of every effort to save it.

It was now clearly seen that if the camp was not moved the Huns would move it, for up to date two of the large hangars had been rendered useless, and the rest were well peppered by splinters, so that steps were taken to build a camp in an adjoining wood, about a mile from the old position, and to construct an Aerodrome adjacent to this. Spaces were cleared at the edge of the wood to accommodate the hangars, and a party of Indian, Chinese, and Italian labourers were employed on levelling off the surface. The camp itself was situated entirely in the wood, a space of one hundred yards being left between each hut. Advantage was also taken of the largest trees near the position chosen, in order to screen the huts as much as possible from the air. All the huts had to be moved from the old camp, and re-erected in the wood, no small undertaking, as the Squadron work had to be carried on as well. When this work was about half-way through, orders were received for another move, this time to VILLESNEUX, a French Aerodrome situated west of CHALONS-SUR-MARNE. The Squadron left on the 29th of March, 1918, arriving at the Aerodrome on the 31st of March. The weather was very bad and the convoy halted at St. DIZIER from the afternoon of the 29th until the morning of the 31st. The weather conditions remained unfavourable for much flying, but altogether the Squadron spent a very pleasant time here, the towns of EPERNEY and CHALONS being within easy reach.

It was known that the stay here was not for long, and it was wondered whether the Squadron would be transferred to one of the

Independent Force Aerodromes at AZELOT or XAFFAVILLERS, or go back to the wood camp at OCHEY, where it was anticipated spending a pleasant time now that the summer months were ahead.   Finally it was arranged for the Squadron to return to OCHEY, the other Aerodromes being not yet ready for occupation.

On the 10th of May it left VILLESNEUX for OCHEY, arriving there on the afternoon of the 12th.   Here the construction of the camp went on as rapidly as possible, eleven huts in all being taken down and re-built.   A road capable of taking the weight of a lorry had also to be constructed through the woods, in order to get water and necessaries up to the camp, the stone being quarried some miles away.   Life in this camp was very pleasant, and everybody was sorry to leave it.   This was inevitable, however, as the Independent Aerodromes were now ready.

The remainder of the Squadron's stay at the forest camp at OCHEY was not marked by any incident worthy of note, except that a change of Commanding Officers took place, Major Burge arriving on the 13th of June, taking over from Major Tempest, who left on the 16th of the same month.

A great deal of attention was being paid here to games of various kinds; medicine ball in particular.

The months of June and July passed very rapidly, the weather was extremely fine, and life in the woods very pleasant.   The camp was now in first class order, and all were sorry to leave it.   But this had to be, as the work which had been going on for over a year in the construction of the Independent Force Aerodromes was rapidly nearing completion.   The Squadron moved in order to occupy one of these Aerodromes on the 10th August.

Good-bye was said to the first of our old friends, the F.E.'s, on 13th August, 1918, when two of them were transferred to the Depot, and the Squadron received its first Handley-Page machine.

The Squadron was now constructed as a Handley-Page Squadron, there being two flights of five machines each, instead of three flights of six machines each.

The Aerodrome was situated about fifteen miles from the lines, where it was thought that it would not be very long before the Huns paid us a visit.   This proved to be correct, for on the 19th of

August, 1918, a small machine came over, and dropped a couple of bombs in the vicinity of the Aerodrome, setting a petrol dump on fire.

Anti-aircraft guns began to make their appearance in the neighbourhood, the air being very often lively with the " woofing " of Archie.

On the 21st the Huns again carried out a raid on the Aerodrome, and dropped somewhere about eight bombs, none of which, however, did any damage.

After this their raids ceased. Whether this was due to their machines being too occupied up North, or to the reported heavy losses is a matter of conjecture. But for an occasional A.A. alert, our nights passed peacefully enough.

A regrettable accident happened here, when three of our officers were killed while taking off on a raid. This was on the 25th August, when a machine, piloted by Lt. Box, with Lt. Inches as observer, and Lt. Boyd as gunner, left the Aerodrome, and crashed, causing the death of these three officers. Their loss was deeply felt by all, and they will ever be remembered by those who knew them.

And now every effort was being made to harass the Hun in his Rhine towns as much as possible. Raids were planned on the large German manufacturing towns, and the introduction of large calibre bombs of 550 lb. and 1,600 lb., bode ill for them in the near future.

Happily for the Hun the sudden cessation of hostilities put a stop to the use of these missiles.

The retreat of the German forces in the West and North saw the end approaching, but raids were carried on with the utmost vigour.

The weather in this part of the country is very unsettled during the Autumn and early Winter, and already this was beginning to make itself felt. While the long evenings were setting in the camp was getting ready for a winter stay. A cinema was introduced by the Commanding Officer, much to the delight of the Squadron, making a pleasant pastime for "dud" evenings. A band was also formed and was being thrashed into shape by Lt. Ward.

The large hut used as the Mess Room for the men was decorated, and a stage put up at one end. The cinema was permanently in this hut, a proper operating cabinet being erected for it.   A Concert Party, made up of Corpl. Bird, Corpl. Bullock, Corpl. Davidson, A.M. Caplin, A.M. Coleman, and A.M. Ford was working hard, having already given one entertainment which was greatly appreciated.

Everything was going as well as it possibly could, but the end was rapidly approaching.   On the evening of the 10th November the Squadron was thrown into a state of excitement by loud cheers and a pyrotechnic display of Very's lights and rockets, which were sent up in great profusion.   All asked "was it the end," but nothing definite could be learned.

On the 11th November it was officially announced that an Armistice with Germany had been signed at 11 o'clock and that all hostilities were to cease.

On the day following, the whole of the Wing paraded, and were addressed by Brigadier General Newall, who gave the salient points of the Armistice.

The work of 100 Squadron from a hostile point of view, was now at an end, and the whole of the Independent Air Force was disbanded, receiving orders to proceed to the North.

On the 16th November, the transport and a certain amount of ground equipment left XAFFAVILLERS for LIGESCOURT, an Aerodrome situated N.W. of ABBEVILLE, travelling by way of VEZELISE, ST. DIZIER, SEZANNE, MEAUX, CLERMONT, AMIENS, ABBEVILLE, arriving at LIGESCOURT at 3.30 p.m. on the 22nd.

The machines left by air on the 16th, arriving at LIGESCOURT the same day, the rest of the personnel travelling by train.

At LIGESCOURT the Squadron settled down to await orders for their final move to the Home Land.

CHAPTER II

THE BIRTH OF 100 SQUADRON, R.A.F.

By Cpl. J. R. Bird.

MY introduction to 100 Squadron was by no means received with enthusiasm. Having just completed 7 days C.B., fined 4 days pay, and Xmas leave stopped, I felt more than delighted when they broke the news to me that I was for "overseas." So with a full pack and the best of luck, I started for Adastral House in a Ford van, to join 100 Squadron, but was pursued with bad luck all the way, for owing to the greasy surface of the road, and the driver being somewhat nervous, the journey was nothing more than a series of "flat spins," and we finished up by knocking a small donkey and barrow underneath a large carrier's van, much to the crowd's amusement. However, I arrived at Headquarters and was told something that brought back memories of the past, I felt like a man receiving his death sentence, "I was for Farnborough." After bucking myself up with a cup of Y.M.C.A. tea, I left civilization and arrived at the birthplace of the Squadron. Here I made several enquiries for the Squadron, but no one knew anything about it. I tramped about for several hours and was being consequently "chewed up" by the "M.P." for walking out without a cane, but at last I found the Equipment Officer, who was the only representative of the Squadron there, and he also "chewed me up" for not reporting before, and at the same time told me the duties and the purpose of the Squadron, which put in a few words, meant we were to be an "Ideal" Squadron and an "Experimental" Squadron in Night Bombing, which I found out later was true to the letter; in other words, Night Flying Squadrons got the benefit of what we paid to learn. After this, our last days in England passed in a dream. It was a series of parades, packing and unpacking of stores, shifting them from one lorry to another, drawing overseas kit, handing it in and drawing it again, vaccination and inoculation galore, some chaps being done twice in the rush, but the two parades I remember most were our " pay parade " and a parade for a march to the station for our 48 hours' embarkation leave. The finish of the leave brought everyone back much more cheerful, even the Disciplinary Sergeant Major was seen to smile. Then one cold bleak morning at 5 a.m., without a soul to cheer or shed a tear, we were marched away to entrain for Southampton Docks. There we were left for eight hours in solitude. At last we boarded the boat for " Sunny France." The space on board was very limited owing to the number of passengers, but I was fortunate enough to get a bunk with four others, but as there was only sleeping accommodation for four, I had to sleep on the floor. After a game of cards we turned in for the night and I made myself as comfortable as possible. which was rather difficult owing to my life-belt. However, we dozed off to sleep and dreamt of V.C.'s and Croix de Guerres. About one o'clock I was rudely awakened by the occupant of the top bunk being violently sea sick, of which I was receiving the full benefit, so I quickly retired to a place of safety while my comrade in distress begged for sudden death; in fact, he wasn't at all particular whether the Germans torpedoed us or not, but we arrived at a place "Somewhere in France," without further mishap and we marched to a place called *A Rest Camp*, but we soon found out that the name was " camouflage." Here we began the Squadron's first experience of how to exist on bully beef and biscuits for 14 days.

This was carried out most successfully, but I am sorry to say no medals were given for it. By this time the Squadron was in financial difficulties and nearly every N.C.O. and man had learnt the noble art of borrowing, and to add to our sorrow several old soldiers who were in the camp told gruesome tales of the " front " and life in general in France, in other words trying to put the " wind up " us, seeming to forget that there were men amongst us who had already seen service with the Infantry in France. But my heart went out to the batmen who were all " rookies."

In a day or so we pushed on again towards our destination, our next stop being Rouen " Rest Camp." Here we met the transport and went through more medical examinations, kit inspections, parades, and were cheered up by being told to make out our "wills" in our pay books, also to improve things we were issued with two kinds of gas masks, namely P.H. helmet and box respirator. These were taken great care of by the troops, who thought of the time when they would be called upon to use same to save their lives, but fortunately they were never required except when an occasional bad tin of Maconochie turned up. We rested here for several days and then pushed on again, this time by road with the transport and arrived at Hesdin, where we were joined by the pilots and machines and the general routine of the Squadron began. The machines were fitted up as "night bombers" in record time and the Squadron congratulated by General Trenchard upon the work.

From here we moved up to Izel-le-Hameau and 100 Squadron introduced themselves to "Jerry" in quick time.

CHAPTER III

"HAPPY LANDINGS"

THIS article, written by Mr. Irvin S. Cobb, an Official American Correspondent on the Western Front, appeared in the columns of *The Saturday Evening Post*, on June 15th, 1918. Mr. Irvin Cobb paid this Squadron a visit during his tour in the Nancy area and here ably describes it and his impressions. All those who were present will now through the medium of his article be able to take themselves back to that memorable evening spent at Ochey. All will thank him most heartily for writing so fully on his visit. This chapter will always be read with great interest and the article will give to members of the Squadron the opportunity of refreshing their memories of the names of a number of brother officers to whom he refers in his article by nickname. His description of the night spent in the mess is true to life, and when it is read by the old members of the Squadron, it will give them opportunity of carrying their memories back to the good old days when one and all were doing their bit in the Great War, and where true comradeship reigned supreme. The article follows :—

"The affair dated from a certain spring noontime, when two of us, writers by trade, were temporarily marooned for the day at the press headquarters of the American Expeditionary Force, because we couldn't anywhere get hold of an automobile to take us for a scouting jaunt along the American sector. All of a sudden a big biplane came sailing into sight, glittering like a silver flying fish. It landed in a meadow behind the town, and two persons, muffled in great coats, decanted themselves out of it and tramped across the half-flooded field toward us. When they drew near we perceived them to be two very young, very ruddy gentlemen, and both unmis-

takably English.   My companion, it seemed, knew one of them, so
there were introductions.

"What brings you over this way?" inquired my friend.

"Well, you see," said his acquaintance, "we were a bit thirsty
—Bert and I—and we heard you had very good beer at the French
officers' club here.   So we just ran over for half an hour or so to
get a drop of drink and then toddle along back again.   Not a bad
idea, eh, what?"

The speaker, I noted, wore the twin crowns of a captain on the
shoulder straps of his overcoat.   His age I should have put at
twenty-one or thereabout, and his complexion was the complexion
of a very new, very healthy cherub.

We showed the way toward beer and lunch, the latter being
table d'hôte but good.   En route my confrere was moved to ask
more questions.

"Anything new happening at the Squadron since I was over
that way?" he inquired.

"Quiet enough to be a bore—weather hasn't suited for our
sort these last few evenings," stated the taller one.   "We got fed
up on doin' nothin' at all, so night before last a squad started across
the border to give Fritzie a taste of life.   But just after we started
the Squadron Commander decided the weather was too thickish and
he signed us back—all but the Young-un, who claims he didn't see
the flare and kept on goin' all by his little self."   He favoured us
with a tremendous wink.

"It seemed a rotten shame, really it did, to waste the whole
evenin'."   This was the Young-un, he of pink cheeks, speaking.
"So I just jogged across the jolly old Rhine until I came to a town,
and I dropped my pills there and came back.   Nice quiet trip it was
—lonely rather, and not a bit excitin'."

Upon me a light dawned.   I had heard of these bombing
Squadrons of the British outfits of young but seasoned flying men,
who, now that reprisal in kind had been forced upon England and
France by the continued German policy of aerial attacks on unpro-
tected and unarmed cities, made journeys from French soil by sky

linc to cncmy diotriotc, thero to spatter down retaliatory bombs upon
such towns as Mainz, Stuttgart, Coblenz, Mannheim, Treves and
Metz.

The which sounded simple enough in the bald telling, but entailed for each separate pair of flyers on each separate excursion
enough of thrill, suspense and danger to last the average man
through all his various reincarnations upon this earth. It meant a
flight by darkness at sixty or seventy miles an hour, the pilot at the
wheel and the observer at the guardian machine gun, above the
tangled skeins of friendly trenches; and a little farther on above and
past the hostile lines, beset for every rod of the way, both going and
coming, by peril of attack from anti-aircraft gun and from speedier,
more agile German flyers, since the bombing airship is heavier and

ON ACTIVE SERVICE.
" A REMINISCENCE OF EVENTIDE."—(*Drawn by Lieut. Rogers.*)

slower than scout planes commonly are. It meant finding the
objective point of attack and loosing the explosive shells hanging
like ripe plums from lever hooks in the frame of the engine body;
and this done it meant winging back again—provided they got back
—in time for late dinner at the home hangars.

Personally, I craved to see more of men engaged upon such
employment. Through lunch I studied the two present specimens
of a new and special type of human being. Except that Bert was
big and the Young-un was short, and except that the Young-un
spoke of dropping pills when he meant to tell of spilling potential
destruction upon the supply depots and railroad terminals of Germany, whereas Bert affectionately referred to his machine as The

Red Hen and called the same process laying an egg or two, there was no great distinction to be drawn between them. Both made mention of the most incredibly daring things in the most commonplace and casual way imaginable; both had the inquisitive nose and the incurious eye of their breed; both professed a tremendous interest in things not one-thousandth part so interesting as what they themselves did; and both used the word "extraordinary" to express their convictions upon subjects not in the least extraordinary, but failed to use it when the topic dealt with their own duties and deserved to excess the adjectival treatment. In short, they were just two well-bred English boys.

Out of the luncheon sprang an invitation, and out of the invitation was born a trip. On a day when the atmosphere was better fitted for automobiling in closed cars than for bombings, we headed away for our billets, travelling in what I shall call a general direction, there being four of us besides the sergeant who drove. Things were stirring along the Front. Miles away we could hear the battery heavies thundering and drumming, and once in a lull we detected the hammering staccato of a machine gun tacking down the loose edges of a fight that will never be recorded in history, with the earnestness and briskness of a man laying a carpet in a hurry.

The Romans taught the French how to plan high roads, and the French never forgot the lesson. The particular road we travelled ran kilometer on kilometer, straight as a lance up the hills and down again across the valleys, and only turned out to round the shoulders of a little mountain or when it flanked a short line of one of the small brawling French rivers. The tall poplars in pairs, always in pairs, which edge it were like lean old gossips bending in toward the centre the better to exchange whispered scandal about the neighbours. Mainly the road pierced through fields, with frequent villages to be passed and a canal to be skirted; but also there were forests where wild boar were reputed to reside and where, as we know, the pheasant throve in numbers undreamed of in the antebellum days before all the powder in Europe was needed to kill men, and while yet some might be spared for killing off birds.

Regarding the mountains a rule was prevalent. If one flank of a mountain was wooded one might be reasonably sure that the farther side would present a patchwork pattern of tiny farms, square sometimes, but more often oblong in shape, each plastered against the steep conformation and each so nearly perpendicular, that we wondered how anybody except a retired paper hanger ever dare try to cultivate it. Let a husbandman's foot slip up there and he would be committing trespass in the plot of the next man below.

OFFICERS' MESS, SHOWING THE FAMOUS BRAZIER.

I shall not tell how far we rode, or whither, but dusk found us, in a place which, atmospherically speaking was very far removed from the French foothills, but geographically not so far. So far as its local colour was concerned the place in point more nearly than anything else I call to mind resembled the interior of a Greek-letter society's chapter house set amid somewhat primitive surroundings. In the centre of the low wide common room, mounted on a concrete box, was a big openwork basket of wrought iron. In this brazier burned fagots of wood, and the smoke went up a metal pipe which widened out to funnel shape at the bottom, four feet above the floor.

23

Such a device has three advantages over the ordinary fireplace. Folks may sit upon four sides of it toasting their shins by direct contact with the heat, instead of upon only one, as is the case when your chimney goes up through the wall of your house. There were illustrations cut from papers upon the walls; there were sporting prints and London dailies on the chairs and trestles; there was a phonograph, which performed wheezily, as though it had asthma, and a piano, which by authority was mute until after dinner; there were sundry guitars and mandolines disposed in corners; there were sofa pillows upon the settees, plainly the handiwork of some fellow's best girl; there were clumsy, schoolboy decorative touches all about; there were glasses and bottles on the tables; there were English non-coms., who in their gravity and promptness might have been club servants, bringing in more bottles and fresh glasses; and there were frolicking, boisterous groups and knots and clusters of youths who, except that they wore the khaki of junior officers of His Majesty's service instead of the ramping patterns affected by your average undergraduates, were for all the world just such a collection of resident inmates as you would find playing the goat and the colt and the skylark in any college fraternity hall on any pleasant evening anywhere among the English-speaking peoples.

SONS OF THE EMPIRE

For guests of honour there were we four, and for hosts there were sixty or seventy members of Night Bombing Squadron Number 100. It so happened that this particular group of picked and sifted young daredevils represented every main division of the Empire's domain, as we were told there were Englishmen, Cornishmen, Welshmen, Scots and Irishmen; also Canadians, Australians, New Zealanders and an Afrikander or two, and a dark youngster from India; as well as recruits gathered in from lesser lands and lesser colonies where the Union Jack floats in the seven seas that girdle this globe.

The ranking officer—a Major by title, and he not yet twenty-four years old—bore the name of a Highland clan, the mere mention of which set me to thinking of whanging claymores and skirling pipes. His next in command was the nephew and namesake of a famous Home Ruler, and this one spoke with the soft-cultured brogue of the Dublin collegian. We were introduced to a flyer bred and reared in Japan, who had hurried to the mother isle as soon as he reached the volunteering age—a shy, quiet lad with a downy upper lip, who promptly effaced himself; and to a young Tasmanian of Celtic antecedents, who, curiously enough, spoke with an English accent richer and more pronounced than any native Englishman in the company used.

I took pains to ascertain the average age of the personnel of the Squadron. I am giving no information to the enemy that he already does not know—to his cost—when I state it to be twenty-two and a half years. With perfect gravity veteran airmen of twenty-three or so will tell you that when a fellow reaches twenty-five he's getting rather a bit too old for the game—good enough for instructing green hands and all that sort of thing, perhaps, but generally past the age when he may be counted upon for effective work against the Hun aloft. And the wondrous part of it is that it is true as Gospel. 'Tis a man's game, if ever there was a man's game in this world; and it's boys with the soft fleece of adolescence on their cheeks that play it best.

A DRAMATIC TOAST

Well, we had dinner; and a very good dinner it was, served in the mess hall adjoining, with fowls and a noble green salad, and good honest-to-cow's butter on the table. But before we had dinner, a thing befell which to me was as simply dramatic as anything possibly could be. What was more, it came at a moment made and fit for dramatics, being as deftly insinuated by chance into the proper spot as though a skilled playmaster had contrived it for the climax of his second act.

Glasses had been charged all round, and we were standing to drink the toast of the British aviator when, almost together, two small things happened. The electric lights flickered out, leaving us in the half glow of the crackling flames in the brazier, its tints bringing out here a ruddy young face and there a buckle of brass or a button of bronze, but leaving all the rest of the picture in flickering shadows; right on top of this a servant entered, saluted and handed to the Squadron Commander a slip of paper bearing a bulletin just received by telephone from the headquarters of a sister Squadron in a near-by sector. The young Major first read it through silently and then read it aloud :—

"Eight machines of Squadron —— made a daylight raid this afternoon. The operation was successfully carried out." A little pause. "Three machines failed to return."

That was all. Three of the machines failed to return—six men, mates to these youngsters assembled here and friends to some of them, had gone down in the wreckage of their aircraft, probably to death or to what was hardly less terrible than death—to captivity in a German prison camp.

Well, it was all in the day's work. No one spoke, nor in my hearing did anyone afterwards refer to it. But the glasses came up with a jerk, and at that, as though on a signal from a stage manager, the lights flipped on, and then together we drank the airmen's toast, which is :—

"Happy landings! "

I do not profess to speak for the others, but for myself I know I drank to the memory of those six blithe boys—riders in the three machines that failed to return—and to a happy landing for them in the eternity to which they had been hurried long before their time.

The best part of dinner came after the dinner was over, which was as a dinner party should be. We flanked ourselves on the four sides of the fire, and tobacco smoke rose in volume as an incense to good fellowship and there were stories told and limericks offered without number. And if a story was new we all laughed at it, and if it was old we laughed just the same. Presently a protesting lad was dragooned for service at the piano. The official troubadour, a youth who seemed to be all legs and elbows, likewise detached himself from the background. Instead of taking station alongside the piano he climbed gravely up on top of it and perched there above our heads, with his legs dangling down below the keys.

Touching on this, the Young-un, who sat alongside me, made explanation :—

"Old Bob likes to sit on the old jingle box when he sings, you know. He says that then he can feel the music going up through him and it makes him sing. He'll stay up there singing like a bloomin' bullfinch till someone drags him down. He seems to sort of get drunk on singin'—really he does. Extraordinary fancy isn't it?"

I should have been the last to drag old Bob down. For, employing a wonderful East Ender whine—old Bob sang a gorgeous Cockney ballad dealing with the woeful case of a simple country maiden, and her smyle it was su-blyme, but she met among others the village squire, and the rest of it may not be printed in a paper having a general circulation; but anyway it was a theme replete with incident and abounding in detail, with a hundred verses more or less and a chorus after every verse, for which said chorus we all joined in mightily.

From this beginning old Bob, beating time with both hands, ranged far afield into his repertoire. Under cover of his singing I did my level best to draw out the Young-un, who it seemed was the Young-un more by reason of his size and boyish complexion than by reason of his age, since he was senior to half his outfit—to draw him out with particular reference to his experiences since the time, a year before, when he quit the line, being then a full captain, to take a berth as observer in the service of the air.

It was hard slogging, though. He was just as inarticulate and just as diffident as the average English gentleman is apt to be when he speaks in the hated terms of shop talk of his own share in any dangerous or unusual enterprise. Besides, our points of view were so different. He wanted to hear about the latest music-hall shows in London with a touch in his voice of what I interpreted as home-sickness. Whereas I wanted to know the sensations of a youth who flirts with death as a part of his daily vocation. Finally I got him under way, after this wise.

" Oh, we just go over the line you know, and drop our pills and come back. Occasionally a chap doesn't get back. And that's about all there is to tell about it. . . Rummiest thing that has happened since I came into the Squadron happened the other night. The Boche came over to raid us, and when the alarm was given everyone popped out of his bed and made for the dug-out. All but Big Bill over yonder. Big Bill tumbled out half-dressed and more than half asleep. It was a fine moonlight night and the Boche was sailing about overhead bombing us like a good one, and Big Bill, who's a size to make a good target, couldn't find the entrance to either of the dugouts. So he ran for the woods just beyond here at the edge of the flying field, and no sooner had he got into the woods than a wild boar came charging at him and chased him out again into the open where the bombs were droppin'. Almost got him, too —the wild boar, I mean. The bombs didn't fall anywhere near him. Extraordinary, wasn't it, having a wild boar turn up like that just when he was particularly anxious not to meet any wild boar, not being dressed for it, as you might say? He was in a towerin' rage when the Boche went away and we came out of the dugouts and only laughed at him instead of sympathizin' with him."

He puffed at his pipe.

"Fritz gets peevish and comes about to throw things at us quite frequently. You see, this camp isn't in a very good place. We took it over from the French and it stands out in the open instead of being on the edge of the forest, where it should be. Makes it rather uncomfy for us sometimes—Fritzie does."

All of which rather prepared me for what occurred perhaps five minutes later when for the second time that night the electric lights winked out.

Old Bob ceased from his caroling, and the mess president, a little sandy Scotchman, spoke up :—

"It may be that the Boche is coming to call on us—the men douse the lights if we get a warning; or it may be that the battery has failed. At any rate, I vote we have in some candles and carry on. This is too fine an evening to be spoilt before it's half over, eh?"

A failed battery it must have been, for no Boche bombers came. So upon the candle being fetched in, old Bill resumed at the point where he left off. He sang straight through to midnight, nearly, never minding the story telling, and the Limerick matching and the laughter and the horse play going on below him, and rarely repeating a song except by request of the audience. If his accompanist at the piano knew the air, all very well and good; if not, old Bob sang it without the music.

They didn't in the least want us to leave when the time came for us to leave, vowing that the fun was only just starting and that it would be getting better towards daylight. But ahead of us we had a long ride, without lights, over pitchy-dark roads, so we got into our car and departed. First, though, we must promise to come back again very soon and must join them in a nightcap glass, they toasting us with their airman's toast, which seemed so well to match in with their buoyant spirits.

When next I passed by that road the hangars were empty of life and the barracks had been torn down. The great offensive had started the week before, and on the third day of it, as we learned from other sources, our friends of Night Bombing Squadron Number 100, obeying an order, had climbed by pairs into their big planes and had gone winging away to do their share in the air fighting, where the fighting lines were locked fast.

There was need just then for every available British aeroplane. The more need because each day showed a steadily mounting list of lost machines and lost airmen. I doubt whether many of those blithesome lads came out of that hell alive, and doubt very much, too, whether I shall ever see any of them again.

So always I shall think of them as I saw them last—their number being sixty or so and the average age twenty-two and a half—grouped at the doorway of their quarters, with the candlelight and the firelight shining behind them, and their glasses raised, wishing to us " Happy landings! "

CHAPTER IV

" DOWN IN HUNLAND "

By Boyd Cable.

IT was cold—bitterly, bitingly, fiercely cold. It was also at intervals wet, and misty, and snowy, as the 'plane ran by turns through various clouds; but it was the cold that was uppermost in the minds of pilot and observer as they flew through the darkness. They were on a machine of the Night Bombing Squadron, and the " Night Fliers" in winter weather take it more or less as part of the night's work that they are going to be out in cold and otherwise unpleasant weather conditions; but the cold this night was, as the pilot put it in his thoughts, " over the odds."

It was the Night-Fliers' second trip over Hunland. The first trip had been a short one to a near objective, because at the beginning of the night the weather looked too doubtful to risk a long trip. But before they had come back the weather had cleared, and the Squadron Commander, after full deliberation, had decided to chance the long trip and bomb a certain place which he knew it was urgent should be damaged as much and as soon as possible.

All this meant that the Fliers had the shortest possible space of time on the ground between the two trips. Their machines were loaded up with fresh supplies of bombs just as quickly as it could be done, the petrol and oil tanks refilled, expended rounds of ammunition for the machine-guns replaced. Then, one after another the machines steered out into the darkness across the 'drome ground towards a twinkle of light placed to guide them, wheeled round, gave the engine a preliminary whirl, steadied it down, opened her out again, and one by one at intervals lumbered off at gathering speed, and soared off up into the darkness.

The weather held until the objective was reached, although glances astern showed ominous clouds banking up and darkening the sky behind them. The bombs were loosed and seen to strike in leaping gusts of flame on the ground below, while searchlights stabbed up into the sky and grouped round to find the raiders, and the Hun "Archies" spat sharp tongues of flame up at them. Several times the shells burst near enough to be heard above the roar of the engine; but one after another the Night-Fliers "dropped the eggs" and wheeled and drove off for home, the observers leaning over and picking up any visible speck of light or the flickering spurts of a machine-gun's fire and loosing off quick bursts of fire at these targets. But every pilot knew too well the meaning of those banking clouds to the west, and was in too great haste to get back, to spend time hunting targets for their machine-guns, and each opened his engine out and drove hard to reach the safety of our own lines before thick weather could catch and bewilder them.

The "Osca" was the last machine to arrive at the objective and deliver her bombs and swing for home, and because she was the last she came in for the fully awakened defence's warmest welcome, and wheeled with searchlights hunting for her, with Archie shells coughing round, with machine-guns spitting fire and their bullets *zizz-izz-ipping* up past her, with "flaming onions" curving up in streaks of angry red fire and falling blazing to earth again. A few of the bullets ripped and rapped viciously through the fabric of her wings, but she suffered no further damage, although the fire was hot enough and close enough to make her pilot and observer breathe sighs of relief as they droned out into the darkness and left all the devilment of fire and lights astern.

The word of the Night-Fliers' raid had evidently gone abroad through the Hun lines, however, and as they flew west they could see searchlight after light switching and scything through the dark in search of them. Redmond, or "Reddie," the pilot, was a good deal more concerned over the darkening sky, and the cold that by now was piercing to his bones, than he was over the searchlights or the chance of running into further Archie fire. He lifted the "Osca" another 500 feet as he flew, and drove on with eyes on the compass and on the cloud banks ahead in turn. Flying conditions do not lend themselves to conversation between pilot and observer, but once or twice the two exchanged remarks, very brief and boiled-down remarks, on their position and the chances of reaching the lines before they ran into " the thick." That a thick was coming was plainly clear to both. The sky by now was completely darkened, and the earth below was totally and utterly lost to sight. The pilot had his compass, and his compass only, left to guide him, and he kept a very close and attentive eye on that and his instrument denoting height. Their bombing objective had been a long way behind the German lines, but Reddie and " Walk " Jones, the observer, were already beginning to congratulate themselves on their nearness to the lines and the probability of escaping the storm, when the storm suddenly whirled down upon them. It came without warning, although warning would have been of little use, since they could do nothing but continue to push for home. One minute they were flying, in darkness it is true, but still in a clear air; the next they were simply barging blindly through a storm of rain which probably poured straight down to earth but which to them, flying at some scores of miles per hour, was driving level and with the force of whip cuts full in their faces. Both pilot and observer were blinded. The water cataracting on their goggles cut off all possibility of sight, and Reddie could not even see the compass in front of him or the gleam of light that illuminated it. He held the machine as steady and straight on her course as instinct and a sense of direction would allow him, and after some minutes they passed clear of the rain-storm. Everything was streaming wet—their faces, their goggles, their clothes, and everything they touched in the machine. Reddie mopped the wet off his compass and peered at it a moment, and then with an angry exclamation pushed rudder and joy-stick over and swung round to a direction fairly opposite to the one they had been travelling. Apparently he had turned completely round in the minutes through the rain—once round at least, and Heaven only knew how many more times. They flew for a few minutes in comparatively clear weather, and then, quite suddenly, they whirled into a thick mist cloud. At first both Reddie and " Walk " thought it was snow, so cold was the touch of the wet on their faces; but even when they found it was no more than a wet mist cloud they were little better off, because again both were completely blinded so far as seeing how or where they were flying went. Reddie developed a sudden fear that he was holding the " Osca's " nose down, and in a quick revulsion pulled the joy-stick back until he could feel her rear and swoop upwards. He was left with a sense of feeling only to guide him. He could see no faintest feature

" WINTER " IN THE VOSGES.

of the instrument-board in front of him, had to depend entirely on his sense of touch and feel and instinct to know whether the " Osca " was on a level keel, flying forward, or up or down, or lying right over on either wing tip.

The mist cleared, or they flew clear of it, as suddenly as they had entered it, and Reddie found again that he had lost direction, was flying north instead of west. He brought the " Osca " round again and let her drop until the altimeter showed a bare two hundred feet above the ground and peered carefully down for any indication of his whereabouts. He could see nothing—blank nothing, below, or above, or around him. He lifted again to the thousand-foot mark and drove on towards the west. He figured

C

that they ought to be coming somewhere near the lines now, but better be safe than sorry, and he'd get well clear of Hunland before he chanced coming down.

Then the snow shut down on them. If they had been blinded before, they were doubly blind now. It was not only that the whirling flakes of snow shut out any sight in front of or around them; it drove clinging against their faces, their glasses, their bodies, and froze and was packed hard by the wind of their own speed as they flew. And it was cold, bone and marrow-piercing cold. Reddie lost all sense of direction again, all sense of whether he was flying forward, or up or down, right side or wrong side up. He even lost any sense of time; and when the scud cleared enough for him to make out the outline of his instruments he could not see the face of his clock, his height or speed recorders, or anything else, until he had scraped the packed snow off them. But this time, according to the compass, he was flying west and in the right direction. So much he just had time to see when they plunged again into another whirling smother of fine snow. They flew through that for minutes which might have been seconds or hours for all the pilot knew. He could see nothing through his clogged goggles, that blurred up faster than he could wipe them clear; he could hear nothing except, dully, the roar of his engine; he could feel nothing except the grip of the joy-stick, numbly, through his thick gloves. He kept the "Osca" flying level by sheer sense of feel, and at times had all he could do to fight back a wave of panic which rushed on him with a belief that the machine was side-slipping or falling into a spin that would bring him crashing to earth. When the snow cleared again and he was able to see his lighted instruments he made haste to brush them clear of snow and peer anxiously at them. He found he was a good thousand feet up and started at once to lift a bit higher for safety's sake. By the compass he was still flying homeward, and by the time—the time—he stared hard at his clock . . . and found it was stopped. But the petrol in his main tank was almost run out, and according to that he ought to be well over the British lines—if he had kept anything like a straight course. He held a brief and shouted conversation with his observer. "Don't know where I am. Lost. Think we're over our lines."

"Shoot a light, eh?" answered the observer, "and try 'n' land. I'm frozen stiff."

They both peered anxiously round as their Verey light shot out and floated down; but they could see no sign of a flare or an answering light. They fired another signal, and still had no reply; and then, "I'm going down," yelled the pilot, shutting off his engine and letting the machine glide down in a slow sweeping circle. He could see nothing of the ground when the altimeter showed 500 feet, nor at 300 nor at 200, so opened the throttle and picked up speed again. "Shove her down," yelled the observer. "More snow coming."

Another Verey light, shot straight down overboard, showed a glimpse of a grass field, and Reddie swung gently round, and slid downward again. At the same time he fired a landing light fixed out under his lower wing-tip in readiness for just such an occasion as this, and by its glowing vivid white light made a fairly good landing on rough grass land. He shut the engine off at once, because he had no idea how near he was to the edge of the field or what obstacles they might bump if they taxied far, and the machine came quickly to rest. The two men sat still for a minute breathing a sigh of thankfulness that they were safe to ground, then turned and looked at each other in the dying light of the flare. Stiffly they stood up, climbed clumsily out of their places, and down on to the wet ground. Another flurry of snow was falling, but now that they were at rest the snow was floating and drifting gently down instead of beating in their faces with hurricane force as it did when they were flying.

Reddie flapped his arms across his chest and stamped his numbed feet. Walk Jones pulled his gloves off and breathed on his stiff fingers. "I'm fair froze," he mumbled. "Wonder where we are, and how far from the 'drome?"

"Lord knows," returned Reddie. "I don't know even where the line is—ahead or astern, right hand or left."

"Snow's clearing again," said Jones. "Perhaps we'll get a bearing then, and I'll go 'n' hunt for a camp or a cottage, or anyone that'll give us a hot drink."

"Wait a bit," said Reddie. "Stand where you are and let's

give a yell. Some sentry or someone's bound to hear us. Snow's stopping all right; but, Great Scott! isn't it dark!"

Presently they lifted their voices and yelled an "A-hoy" together at the pitch of their lungs. There was no answer, and after a pause they yelled again, still without audible result.

"Oh, curse!" said Jones shivering. "I'm not going to hang about here yelping like a lost dog. And we might hunt an hour for a cottage. I'm going to get aboard again and loose off a few rounds from my machine-gun into the ground. That will stir somebody up and bring 'em along."

"There's the line," said Reddie suddenly. "Look!" and he pointed to where a faint glow rose and fell, lit and faded, along the horizon. "And the guns," he added, as they saw a sheet of light jump somewhere in the distance and heard the *bump* of the report. Other gun flashes flickered and beat across the dark sky. "Funny," said Reddie; "I'd have sworn I turned round as we came down, and I thought the lines were dead the other way."

The observer was fumbling about to get his foot in the step. "I thought they were way out to the right," he said. "But I don't care a curse where they are. I want a camp or a French cottage with coffee on the stove. I'll see if I can't shoot somebody awake."

"Try one more shout first," said Reddie, and they shouted together again.

"Got 'im," said Reddie joyfully, as a faint hail came in response, and Jones took his foot off the step and began to fumble under his coat for a torch. "Here!" yelled Reddie. "This way! Here!"

They heard the answering shouts draw nearer, and then, just as Jones found his torch and was pulling it out from under his coat, Reddie clutched at his arm. "What—what was it——" he gasped. "Did you hear what they called?"

"No, couldn't understand," said Jones in some surprise at the other's agitation. "They're French, I suppose; farm people, most like."

"It was *German*," said Reddie hurriedly. "There again, hear that? *We've dropped in Hunland.*"

"Hu-Hunland!" stammered Jones; then desperately, "It can't be. You sure it isn't French—Flemish, perhaps?"

"Flemish—here!" said Reddie, dismissing the idea, as Jones admitted he might well do, so far south in the line. "I know little enough German, but I know French well enough; and that's not French. We're done in, Walk."

A "HANDLEY PAGE."

"Couldn't we bolt for it?" said Walk, looking hurriedly round, "It's dark, and we know where the lines are."

"What hope of getting through them?" said Reddie, speaking in quick whispers. "But we've got a better way. We'll make a try. Here, quickly, and quiet as you can—get to the prop. and swing it when I'm ready. We'll chance a dash for it."

Both knew the chances against them, knew that in front of the machine might lie a ditch, a tree, a hedge, a score of things that would trip them as they taxied to get speed to rise; they knew too that the Germans were coming closer every moment, that they might be on them before they could get the engine started, that they would probably begin shooting at the first sound of her start. All these things and a dozen others raced through their minds in an instant; but neither hesitated, both moved promptly and swiftly. Reddie clambered up and into his seat; Walk Jones jumped to the propeller, and began to wind it backwards to " suck in " the petrol to the cylinders. " When she starts, jump to the wing-tip and try 'n' swing her round," called Reddie in quick low tones. " It'll check her way. Then you must jump for it, and hang on and climb in as we go. Yell when you're aboard. All ready now."

A shout came out of the darkness—a shout and an obvious question in German. " Contact," said Walk Jones, and swung the propeller his hardest. He heard the whirr of the starter as Reddie twirled it rapidly. " Off," called Jones as he saw the engine was not giving sign of life, and " Off " answered Reddie, cutting off the starting current.

Another shout came, and with it this time what sounded like an imperative command. Reddie cursed his lack of knowledge of German. He could have held them in play a minute if— " Contact," came Walk's voice again. " Contact," he answered, and whirled the starter madly again. There was still no movement, no spark of life from the engine. Reddie groaned, and Walk Jones, sweating despite the cold over his exertions on the propeller, wound it back again and swung it forward with all his weight. His thick leather coat hampered him. He tore it off and flung it to the ground, and tried again. The shouts were louder now and coming from different points, as if a party had split up and was searching the field. A couple of electric torches threw patches of light on the ground, lifted occasionally and flashed round. One was coming straight towards them, and Reddie with set teeth waited the shout of discovery he knew must come presently, and cursed Walk's slowness at the "prop." Again on the word he whirled the starter, and this time " Whurr-r-r-rum," answered the engine, suddenly leaping to life; " Whur-r-r-ROO-OO-OO-OOM-urr-r-r-umph," as Reddie eased and opened the throttle. He heard a babel of shouts and yells, and saw the light-patches come dancing on the run towards them. A sudden recollection of the only two German words he knew came to him. " Ja wohl," he yelled at the pitch of his voice, " Ja wohl "; then in lower hurried tones, " Swing her,

Walk; quick, swing her," and opened the engine out again. The running lights stopped for a minute at his yell, and Walk Jones jumped to the wing-tip, shouted "Right!" and hung on while Reddie started to taxi the machine forward. His weight and leverage brought her lumbering round, the roar of engine and propeller rising and sinking as Reddie manipulated the throttle, and Reddie yelling his "Ja wohl," every time the noise died down. "Get in, Walk; get aboard," he shouted, when the nose was round and pointing back over the short stretch they had taxied on landing, and which he therefore knew was clear running for at least a start. He heard another order screamed in German, and next instant the *bang* of a rifle, not more, apparently, than a score of yards away. He kept the machine lumbering forward, restraining himself from opening his engine out, waiting in an agony of apprehension for Walk's shout. He felt the machine lurch and sway, and the kicking scramble his observer made to board her, heard next instant his yelling "Right-oh!" and opened the throttle full as another couple of rifles bang-banged. The rifles had little terror either for him or the observer, because both knew there were bigger and deadlier risks to run in the next few seconds. There were still desperately long odds against their attempt succeeding. In the routine method of starting a machine, chocks are placed in front of the wheels and the engine is given a short full-power run and a longer easier one to warm the engine and be sure all is well; then the chocks are pulled away and she rolls off, gathering speed as she goes, until she has enough for her pilot to lift her into the air. Here, their engine was stone cold, they knew nothing of what lay in front of them, might crash into something before they left the ground, might rise, and even then catch some house or treetop, and travelling at the speed they would by then have attained—well, the Lord help them!

Reddie had to chance everything, and yet throw away no shadow of chance. He opened the throttle wide, felt the machine gather speed, bumping and jolting horribly over the rough field, tried to peer down at the ground to see how fast they moved, could see nothing, utterly black nothing, almost panicked for one heart-stilling instant as he looked ahead again and thought he saw the blacker shadow of something solid in front of him, clenched his teeth and held straight on until he felt by the rush of wind on his face he had way enough, and pulled the joy-stick in to him. With a sigh of relief he felt the jolting change to a smooth swift rush, held his breath, and with a pull on the stick zoomed her up, levelled her out again (she should clear anything but a tall tree now), zoomed her up again. He felt a hand thumping on his shoulder, heard Walk's wild exultant yell—" 'Ra-a-ay!" and, still lifting her steadily, swung his machine's nose for the thumping lights that marked the trenches.

They landed safe on their own 'drome ground half an hour after. The officer whose duty it was for the night to look after the landing-ground and light the flares in answer to the returning pilots' signals, walked over to them as they came to rest.

"Hullo, you two," he said. "Where the' blazes you been till this time? We'd just about put you down as missing."

Reddie and Walk had stood up in their cockpits and, without a spoken word, were solemnly shaking hands.

Reddie looked overboard at the officer on the ground. "You may believe it, Johnny, or you may not," he said, "but we've been down into Hunland."

"Down into hell!" said Johnny. "Quit jokin'. What kept you so late?"

"You've said it, Johnny," said Reddie soberly. "Down into hell—and out again."

They shook hands again, solemnly.

100 SQUADRON LAMENT

BY CPL. J. R. BIRD.

For months in England, on the spree,
With the Squadrons on H.D.,
Count Zeppelin's crimes were an awful length,
But we struck six airships off his strength.

And we brought them down in flames,
And we brought them down in flames,
And we brought them down in flames,
And they haven't been there since.

Then some " brass hat " at Adastral House
Tried his best to start a grouse,
To form " One Hundred " for overseas,
He picked his men from the best H.D.'s,

And they sent us out to France,
And they sent us out to France,
And they sent us out to France,
To show them how to bomb.

We landed on the Western Front,
From ISEL LE HAMEAU was our first stunt,
And we soon ken from Jerry's moans,
That he didn't like the Aeros with the skull and cross-bones.

For they blew up all his railways,
For they blew up all his railways,
For they blew up all his railways,
And ammunition dumps.

Our pilots got well known round there,
So they moved us up to a place called AIRE.
And we bombed his 'dromes till the Hun wished he
Could run across the Major they called Christie.

We " wrote off " his best 'drome,
We " wrote off " his best 'drome,
And also the Menin Road.
We " wrote off " his best 'drome,

100 SQUADRON

Then Jerry, just to show his spite,
Bombed London with his planes at night.
The people said—"You silly clowns,
Why not go and bomb his towns?"

        So they pushed us off to Ochey,
        So they pushed us off to Ochey,
        So they pushed us off to Ochey,
        To get square with the Hun.

Well, Jerry must have thought the same,
And he tried his best to stop the game.
We all remember that fine night,
That brought the Squadron their first fright.

        For he tried to wipe out Ochey,
        For he tried to wipe out Ochey,
        ·For he tried to wipe out Ochey,
        But the Café stands there yet.

The "wind up" there, no man could stick,
And everyone paraded sick.
Then someone said t'would be "the goods,"
To move up further in the woods.

        And everyone was happy,
        And everyone was happy,
        And everyone was happy,
        For there was rest, sweet rest.

When we got rid of our F.E.'s,
We got to work with the twin H.P.'s.
And "Jerry" said by what we hear,
That the only one he had to fear,

        Was good old "100 Squadron,"
        Was good old "100 Squadron,"
        Was good old "100 Squadron,"
        We hope to meet again.

CHAPTER V

A SHORT NIGHT RAID

By Lieut. W. A. Barnes.

"Last night an enemy dump at ———— was successfully attacked."

SUCH announcements as this have appeared so frequently in the Press as to have become quite a commonplace, and even perhaps a little tiresome to the average reader.

They appear to be just the dull official record of an equally dull piece of routine work. But in reality such is far from being the case, for bombing dumps often proves the most exciting, and is certainly the most spectacular form of all night bombing work.

Not only is it the most interesting, but the importance of its effect upon enemy plans and operations can hardly be exaggerated.

There not being enough moonlight for a long raid on this particular night, the target given us was a German ammunition dump. Although dumps are usually situated but a short distance from the lines, they are by no means easy targets to find at night, for they are seldom situated near any definite land-marks, and are invariably well camouflaged.

We had carefully studied an aerial photograph of the target before setting out, and noted a few peculiarities of its surroundings which would aid us in picking it up.

After gaining height we struck a compass course for our objective, and at the end of about thirty minutes' flying, could just make out the faint outline of sheds. From the landmarks we had noted, we were practically certain we had arrived over our objective, but to make absolutely sure we let out a parachute flare to light up the ground.

This promptly dispelled all doubt, for searchlights opened up, and a hail of machine-gun bullets and "flaming-onions" leapt up from the ground. "Archie" had been active for some time, but the shells were bursting well above us and we were in little danger, save from a direct hit.

The parachute flare proved a friend indeed, for both searchlights and machine-guns concentrated upon it, giving us just time to dive swiftly, release our bombs, switch on the engine and climb away.

When clear away and turning to observe results, we were spectators of one of the finest firework displays I have ever seen.

Ammunition was exploding at a record speed, dense clouds of smoke were rising, and highly coloured flames were leaping up to a great height from the ground.

We watched this fascinating exhibition for some minutes, until the "cough" of an "Archie" burst near by reminded us that we were still in the danger zone, when with one last look, and a grin of satisfaction from pilot to observer, we turned and made for home.

" ESCAPE "

The following is a narrative of the escape of two officers (Lieut. L. D. Kirk and 2/Lieut. W. Richards) on the night of 27-28th May, 1918 :—

" These officers left on a bombing raid for KREUZWALD between 10 and 11 o'clock, when near ST. AVOLD the machine was hit by anti-aircraft fire and a few minutes later the engine cut out absolutely dead.

" Realizing that a Holt flare would attract the attention of the enemy, Lieut. Kirk landed without lighting one, and succeeded in pancaking his machine safely.

" 2/Lieut. Richards was rendered unconscious for a few minutes, but Kirk took hold of him by the arms and helped him to his feet, and they both made off in a south-westerly direction.

" After about half an hour's walking they approached a battery of heavy guns. With great daring and presence of mind they managed to pass through this, actually crossing over one of the gun emplacements. They continued in a south-westerly direction, alternately running and walking.

" They then came to a communication trench, which they negotiated successfully, but they had to leave their Sidcot suits in the barbed wire, as they found it impossible to get through it owing to these being too cumbersome.

" They heard Germans speaking in the trench, and had to lie down for a considerable time, staying where they were until all was quiet again.

" By this time it was getting light, so they crawled to a hedge in ' No Man's Land ' and lay hidden here for the whole of the day, enduring great privations of hunger—as they had nothing but a small stick of chocolate—and thirst.

" From where they were they could see German shells bursting several kilos away in the direction of the French lines, so they made their plans accordingly, knowing that where these shells were bursting must be friendly territory. As soon as it was getting dark they left their hiding place and proceeded on their way.

" They then got to the river and followed it for some time, having to get through numerous wire entanglements.

" They then made for a wood, but were challenged and fired at by outposts of sentries. After this they kept to the open, hiding every now and then in the long grass. During all this time they were continually being fired at both by rifles and machine guns.

" Their next obstacle was the river. Kirk being a poor swimmer, Richards swam across to the other side to see if everything was clear, as they suspected barbed wire being in the river. He then swam back again and informed Kirk that everything was O.K. Kirk then swam for the other side, while Richards waited to see him safely there before again making the attempt himself.

" After crossing the river, being absolutely perished with cold, they made off at their utmost speed, but were impeded by wire. They were challenged by a sentry, apparently French, but not being sure, Richards answered "Pardon," and they ran for their lives.

" Sighting ' C ' Lighthouse they made towards it, and eventually arrived at LIXIERES, where they found a French soldier. From him they enquired their whereabouts, and were taken to the nearest French Head Quarters.''

A FORCED LANDING AT NIGHT

By Lieut. W. A. Barnes.

We were flying peacefully along, both pilot and observer possessed with that wonderful feeling of exhilaration that comes to all flying men after having crossed the lines on the homeward journey. In twenty minutes we should reach the aerodrome, and all the comfort it meant after a long night's work. No more had we to fear being brought down, or having to descend on the enemy side of the line. No longer was it necessary to indulge in all kinds of aerobatics to elude the wily searchlights, and not again that night should we hear that hateful " wouf, wouf " of the Hun Archie, as it burst near at hand.

My observer had just leaned over from the front seat, shouted " cheerio," and pushed a chocolate into my mouth, his usual reward for piloting him safely back across the lines, when " clank, clank " went the engine, and the whole machine began to shiver. I tried to coax it, but it simply " clanked " more viciously, the pointer of the revolution counter wagged from side to side, and it quickly became apparent that we were in for a forced landing.

We were now at five thousand feet, and with what little power the engine was still giving, we could at most only keep in the air for seven or eight minutes, and travel about the same number of miles.

There was not a moment to be lost, and so I shouted through the telephone to my observer to start dropping parachute flares when we reached four thousand feet. These flares are composed of a magnesium compound attached to a parachute, and when launched from a machine they burn brilliantly in the air, and take some time to reach the earth. Thus they light up the ground, and enable the pilot to choose the best spot to land upon.

Out dropped the first flare and lit up beautifully, but all we could see beneath us was woodland, with a river running through it. I had heard of pilots bringing their machine down slowly on to the

46

top of a wood, and landing without sustaining injury to themselves. Should I try to do the same if necessary? or should I risk the river? were the thoughts which flashed through my mind.

Lower and lower we came, the engine now clanging and banging like so many tins being rattled together, it was still giving us a little forward speed, however, which might prove very useful.

OCHEY AERODROME.

As we came lower we could see a clearing beyond the wood, but whether we could reach it was a matter of grave doubt. Of course, even if we did it might contain obstacles which would crash the machine on landing, but we would much rather risk this than take our chance on either the wood or the river.

We were now down to two hundred feet, it was too late to try the river, and it was now one of two things, the clearing, or the wood. The clearing could now be seen quite well, and it looked perfectly level in the moonlight, but then the ground always does.

Lower and lower we glided. Thank goodness! Yes, we were going to clear the wood by the narrowest of margins. In a few seconds the wheels of the machine had touched the ground, but oh! would it never pull up? An awful bump which threw us both out of our seats settled the question, and the machine came to an abrupt standstill.

We hastily jumped out, and found that we had struck a partly dug trench, which had been the cause of our sudden halt. After congratulating each other on our escape, and lighting cigarettes, I examined the machine, and found the undercarriage and centre section struts broken. In the meantime my observer had fished his Thermos flask out of the machine, and presented me with a steaming cup of coffee, with a "Cheerio, old man, here's to soft landings."

BOMBING A TRAIN

By Lieut. W. A. Barnes.

Bombing a moving train has many of the characteristics of big game hunting, and is perhaps the most sporting target in the whole of night bombing work.

The results, too, especially just before an offensive, often have far-reaching effects, for it impedes the work of massing together both men and material, and delays food and ammunition in being brought up to the front line.

An offensive by the Germans was expected, and the orders for the night were to bomb and machine gun a variety of targets behind the lines, which doings were calculated to harass the enemy and upset his plans.

We were told to pay particular attention to trains running towards the lines, for these would undoubtedly contain men and munitions that were being massed for the attack.

Leaving the aerodrome with a full load of small, high-explosive bombs, each of which was capable of derailing a train, we headed straight for a railway junction, some ten miles behind the lines. We were well acquainted with the whereabouts of this junction, from experience of former raids.

Arriving over it at 4,000 feet, we could see the rails quite plainly as they shone in the moonlight, and we circled round it to wait and watch events.

We had not long to wait before down below we saw a faint glow and a trail of white smoke, which showed up well against the black background of earth. It was a train, and travelling towards the lines.

With engine cut completely off, we dived swiftly towards it, and, as we neared it, turned quickly round and took up a position behind it. Lower and lower we glided until the carriages became quite visible. We continued to glide down, however, until we were low enough to be absolutely certain of obtaining direct hits. Switching on the engine and throttling back, until the speed of our machine was only a trifle faster than that of the train, we flew parallel above it, and gradually overtook it.

As the carriages slowly passed beneath us we released three bombs in quick succession, and the force of the resulting explosions shook our machine from head to stern.

With throttle full open we quickly climbed to a height, and let off a parachute flare to aid us in observing the result. This was hardly necessary, for the clouds of smoke and sparks that were arising from the ground told their tale. By the light of the flare, however, we saw a heap of burning wreckage that had once been a train.

We did not gaze on the results of our handiwork long, but flew off to search for other suitable targets upon which to drop the remainder of our bombs.

D

CHAPTER VI

ON OPERATIONS

IT is here intended to give a resumé of the whole of the operations undertaken, and at the same time include any points of interest in the Squadron's work. Some brief notes, dealing with the machines and other items, it is thought would be of interest to readers before a resumé of the Squadron's operations is given. The Squadron was equipped with the F.E.2B. machine on landing in France, and served with this type up to the end of August, 1918. It can truthfully be stated here that there was no machine that served its country so well as did this type. Perhaps this was due to the fine material which was always available to fly it, and that it was this factor which was largely responsible for the magnificent work it performed. Be all that as it may, it was undoubtedly a most excellent machine for night bombing, and the whole personnel of the Squadron made the best of the machine and did it more than credit. The limit of its carrying capacity in bombs was a decided drawback to pilots and observers out for a really good strafe. Especially was this disappointing when over targets, and having just three 112 lb. bombs to drop, without the good fortune to obtain a bull's-eye with just one. The machine was far too slow when amongst the enemy's A.-A. guns and searchlights. This made it not a little disquieting to its occupants, who under such circumstances were wont to discharge their wrath upon the inventors, for being so inconsiderate and lacking in imagination. As a redeeming influence for overcoming this discomfort pilots were left to trust in the name of the girl they left behind them. To make it more clear, it would be as well to mention that the nose of each machine bore in block letters a girl's Christian name, and in some cases nicknames, which were obviously of importance to the pilot only. So much for the machine.

The Squadron first introduced itself to the Hun on the night of 5-6th April, 1917. On this night the Squadron's full complement of machines (eighteen) attacked the hostile Aerodrome at DOUIA, which at this time was a veritable nest of what one might almost describe as the flower of the German Flying Corps, known as the "Richtofen Circus." The results of this raid, together with those obtained during a second attack on the night following, were excellent, and portended well for the future success of the Squadron. The introduction to the Hun was well executed and came to him with sudden unexpectedness, as it was the first night bombing raid undertaken on a large scale in France. Below is published an extract from Capt. von Richtofen's book, "Der Rote Kampf-flieger" (The Red Fighting Airman), which refers solely to the two attacks mentioned above carried out on DOUIA Aerodrome by the Squadron.

The story is painted in highly rich colours and was intended, of course, for home consumption. However, it will be read with great interest by those who took part in the raids in question. . Capt. von Richtofen here pays the Squadron a just tribute in speaking so highly of the individual bravery of the pilots and observers, and his narrative rather bears witness to his own sporting instincts. When this narrative was published it is regretted that he could not have included the nett results of 'the raids, but photographs taken after the raids showed considerable damage, several hangars being destroyed. He fails to add that the aerodrome was speedily evacuated. His reference to three machines having been brought down in the second night of the attack is incorrect, one machine only on each of the two nights failing to return.

"BRITISH BOMBING ON OUR AERODROME"

"Nights when the moon is full are the best for night flying. In the moonlight nights of early April our friends the British were especially active. This was, of course, in connection with the battle of Arras. They must have discovered that we had settled ourselves in a most beautiful big new aerodrome, DOUAI. One night when we were sitting in the Casino the telephone bell rang, and we were informed that the British were on the way. Great excitement prevailed, of course. We had dug-outs provided by the excellent Simon, our building officer. So down we went, and then certainly we did hear the sound of engines, at first quite soft, but nevertheless quite unmistakable. The anti-aircraft guns and searchlights seemed also to have had the message, they also gradually got busy. The foremost of the enemy were still much too far off to be attacked. We were fearfully excited, but knew all the time that the British would not be able to find our aerodrome, which was not so easy, as we were not near any broad highroad, water, or railway line, which form the best guides at night.

" The Englishman was flying very high. First he circled round the aerodrome and we began to think that he was looking for some other objective. All at once, however, he shut off his engine, and came down. 'Now for the real things,' said Wolff. We fetched our rifles, and began to fire at the Englishman. We could not see him yet, but the noise he made alone calmed our nerves. At last he was caught in the beam, and the whole aerodrome shouted with surprise, for it was quite an old machine. We recognised the type at once. He was not more than a kilometre away, and was flying straight for our aerodrome, and coming still lower. Then he shut off his engine again, and came straight for us. 'Thank goodness, he's chosen the other side of the aerodrome,' said Wolff. But it wasn't long before the first dropped, and then there came a rain of small bombs. It was a fine display of fireworks, and might have impressed a rabbit. I believe that night bombing has a merely moral effect. If a man gets hit it is very unpleasant for him, of course, but not for other people. We thought it great fun, and hoped the British would come over often. So this old lattice-tail dropped his bombs, and that from a height of 50 metres. It was a regular bit of impertinence, as I pride myself on being able to hit a bull in the light of the full moon at 50 metres, and why should I not hit an Englishman? It would have been quite a change to bring the man down from below. When the Englishman had gone we went back again into the Casino, and discussed how to prepare a reception for the raiders the next night. Next day the servants, etc., were all very busy planting stakes in the ground near the Casino and officers' quarters, to act as machine-gun platforms. We practised with captured British machine guns, fitted night sights to them, and were very much excited as to what would happen. I will not divulge the number of machine guns, but there were enough to go round.

"We were again sitting in the Casino. Night-flyers were the topic of the conversation. A servant rushed in, shouting that they were coming, and disappeared, somewhat lightly clad, into the nearest dug-out. Each of us dashed to his machine gun, and a few good shots amongst the other ranks were similarly armed, the rest having rifles. The pursuit flight was at all events armed to the teeth, and ready to receive the raiders.

"The first one came very high, as on the preceding night, and then came down to 50 metres, coming this time straight for our quarters, much to our delight. He was caught in the beam, and was not more than three hundred metres from us. The first man opened fire and all the others followed suit. A storming attack could not have been better beaten off than this attack by a single impertinent airman at a height of fifty metres. He was received by a murderous fire. He could not hear the machine gun fire, of course, owing to the noise of his engine, but he saw the flashes, and must have been a jolly good man, for he kept straight on his course. He flew directly over us. When he was directly over we naturally made a rush for the dug-out, as to be killed by one of these petty bombs would have been a poor sort of death for a fighting airman. As soon as he was away back we ran to the machine guns, and at him again. Friend Schafer asserted, of course, that he had hit the man. Schafer is quite a good shot. Still in this case I did not believe him. We had achieved something, for the enemy dropped his bombs rather aimlessly owing to our shooting. One of them, it is true, had exploded only a few yards away from the ' petit rouge,' but had not hurt it.

"During the night the fun recommenced several times. I was already in bed fast asleep, when I heard in a dream anti-aircraft firing. I woke up and discovered that the dream was reality. One of the Englishmen flew at so low an altitude over my habitation that

("Petit Rouge" refers to Richtofen's pet machine.)

in my fright I pulled the blanket over my head.   The next moment I
heard an incredible bang just outside my window.   The panes had
fallen a victim to the bomb.   I rushed out of my room in my shirt
in order to fire a few shots after him.   They were firing from everywhere.   Unfortunately, I had overslept my opportunity.   The next
morning we were extremely surprised and delighted to discover that
we had shot down from the ground no fewer than three Englishmen.
They had landed not far from our aerodrome, and had been made
prisoners.   As a rule we had hit the engines, and had forced the
airmen to come down on our side of the front.   After all, Schafer
was possibly right in his assertion.   At any rate, we were satisfied,
for they preferred avoiding our aerodrome.   It was a pity that they
gave us a wide berth, for they gave us lots of fun.   Let us hope
that they come back to us next month.''

Following the successful operations referred to, we now
took an active part in the Battle of Vimy Ridge and Arras
during the period of April to May.   The chief targets of attack
during these and subsequent battles were (1) railway junction and
trains, (2) convoys and troops on roads.   Aerodromes were also
targets for attack, which had for its object the attainment of the
mastery in the air, a very essential acquirement for ensuring successful operations on the ground.   The operations reports shown
further on will give to readers some idea of the extent of these
operations, and what far-reaching results this bombing may have,
and the help it affords to the other arms of the fighting forces.   The
persistent attacks on the enemy's communications played no small
part in helping our Armies to gain their successes at the battles.
During these operations a number of trains were wrecked, considerable damage done to railway stations, and motor transport on roads
was severely handled.   Subsequent reports received regarding these
attacks proved beyond doubt that the destruction among the
enemy's railway communications was great, and was causing him
alarm, and was having a far-reaching effect upon the battles then
being fought.   Several stories of interest on night bombing raids
are included in this book, but one in particular may be referred to
here, as it originated from an incident which occurred on the night
of 9/10th April, 1917.   It will be seen in the operations report on

the night in question that a certain pilot landed behind the enemy's lines in a snowstorm, and after realizing his position, took off again and returned safely to our lines. The story has been ably produced by "Boyd Cable," and is published with his kind permission in these records.

Following close on the heels of the Battle of ARRAS, came the Battle of MESSINES in June, 1917; followed by the third Battle of YPRES, which covered practically the whole period of July to October, 1917.

During these battles we again took an active part, as operations will show, and its work throughout these battles was consistently brilliant; as in the former battles the targets attacked were identically the same in nature, but differed in respect to places, these latter of course being usually behind the front on which the battle was taking place. It is somewhat difficult in the absence of Intelligence Reports to add many details to those already contained in the Operations Reports further on, and it would be interesting if the data regarding actual results of these raids could be obtained, but in view of the long lapse of time which inevitably would be caused before this data could be obtained, and the consequent difficulties in obtaining it, this chapter must remain incomplete. During the offensive which our armies were undertaking at YPRES through the months of July to October, the following letter addressed to the O.C. Squadron was received from the G.O.C., the Royal Flying Corps (as it then was): "Please congratulate all pilots and observers on their splendid work last night, when the night was particularly dark. This bombing by No. 100 Squadron is according to the prisoners' statements of the greatest use to our operations." The particular night referred to was the night of 21/22 August, 1917, full details of which will be found in the chapter containing the Operations Reports. Many similar congratulatory letters and telegrams were received from time to time on our many successes, but this serves the purpose of showing that the fine work of the Squadron was not without praise; and the bombing bearing fruit, as the following reports will make clear. Two reports were received regarding the attack carried out on the night of 3/4th July, 1917, one of which stated three hangars, the other four hangars as having been destroyed. Both reports, however, stated that thirty new machines were burnt. The damage was estimated at one million francs.

This was a very notable achievement and one of which we might justly be proud. The reports added that the enemy aviators after this raid were forced to fly to another Aerodrome every evening and spend the night there. During the same period under review reports were received confirming the blowing up of a number of the ammunition dumps in the COURTRAI area, which resulted in considerable damage being done. A story by an eye-witness of his impressions on seeing an ammunition dump going up will be found in the chapter containing short stories, where he ably describes the effect as seen from the air.

After the third Battle of YPRES, which terminated in October, 1917, the Squadron was moved to OCHEY. At this time the enemy's raids into England were becoming frequent, and more violent, and it was therefore necessary to take stringent measures to counteract this offset, so as to give the enemy a taste of his own medicine. The work of bombing the enemy in his own country was eagerly sought for by all ranks, and it was not long before the enemy was made to realize that two could play the same game, but it was necessary to hit him harder, which being achieved it was known that he would soon be crying out for the cessation of the bombing of open towns. He was soon brought to his knees, and the bombing of towns in England was speedily brought to an abrupt end. The bombing of Germany was not allowed to lapse on this score, but eventually played a very great part in bringing hostilities to an end much quicker than otherwise would have been the case. The moral effect upon the civilian population apart from the material damage caused, was one of the decisive factors in the success of our arms.

The honour of being the first Squadron in the Independent Force under General Trenchard, was a fitting finish to its Active Service career. Although we were not equipped with the Handley-Page machines until the end of August, 1918, many raids into Germany were undertaken by the F.E.2B. machines, and more credit is due for performing such long distance raids on this type. It served also as a useful asset in combating the enemy's aerial activity down in this region, which was undoubtedly concentrated for defensive purposes against the Squadrons operating into the heart of their country. This again proved a most useful asset to our armies in the field, for the enemy was forced to withdraw valuable units from their Flying Services from other parts of the front, and the quantity of anti-aircraft defences in the way of guns, searchlights, and personnel to man them for the defence of their towns, proved a great drain on their resources. We were successful as previously stated, in keeping the enemy's night flying units from becoming anything approaching a menace. When equipped with the Handley-Page machine the Squadron set out to attack towns in the heart of Germany, which it had for so long looked forward to doing, but although a short time only was allowed to carry this work through, it accomplished many raids on German towns.

It was not long after we arrived at OCHEY, that the enemy really set out to attack us with extreme violence. The Squadron, however, were not to be beaten, and his attacks were overcome by highly successful counter-attacks on his chief Aerodrome in this sector. The Aerodrome referred to was FRESCATY. These attacks were carried out on the nights 26/27th February, and 23/24th March, 1918, and resulted in the destruction of one large shed, and sixteen machines. This appeared to close the enemy's activities for at any rate some few months, and we were allowed freedom of action once more. His attacks, however, afforded us many an amusing incident, which those who witnessed them will ever remember. His methodical bombing of the empty hangars at OCHEY, for practically months after we had moved to a more camouflaged part of the Aerodrome, was distinctly humorous, and to add to the humour he did not succeed in finding out this "Ruse de Guerre" until a few days after we had moved once again to another Aerodrome, when he persisted in his methodical bombing of more empty hangars.

Prior to the attack on FRESCATY Aerodrome, operations had been proceeding on German towns with visibly good effect, the most important among them being TREVES (TRIER) on 24/25th January, and 18/19th February, 1918. Taking into consideration the type

AN AERIAL PHOTOGRAPH OF OCHEY AERODROME TAKEN AFTER AN ENEMY BOMBING RAID. THE HANGARS ON THE LEFT OF THE PICTURE ARE THOSE WHICH WERE OCCUPIED BY THE SQUADRON, AND THE HANGARS IN THE FOREGROUND ARE THOSE OCCUPIED BY A FRENCH SQUADRON. THE BURSTS OF THE BOMBS CAN BE CLEARLY SEEN.

of machine on which these raids were done, the distance covered to reach this target was considerable, and pilots and observers who took part in these raids are to be complimented on their achievement, and the mechanics are also to be complimented upon their efficient work, which enabled these machines to so successfully accomplish their task.

During the next month a notable success was achieved on the night of 24/25th March, 1918, when METZ was attacked, and subsequent information showed that the damage was considerable,

thc worst bcing thc dostruction of thc Boulovard in front of
the station, where damage to material was said to exceed two million francs.   An ammunition train was blown up in the station, and
the extensive material damage can be attributed to this occurrence.

OCIIEY :
SHOWING CAMOUFLAGED HANGARS ON EDGE OF WOOD.

At the end of March the Squadron was moved temporarily to an
Aerodrome near RHEIMS.   It will be well remembered that at this
time the enemy opened his last attack for the final bid for the world
power.   Here a number of raids were undertaken in the
sector behind the RHEIMS-AMIENS front.   The targets attacked
were among the enemy's most important lines of communication,
and so assisted to stem the tide of the German invasion.

BOULAY Aerodrome, which now came into prominence, will
remain an everlasting memory to the old Squadron.   Here the
enemy concentrated his Night Flying machines (chiefly Gothas and
Friedrichafens), but we never allowed them to become really

dangerous opponents.   By systematic attacks on this Aerodrome, and great perseverance on the part of the pilots and observers, the enemy were held.   On several occasions enemy machines were caught either landing or taking off, and individual pilots and observers showed their true sporting and courageous instincts by coming down to a very low altitude to do their execution.   At least three enemy aeroplanes are known to have been destroyed by being brought down, and twelve out of a total of twenty-two hangars on this aerodrome were shown on photographs to have received appreciable damage from the attacks which had been carried through to the end of August, but the enemy's losses in actual machines, which must have been heavy, have not been ascertained.   According to prisoners' statements, however, this is more than confirmed.   It is interesting to note that no fewer than eighteen and a half tons of bombs were dropped by the Squadron on this target.

Although the Aerodromes were frequently allotted as targets for attack, the work of bombing Germany was not allowed to lapse.

The most successful operation undertaken at this time was undoubtedly that on the HAGENDINGEN STEEL WORKS, on the night of 16/17 July.   Appreciable damage was done to the works, and the photographs taken next day showed : (1) A direct hit on the Central blowing station; (2) the roof of a workshop alongside the rolling mills burnt out.   The factory was not working when the photograph was taken, and the cessation of work undoubtedly resulted from the hit on the central blowing station.   Some time elapsed before the factory was again in full swing.   The Squadron thus added another leaf to its laurels, and considering how well defended this factory was, with its numerous anti-aircraft guns, searchlights, and other forms of frightfulness, those who took part in this particular raid can justly be proud of achieving such fine results.

A most successful raid was undertaken by one of our machines on the Chemical Works at SAARALBEN, where extensive damage was caused.   Full details of this achievement will be found in the Operations Reports on the night of 22/23rd August, 1918.

The work of the Independent Force has now become well known, and the enemy was the first to recognize its importance.   It was a great honour to have belonged to such a Force, and for the Squadron to come once again under the command of Major-General Sir Hugh Trenchard, with whom it had been so closely associated during the months it spent in the Northern sector of the Western front, when he was commanding the Royal Flying Corps in the field. We will always remember him as one who took a great interest in its career, and for his personal appreciation of its many successes. Amongst its successes may be here recorded the particularly fine effort of carrying out raids on no fewer than thirteen consecutive nights (eleven consecutive nights being its next best). This was accomplished in the latter part of July and early August, 1918. The strain upon pilots and observers who took part in these raids, and the exceptionally hard work which this entailed on the part of the ground personnel, makes its achievement rank as one of the best in the annals of the old Squadron.

This chapter will now be brought to a close with the Battle Honours so richly and deservedly earned. History will have recorded these battles amongst the greatest ever fought, and the old Squadron will rank amongst the greatest of the flying units in the world war.

BATTLE HONOURS

VIMY. April, 1917.
ARRAS. April to May, 1917.
MESSINES. June, 1917.
3rd Battle of YPRES culminating in the battle of
PASSCHENDALE. July to October, 1917.
AMIENS. April, 1918.
ST. MIHIEL. September, 1918.
ARGONNE. October to November, 1918.

To these Battle Honours must be added its one continuous battle against the heart of Germany, which stretched over a period of one year. The first to bomb Germany, it was also given the satisfaction of knowing that it was the last, for on the night of the armistice coming into force, the last machine to return from a raid was that of No. 100 Squadron.

The following are some of the largest industrial towns in Germany which were bombed by the Squadron :—FRANKFORT, MANNHEIM (LUDWIGSHAFEN), OFFENBERG, KAISERSLAUTERN, KARLSRUHE, SAARBRUCKEN (BURBACH WORKS), EHRANGE, TRIER.

One regret will always remain, that we were robbed at the last minute of being the first to have bombed BERLIN, preparations for which were almost completed when the Armistice was signed.

During the whole of its Active Service career on the Western Front, no fewer than two hundred and thirteen raids were carried out, with a total of one hundred and eighty-five tons of bombs dropped.

Approximately four hundred and fifty thousand rounds of machine-gun ammunition were expended during these raids.

A total of five enemy machines were brought down and probably destroyed.

The following messages were received at the termination of hostilities :—

THE KING'S MESSAGE :

The following message received by Lord Weir from His Majesty the King :—

" In this supreme hour of victory, I send greetings and hearty congratulations to all ranks of the Royal Air Force. Our aircraft have been ever in the forefront of the battle. Pilots and observers have consistently maintained the ever-changing fortunes of the day and in the war zone our dead have been always beyond the enemy's lines or far out at sea. Our far flung Squadrons have flown over home waters and foreign seas, the Western and Italian battle line, Rhineland, the Mountains of Macedonia, Gallipoli, Palestine, the Plains of Arabia, Sinai and Darfar. The birth of the Royal Air Force with its wonderful expansion and development will ever remain one of the most remarkable achievements of the great war. Everywhere by God's help, officers, men and women of the Royal Air Force have splendidly maintained our just cause and the value of their assistance to the Navy and Army and to home defence has been incalculable. For all their magnificent work, self-sacrifice and devotion to duty, I ask you on behalf of the Empire to thank them all."

100 SQUADRON

SECRETARY OF STATE TO THE AIR MINISTRY:

Following received from Lord Weir addressed to General Trenchard, begins :—

"On this historic occasion I shall be glad if you will convey to all ranks my deep and hearty congratulations at the glorious outcome of all their great efforts. I realise most keenly how arduous their work has been and the unexampled courage and endurance demanded from pilots and observers in the very special character of their work. Let them all remember and cherish the thought that they have each and all played a very considerable and quite definite part in bringing about the demoralisation of the enemy. Their glorious work will never be forgotten and their record as the only force which ever hit Germans in Germany will long endure."

GENERAL OFFICER COMMANDING INDEPENDENT AIR FORCE:

The following message was received from General Trenchard, General Officer Commanding Independent Air Force :—

"Am very sorry I cannot come and say Good-bye to you all. I am very proud to have commanded such fine Squadrons as you have shown yourselves to be. I wish you the best of luck in whatever you do in the future and shall always be pleased to see or hear from any of you. Good-bye and Good Luck.—H. Trenchard."

FROM G.O.C. 8th. Bde. R.A.F.

> 8th Brigade,
> R.A.F.,
> France, 17th Feb., 1918.

My Dear Burge,—

Now that demobilization is in progress and No. 100 Squadron will have no further opportunity of adding to its laurels during the present war, I should like to take this opportunity of congratulating you and all ranks of your Squadron on the splendid work they have done.

As the first British Night Bombing Squadron in France, No. 100 very soon earned a great reputation, which it has not only maintained, but has added to consistently up to the very last day of hostilities.

100 SQUADRON

It has been my good fortune to have had No. 100 Squadron under my command in the 9th Wing, 41st Wing, and the 8th Brigade and I shall never forget the courage and cheerful determination with which its members have carried out all operations assigned to them.

The recent tour of the objectives attacked by the 8th Brigade and the Independent Force, gives ample proof of the fine spirit displayed and also of the splendid results achieved in consequence.

The annals of 100 Squadron will be a fitting memorial to those who have given their lives for their country and will prove a source of inspiration, alike to those remaining in the service and to those returning to civil life.

The very best of luck to you all.

Yours sincerely,

C. Newall

Major W. J. Tempest, D.S.O., M.C.,

Commanded the squadron from 11th December, 1917, to 12th June, 1918.

OPERATION REPORTS

Date.—5/6th April, 1917.　　　　　　　*Objective.*—Douai Aerodrome.

Taking Part :—

Pilots.

Lieut. Holmes.
　　,,　Fenwick.
2nd-Lieut. Richards.
　　,,　　M. H. Butler.
　　,,　　Nock.
Capt. McClaughry.
2nd-Lieut. Chaplin.
Capt. Sowrey.
2nd-Lieut. L. Butler.
Capt. Collison.
Lieut. Scholte.

Observers.

2nd-Lieut. Young.
Corpl. Waite.
2nd Air Mech. Barnes.
2nd-Lieut. Housden.
　　,,　　　Harrington.
　　,,　　　Murch.
2nd Air Mech. Guyat.
　　,,　　　Hodson.
　　,,　　　Robb.
　　,,　　　Hawkins.
2nd-Lieut. Young.

Bombs Dropped.—128 20 lb. and 4 40 lb.

Results.—All bombs were dropped on and around hangars. Some very good shooting done. 4 sheds seen burning when last machine left.

Casualties.—One machine missing 2nd-Lieut. Richards, pilot ; 2nd Air Mech. Barnes, observer.

Date.—7/8th April, 1917.　　　　*Objective.*—Douai Railway Station and Sidings.

Taking Part :—

Pilots.

Lieut. Holmes.
Capt. McClaughry.
　　,,　Collison.
2nd-Lieut. Boret.
　　,,　　Worrall.
　　,,　　Marshall.
　　,,　　L. Butler.
　　,,　　Blayney.
Capt. Sowrey.

Observers.

2nd Air Mech. Ekins.
2nd-Lieut. Murch.

2nd Air Mech. Caplin.
1st Air Mech. Hunter.
Act.-Corpl. Waite.
2nd Air Mech. Robb.
2nd-Lieut. Housden.
2nd Air Mech. Crickmore.

Bombs Dropped.—96 20 lb. and 2 40 lb.

Results.—8 20 lb. on the Railway Station and Sidings, 6 20 lb. in neighbourhood of Station. 60 20 lb. on Aerodrome. O.K. hits on 3 Bessoneau Hangars. 22 20 lb. and 2 40 lb. dropped on Aerodrome. One hangar hit.

Casualties.—One machine missing 2nd-Lieut. L. Butler ; 2nd Air Mech. Robb, observer.

100 SQUADRON

Date.—8/9th April, 1917.　　　　　　*Objective.*—Douai. Arras Railway Line.

Taking Part :—

Pilot.　　　　　　　　　　　　　　*Observer.*

2nd-Lieut. Boret.　　　　　　　　2nd Air Mech. Caplin.

Bombs Dropped.—8 20 lb.

Results.—2 20 lb. on train.
　　　　6 20 lb. on lighted Railway Station.

Date.—9/10th April, 1917.

Objective.—Trains and Lighted Railway Stations in neighbourhood of Douai.

Taking Part :—

Pilots.　　　　　　　　　　　　　*Observers.*

Capt. McClaughry.　　　　　　　2nd-Lieut. Murch.
Lieut. Holmes.　　　　　　　　　　,,　　Housden.
2nd-Lieut. Boret.　　　　　　　　2nd Air Mech. Caplin.
Capt. Sowrey.　　　　　　　　　　　,,　　Crichmore.
Lieut. Worrall.　　　　　　　　　1st Air Mech. Hunter.
　,,　Fenwick.　　　　　　　　　2nd Air Mech. Lem.

Bombs Dropped.—40 20 lb.

Results.—O.K. hits on :—

　　1 train—thought to be passenger—wrecked.
　　1　,,　—goods—set on fire and wrecked.
　　1　,,　—supposed goods—believed derailed.
　　1　,,　—mixed goods and passenger.
　　Douai Station bombed and hit several times.

Remarks.—All machines returned safely. 3 had forced landings our side of the lines ; 2 due to snowstorms and 1 due to engine trouble. One of these pilots, Lieut. Fenwick and observer, 2nd Air Mech. Lem, landed originally well behind the enemy's lines, locality unknown, owing to losing bearings in a snowstorm. Pilot realised position, re-started engine and returned, but was driven down again by snowstorm this side of lines.

Date.—13/14th April, 1917.　　　　*Objective.*—Trains on Railways, radiating from Douai.

Taking Part :—

Pilots.　　　　　　　　　　　　　*Observers.*

2nd-Lieut. Boret.　　　　　　　　2nd Air Mech. Caplin.
　,,　　Nock.　　　　　　　　　2nd-Lieut. Harrington.
　,,　　Kemp.　　　　　　　　2nd Air Mech. Hawkins.
Lieut. Scholte.　　　　　　　　　Corpl. Airey.
2nd-Lieut. Marshall.　　　　　　1st Air Mech. Hunter.
　,,　　Blayney.　　　　　　　2nd Air Mech. Griffiths.

Bombs Dropped.—37 20 lb.

Results.—Train hit and derailed just N. of Douai.
　　8 bombs dropped on Railway Track between Vitry and Douai ; also on M.T. column in neighbourhood.
　　8 bombs dropped on Somain Station.

100 SQUADRON

Date.—17/18th April, 1917.   *Objective.*—Trains on Railway Lines, radiating from DOUAI.

Taking Part :—

Pilots.
2nd-Lieut. Nock.
,,   Kemp.
Capt. Collison.

Observers.
2nd-Lieut. Harrington.
2nd Air Mech. Hawkins.
—

Bombs Dropped.—25 20 lb. and 20 Pom-Pom shells fired.

Results.—1 train just East of DOUAI shelled by Pom-Pom. Hits observed on engine with
   apparent effect.
   One M.T. Park alongside a road near CANTIN, consisting of approximately 100 to
   200 vehicles, with head-lamps alight, bombed and struck. Destruction of some
   vehicles observed.
   Two M.T. Columns near BREBIERES bombed. Hits observed.

METZ-SABLON.   VIEW OF THE RAILWAY TRIANGLE.

Date.—23/24th April, 1917.   *Objective.*—Trains on Railway Lines, radiating from DOUAI.

Taking Part :—

Pilots.
2nd-Lieut. Nock.
,,   Kemp.
,,   M. L. Butler.
,,   Blayney.
,,   Chaplin.
Lieut. Harman.

Observers.
2nd-Lieut. Harrington.
2nd Air Mech. Crickmore.
2nd-Lieut. Housden.
2nd Air Mech. Griffiths.
,,   Guyat.
,,   Lem.

Bombs Dropped.—38 20 lb.

Results.—PON-A-VENDIN Station bombed. •
   Engine repair shop at side of railway line N.E. of LENS bombed.
   Railway track bombed and struck East of DOUAI; also East of LENS.
   One M.T. Column bombed on road running South from LENS. Hits reported.
   Supply Depot, presumably alongside the LENS-BREBIERES railway line, bombed with
   apparent effect.

Results.—One pilot flew almost an hour at a low altitude (about 500 to 800 ft.) over LENS
   and neighbourhood, causing apparently a stoppage of railway traffic.

100 SQUADRON

Date.—26/27th April, 1917.

Objective.—Trains and Railway Stations on the lines radiating from DOUAI.

Taking Part :—

Pilots.	*Observers.*
Lieut. Fenwick.	2nd Air Mech. Wise.
2nd-Lieut. Blayney.	,, Guyat.
,, Eccles.	,, Hawkins.
Lieut. Worrall.	1st Air Mech. Hunter,
2nd-Lieut. Kemp.	2nd Air Mech. Crickmore.
Lieut. Harman.	,, Lem.
2nd-Lieut. Bulter.	2nd-Lieut. Housden.

Bombs Dropped.—48 20 lb.

Results.—Two trains bombed, hit, derailed at BREBIERES.
One train bombed and hit, believed derailed near DECHY.
Edge of Station and M.T. Column alongside same bombed and hit.
Hits recorded on railway track at BREBIERES Junction.
Small convoy of M.T. vehicles on the ARRAS-CAMBRAI main road, bombed and hit.

Date.—29/30th April, 1917. *Objective.*—Trains on railways on lines, radiating from DOUAI.

Taking Part :—

Pilots.	*Observers.*
Lieut. Tempest.	2nd-Lieut. Murch.
Capt. Collison.	,, Housden.
,, McClaughry.	—
2nd-Lieut. Kemp.	2nd Air Mech. Crickmore.

Bombs Dropped.—32 20 lb.

Results.—8 bombs dropped on first Station N. of DOUAI believed DORIGNIES. Bombed from 100 ft.
8 bombs dropped on train just E. of OIGNIES, believed hit.
Train bombed, hit and rear portion of same believed derailed between DOUAI and SOMAIN.
Train bombed, hit, and rear portion derailed and piled up leaving sidings just E. of DORIGNIES.

Date.—2/3rd May, 1917.

Objective.—(1) VALENCIENNES Goods Station.
(2) Trains in Station or on lines radiating from SOMAIN Junction.

Taking Part :—

Pilots.	*Observers.*
Lieut. Holmes.	—
Capt. McClaughry.	—
2nd-Lieut. Boret.	—
Lieut. Tempest.	2nd-Lieut. Murch.
,, Harman.	,, Harrington.
2nd-Lieut. Eccles.	—
,, Chaplin.	—
,, Blayney.	—

Bombs Dropped.—8 112 lb. and 22 20 lb.

Results.—Large sheds at VALENCIENNES Goods Station hit, with 4 112 lb. bombs, 2 of which were seen to definitely explode with considerable success ; bombed from 500 ft.
2 Trains bombed, hit and piled up near SOMAIN Junction.
1 Train bombed, hit and derailed near CANTIN.
1 Train bombed, hit and derailed at the crossing just W. of ESCAUDIN.
In addition the main line between VALENCIENNES and SOMAIN was bombed with success, 1 112 lb. bomb falling in LA GOULES Station.

100 SQUADRON

Date.—3/4th May, 1917.

Objective.—Bombing trains and station on the route VITRY, BREBIERES, QUIERY, HENIN, LIBTARD, BILLY-MONTIGNY.

Taking Part :—

Pilots.	Observers.
Lieut. Worrall.	Corpl. Hunter.
2nd-Lieut. Eccles.	2nd Air Mech. Hawkins.
Capt. Sowrey.	—
2nd-Lieut. Butler.	2nd-Lieut. Housden.
,, Kemp.	2nd Air Mech. Caplin.
Lieut. Fenwick.	,, Wise.
Capt. Collison.	,, Ekins.

Bombs Dropped.—40 20 lb.

Results.—6 bombs dropped from a height of 1,000 ft., on sheds at LENS Station, hits observed.
    4 bombs dropped from a height of 100 ft. on train which was hit and believed derailed.
    4 bombs dropped from a height of 50 ft. on a train which was hit and derailed.
    2 bombs dropped from a height of 100 ft. on a train just S. of BEAUMONY.
    6 bombs dropped from 1,500 ft. on MERICOURT Station, which at the time had trains at rest in it with steam up, hits observed on trains.
    4 bombs dropped from 500 ft. on CARVIN Aerodrome.
    4 bombs dropped from 500 ft. on a train just N. of COURRIERES.

Date.—4/5th May. *Objective.*—Bombing of trains on lines radiating from DOUAI.

Taking Part :—

Pilot.	Observer.
Lieut. Fenwick.	2nd Air Mech. Wise.

Bombs Dropped.—8 20 lb.

Results.—One train hit and derailed.

Date.—6/7th May, 1917.   *Objective.*—DORIGNIES Aerodrome.

Taking Part :—

Pilots.	Observers.
Lieut. Tempest.	2nd-Lieut. Murch.
,, Worrall.	Corpl. Hunter.
2nd-Lieut. Boret.	2nd Air Mech. Caplin.
,, Prosser.	2nd-Lieut. Harrington.
,, Eccles.	,, Housden.
,, Kemp.	2nd Air Mech. Crickmore.
,, Nock.	,, Cuss.
Lieut. Harman.	,, Lem.

Bombs Dropped.—52 20 lb. and 6 40 lb.

Results.—42 bombs were dropped from an average height of 400 ft. and some of the hangars were seen to be ablaze, but an accurate report is impossible.
    2 or 3 bombs were dropped on a large factory near the Aerodrome, which caused a large fire.

Casualties.—One machine missing, 2nd-Lieut. Holmes, pilot; 2nd Air Mech. Ekins, observer. One pilot wounded, 2nd-Lieut. Eccles.

100 SQUADRON

Date.—9/10th May, 1917. *Objective.*—Dorignies Aerodrome.

Taking Part:—

Pilots.	*Observers.*
Capt. Collison.	—
Lieut. Worrall.	Act.-Corpl. Hunter.
Capt. Sowrey.	—
,, McClaughry.	—
2nd-Lieut. Blayney.	2nd-Lieut. Murch.
,, Boret.	2nd Air Mech. Caplin.

Bombs Dropped.—22 20 lb. and 4 112 lb. and 2 40 lb.
Results.—14 20 lb. and 4 112 lb. on Aerodrome, results unknown.
   8 20 lb. and 2 40 lb. on other targets.
Date.—11/12 May, 1917.

Objective.—Trains in movement on railway lines radiating from Douai.

Taking Part:—

Pilots.	*Observers.*
2nd-Lieut. Nock.	—
Lieut. Worrall.	Corpl. Hunter.
,, Tempest.	2nd-Lieut. Murch.

Bombs Dropped.—1 112 lb. and 16 20 lb.
Results.—8 20 lb. dropped from 500 ft. on a train on Douai-Seclin line, hits observed.
   8 20 lb. dropped on train on Lille-Tournai line.
   1 112 lb. from 1,500 ft. on a searchlight N.W. of Douai.

Date.—26/27th May, 1917.
Objective.—(1) St. Sauveur Station, Lille. (2) Don Railway Station.

Taking Part:—

Pilots.	
Lieut. Worrall.	—
2nd-Lieut. Boret.	—
,, Castle.	—
,, Harper.	—

Bombs Dropped.—8 112 lb.
Results.—8 112 lb. dropped on Don Station, results unobserved.

Date.—27/29th May, 1917.
Objective.—(1) St. Sauveur Station, Lille. (2) Don Railway Station.

Taking Part:—

Pilots.	*Observers.*
Capt. McClaughry.	—
2nd-Lieut. Kemp.	2nd-Lieut. Housden.
Lieut. Tempest.	,, Harrington.
2nd-Lieut. Castle.	2nd Air Mech. Wise.
,, Blayney.	—
,, Nock.	—
Lieut. Harman.	—
2nd-Lieut. Harper.	—
Lieut. Brooks.	—

Bombs Dropped.—1 230 lb., 15 112 lb., 2 40 lb, and 10 20 lb.
Results.—1 230 lb. dropped on St. Sauveur Station.
   Remainder on Don Station, causing a fire.
Remarks.—2nd-Lieut. Castle leading the raid, dropped his phos. bomb from 500 ft. with good
   effect. At this juncture he was wounded in the arm by a piece of Pom-Pom
   shell, but succeeded in bringing machine back to Aerodrome safely.
Casualties.—2nd-Lieut. Castle wounded.

100 SQUADRON

Date.—29/30th May, 1917.

Objective—Trains, Lighted Railway Stations on Railway Lines around LILLE.

Taking Part :—

Pilots.	Observers.
Capt. McClaughry.	Corpl. Hunter.
2nd-Lieut. Boret	—
,, Harper.	—
Capt. Sowrey.	—
,, Birley.	—
Lieut. Tempest.	—
,, Harman.	—
,, Worrall.	—

METZ-SABLONS.   SHOWING PORTION OF DAMAGE DONE ON NIGHT OF
24/25TH MARCH, 1918.

Bombs Dropped.—18 112 lb.

Results.—1 train bombed from 800 ft., hit and piled up near TRESSINS, on LILLE-TOURNAI
line.
1 train bombed, hit, from 800 ft. at WASQUEHALN, near LILLE.
1 Camp or Depot alongside railway line about half-way between LILLE and LA
BASSE, bombed and hit from 1,500 ft.
ASCQ Station bombed and hit with 2 bombs from 1,000 ft.
Aerodrome believed to be TOURMIGNIES, bombed from 500 ft.
1 bomb hit group of hangars, 1 bomb on group of active machine guns and
searchlights, which immediately ceased.
1 bomb on TOURNAI Railway Station, from 1,500 ft.

Remarks.—One pilot, Lieut. Worrall, landed and crashed his machine near STEENWERCK,
after having been wounded in forearm by a tracer bullet.

Casualties.—2nd-Lieut. Worrall wounded.

100 SQUADRON

Date.—31st May/1st June, 1917.

Objective.—(1) ORCHIES Goods Station and Sidings, (2) FAIENCERIES-ORCHIES.

Taking Part :—

Pilots.	Observers.
Capt. Sowrey.	—
,, McClaughry.	2nd-Lieut. Murch.
Lieut. Tempest.	—
2nd-Lieut. Blayney.	Corpl. Guyat.
,, Kemp.	1st Air Mech. Crickmore.
Lieut. Harman.	—
2nd-Lieut. Boret.	—
,, Nock.	—
,, Carpenter.	Corpl. Hunter.
,, Harper.	—
,, Chaplin.	2nd Air Mech. Hawkins.

Bombs Dropped.—1 230 lb., 20 112 lb. and 8 20 lb.

Results.—1 230 lb. and 8 112 lb. bombs dropped on FAIENCERIES, of which the former and 6 of the latter were direct hits.
    11 112 lb. bombs dropped on goods yard and sidings.

   TEMPLEUVE goods sidings bombed with six 20 lb. from 1,500 ft.

Remarks.—Several Pilots report having seen the 230 lb. explode with extreme violence in the FAIENCERIES, blowing out portions of the structure. 6 112 lb. followed from a lower altitude with visibly good effect.

Date.—2/3rd June, 1917.

Objective.—Trains on lines : LILLE-TOURNAI, LILLE-ROUBAIX-MOUSCRON, MOUSCRON-COURTRAI.

Taking Part :—

Pilots.	Observers.
Capt. Sowrey.	—
2nd-Lieut. Blayney.	2nd Air Mech. Hawkins.
,, Prosser.	Corpl. Guyat.
Lieut. Harman.	—
2nd-Lieut. Boret.	—
,, Carpenter.	Corpl. Hunter.

Bombs Dropped.—10 112 lb. and 8 20 lb.

Results.—2 bombs on train near COMINES.
    2 bombs on train near WERVICQ.
    2 bombs on train near LA MADELEINE.
    2 bombs on rolling stock at MENIN Station.
    2 bombs on cross roads at WARNETON.
    8 20 lb. from 1,500 ft. on a train near WASQUEHAL.

100 SQUADRON

Date.—3/4th June, 1917.

Objective.—Trains on LILLE-COMINES AND MENIN-COURTRAI lines. MENIN Station.

Taking Part :—

Pilots.	Observers.
Capt. Sowrey.	—
,, McClaughry.	—
2nd-Lieut. Nock.	—
,, Boret.	Corpl. Guyat.
,, Prosser.	—
Lieut. Harman.	2nd-Lieut. Stedman.
2nd-Lieut. Kemp.	1st Air Mech. Crickmore.
,, Harper.	2nd Air Mech. Hawkins.
,, Blayney.	2nd-Lieut. Murch.
,, Turnbull.	2nd Air Mech. Lem.
,, Carpenter.	—
,, Allan.	2nd Air Mech. Griffiths.

Bombs Dropped.—19 112 lb. and 12 20 lb.

Results.—Train (believed troop) bombed and wrecked from 1,500 ft., between QUESNOY and COMINES.
    2 112lb. bombs dropped on train in siding just south of QUESNOY.
    1 112 lb. bomb on AVELCHEN Junction.
    2 112 lb. bombs on COURTRAI Station from 600 ft., rolling stock hit, subsequent explosions seen.
    4 20 lb. bombs from 500 ft. on 2 trains in COURTRAI Station.
    10 112 lb. and 8 20 lb. were dropped on MENIN Goods Station and sidings from an average height of 800 ft. All bombs seen to explode on objective, which was apparently set on fire.

Remarks.—A reconnaissance was carried out over RUBAIX which proved very successful. Two pilots report that a number of explosions were produced by their bombs, followed by a volume of smoke in MENIN Station. A third pilot reports a large fire had broken out on his arrival. The occupants of the last two machines which passed over MENIN on their way to COURTRAI two hours later state that the Station was clearly on fire.

Date.—4/5th June, 1917.

Objective.—Trains on lines LILLE-COMINES, WERVICQ, MENIN-COURTRAI. Transport on the LILLE-COMINES Road. ROULERS Railway Station.

Taking Part :—

Pilots.	Observers.
2nd-Lieut. Harper.	Lieut. Lockhart.
,, Kemp.	,, Price.
Lieut. Harman.	,, Stedman.
2nd-Lieut. Boret.	—
,, Blayney.	,, McNaughton.
,, Turnbull.	Corpl Hunter.
Capt. Collison.	Lieut. Godard.
2nd-Lieut. Carpenter.	—

Bombs Dropped.—1 230 lb. and 14 112lb.

Results.—1 230 lb. and 6 112 lb. on ROULERS Station, direct hits.
    4 112 lb. dropped on trucks in COMINES Station, explosions seen.
    2 112 lb. dropped from 1,000 ft. on train between ROULERS and MENIN.

100 SQUADRON

Date.—5/6 June, 1917.

Objective.—WERVICQ Station and railway line to west of same. ROULERS Station. Trains on lines COURTRAI-MENIN, LILLE-COMINES, TOURCOING-MENIN.

Taking Part :—

Pilots.	Observers.
Capt. Sowrey.	—
,, McClaughry.	2nd-Lieut. Murch.
,, Collison.	Lieut. Godard.
2nd-Lieut. Blayney.	Corpl. Guyat.
,, Nock.	—
Lieut. Harman.	Lieut. Stedman.
2nd-Lieut. Carpenter.	—
,, Allen.	—
,, Kemp.	—
,, Harper.	2nd Air Mech. Hawkins.
,, Turnbull.	2nd-Lieut. Harrington.

Bombs Dropped.—21 112 lb. and 1 230 lb.

Results.—2 112 lb. bombs dropped from 1,500 ft. on a train between MOUSCRON and HEGNES.
    2 112 lb. from 700 ft. on trains entering MENIN Station.
    2 112 lb. on ROULERS Station.
    2 112 lb. on a train 1 mile north of ROULERS. Wrecked.
    2 112 lb. on a train near MENIN.
    2 112 lb. at a train at CROIX.
    2 112 lb. on a train at COURTRAI Junction.
    2 112 lb. on a train half-way between MENIN and ROULERS.
    1 230 lb. on WERVICQ Station.
    5 112 lb. in and around WERVICQ Station.

Date.—6/7th June, 1917.

Objective.—The following Stations :—COURTRAI, HALLUIN, INGLEMUNSTER, COMINES.

Taking Part :—

Pilots.	Observers.
Capt. Sowrey.	—
2nd-Lieut. Boret.	—
,, Nock.	—
Capt. McClaughry.	2nd-Lieut. Murch.
,, Collison.	Lieut. Godard.
2nd-Lieut. Turnbull.	2nd-Lieut. Harrington.
,, Blayney.	Lieut. McNaughton.

Bombs Dropped.—3 230 lb. and 8 112 lb.

Results.—1 230 lb. bomb from 2,600 ft. on WERVICQ Station.
    2 112 lb. bombs from 900 ft. on track close to WERVICQ Station.
    1 230 lb. bomb from 600 ft. on supply dump along WARNETON-COMINES line.
    2 112 lb. from 2,800 ft. on track and buildings near WARNETON Station.
    1 230 lb. bomb on QUESNOY Station.
    4 230 lb. bombs track 4 miles south-west of ROULERS from 2,000 ft.

100 SQUADRON

Date.—6/7th June, 1917.

Objective.—Bombing of WERVICQ, QUESNOY and WARNETON Stations.

Taking Part :—

Pilots.	Observers.
Capt. Sowrey.	—
2nd-Lieut. Boret.	—
,, Nock.	—
Capt. McClaughry.	2nd-Lieut. Murch.
,, Collison.	Lieut. Godard.
2nd-Lieut. Turnbull.	2nd-Lieut. Harrington.
,, Blayney.	Lieut. McNaughton.

Bombs Dropped.—3 230 lb. and 8 112 lb.

Results.—1 230 lb. dropped on supply dump between WARNETON and COMINES.
　　1 230 lb. dropped on WERVICQ Station from 600 ft.
　　1 230 lb. near QUESNOY Station.
　　2 112 lb. on hostile batteries just south of WARNETON from 1,200 ft.　Batteries ceased fire.
　　2 112 lb. on track 4 miles south-west of Roulers.
　　2 112 lb. on WERVICQ Station from 900 ft.
　　2 112 lb. on WARNETON Station.

Date.—7/8th June, 1917.

Objective.—Bombing of MENIN-COURTRAI-WARNETON Railway Stations.　Trains on lines :
　　MENIN-COURTRAI, MENIN-COMINES, MENIN-ROULERS.

Taking Part :—

Pilots.	Observers.
Capt. Collison.	Lieut. Thompson.
2nd-Lieut. Boret.	—
,, Prosser.	Lieut. Lockhart.
,, Harper.	,, Price.
,, Turnbull.	2nd-Lieut. Harrington.
,, Allen.	—
Lieut. Harman.	Lieut. Stedman.
2nd-Lieut. Blayney.	,, McNaughton.
,, Carpenter.	—
,, Stainer.	Corpl. Hunter.
Major Christie.	—
2nd-Lieut. Nock.	—
Capt. Sowrey.	—
,, McClaughry.	2nd-Lieut. Murch.

Bombs Dropped.—3 230 lb., 22 112 lb., and 8 20 lb.

Results.—12 112 lb. on MENIN Station.
　　2 112 lb. on COURTRAI Goods Yard.
　　3 230 lb. and 4 112 lb. on dump at WARNETON Station.　Dump exploded, seen and heard for miles around.
　　2 112 lb. on train leaving MENIN Station.
　　8 20 lb. on rolling stock in WERVICQ Station.

100 SQUADRON

Date.—8/9th June, 1917.

Objective.—Bombing of COURTRAI Station and Trains on COURTRAI-MOUSCRON line.

Taking Part :—

Pilots.	Observers.
2nd-Lieut. Nock.	—
,, Carpenter.	—
,, Boret	—
,, Prosser.	Leut. Stedman.
,, Harper.	,, Lockhart.
Capt. Collison.	2nd Air Mech. Hawkins.
,, Sowrey.	—

Bombs Dropped.—1 230 lb. and 12 112 lb.

Results—8 112 lb. bombs dropped in neighbourhood of COMINES Station.
    1 230 lb. on WARNETON-COMINES dump.
    2 112 lb. on WARNETON Station.
    2 112 lb. in neighbourhood of WARNETON Station.

Date.—26/27th June, 1917.   *Objective.*—PROVIN Aerodrome.

Taking Part :—

Pilots.	Observers.
Lieut. Tempest.	2nd-Lieut. Murch.
,, Harman.	Lieut. Stedman.
2nd-Lieut. Turnbull.	2nd-Lieut. Harrington.
Capt. Collison.	Lieut. McNaughton.
2nd Lieut. Richardson.	Corpl. Guyat.
,, Kemp.	Lieut. Price.
,, Borea.	—
,, Lewis.	Lieut. Thompson.
,, Kent.	2nd Air Mech. Lem.
Capt. Holland.	—

Bombs Dropped.—5 230 and 6 112 lb.

Results.—All bombs dropped on and around Aerodrome.   Visibility rendered observations difficult.

Date.—27/28th June, 1917.   *Objective.*—RECKEM Aerodrome.

Taking Part :—

Pilots.	Observers.
Capt. Holland.	—
2nd-Lieut. Lewis.	Lieut. Thompson.
,, Borea.	—
Lieut. Harman.	Lieut. Stedman.
2nd-Lieut. Kent.	2nd Air Mech. Hawkins.
,, Turnbull.	2nd Air Mech. Lem.
,, Prosser.	Sergt. Doyle.

Bombs Dropped.—12 112 lb.

Results.—10 112 lb. dropped on and around hangars. Results unknown.
    2 112 lb. dropped on MENIN Station from 800 ft. O.K. hit.
Casualties.—One Pilot, Capt. Holland, hit by A.A. and crashed and was rather burned by one of his phosphorus bombs exploding.

100 SQUADRON

Date.—2/3rd July, 1917.   *Objective.*—ENGEL Sidings and Sheds. LEUGENBOOM Gun.

Taking Part :—

Pilots.	Observers.
Capt. Sowrey.	—
Lieut. Tempest.	2nd-Lieut. Murch.
2nd-Lieut. Kemp.	Lieut. Price.
,, Richardson.	2nd-Lieut. Housden.
,, Lewis.	Lieut. Thompson.
,, Turnbull.	,, Stedman.
,, Kent.	Corpl. Hunter.
,, Boret.	—

Bombs Dropped.—7 230 lb. and 10 112 lb.

Results.—5 130 lb. and 6 112 lb. bombs dropped near Gun, but actual results cannot be definitely stated.

1 230 lb. and 2 112 lb. dropped on ENGEL Transport Shed. Results unobserved.

2 112 lb. dropped southern end of sidings.

1 230 lb. dropped on Sidings, direct hit.

Date.—3/4th July, 1917.

Objective.—RAMILIES CHIN Aerodrome.
CHATEAU DU SART Aerodrome.

Taking Part :—

Pilots.	Observers.
2nd-Lieut. Blayney.	Corpl. Guyat.
,, Lewis.	Lieut. Thompson.
,, Kent.	Corpl. Hunter.
,, Boret.	—
,, Turnbull.	Lieut. Stedman.
2nd-Lieut. Richardson.	Lieut. Housden.
Lieut. Tempest.	2nd-Lieut. Murch.
Capt. Collison.	Lieut. McNaughton.
2nd-Lieut. Prosser.	Sergt. Doyle.
Capt. Sowrey.	—

Bombs Dropped.—5 230 lb. and 10 112 lb.

Results.—1 230 lb. and 2 112 lb. dropped from 800 ft. on RAMILIES CHIN Aerodrome. Direct hit obtained by 1 112 lb. and hangar set on fire.

1 230 lb. dropped from 600 ft. on railway trucks N.E. of LILLE.

2 112 lb. dropped from 2,500 ft. on enemy communication trenches near FORT CARNOT.

1 230 lb. from 1,400 ft. on railway track near ASCQ.

2 112 lb. from 900 ft. on hostile aerodrome on which there were night flying lights visible.

2 112 lb. from 1,100 ft. on FORT CARNOT.

1 230 lb. from 900 ft. on hostile transport on main road leading Westwards from LILLE.

1 230 lb. on CHATEAU DU SART Aerodrome.

Date.—5/6th July, 1917.   *Objective.*—HEULE Aerodrome.

Taking Part :—

Pilots.	Observers.
Lieut. Tempest.	2nd-Lieut. Murch.
2nd-Lieut. Lewis.	Lieut. Thompson.

Bombs Dropped.—16 20 lb.

Results.—6 20 lb. dropped from 1,000 ft. on objective.

2 20 lb. dropped from 500 ft. on train half way between COURTRAI and ISEGHEM.

8 20 lb. dropped from 900 ft. on a train near WERVICQ.

100 SQUADRON

Date.—6/7th July, 1917.   *Objective.*—HEULE Aerodrome.

Taking Part :—

Pilots.	*Observers.*
2nd-Lieut. Carpenter.	Corpl. Hunter.
,, Nock.	—
,, Blayney.	Corpl. Guyat.
,, Kemp.	Lieut. Price.
Capt. Collison.	—
,, Sowrey.	—
2nd-Lieut. Turnbull.	Lieut. Stedman.
,, Kent.	2nd Air Mech. Lem.
,, Boret.	—
Lieut. Tempest.	2nd Air Mech. Murch.
2nd-Lieut. Lewis.	Lieut. Thompson.
,, Richardson.	2nd-Lieut. Housden.

Bombs Dropped.—1 230 lb. and 98 20 lb.

Results.—All the 20 lb. bombs were dropped on the objective, actual results unknown. Several pilots were confident that their bombs hit the hangars.

The 230lb. was dropped on BISSECHEN Aerodrome, which was lit up at the moment for night flying purposes.

Casualties.—One machine crashed. Pilot, 2nd-Lieut. Richardson and Observer 2nd-Lieut. Housden admitted to hospital injured.

Date.—7/8th July, 1917.   *Objective.*—BISSEGHEN Aerodrome.

Taking Part :—

Pilots.	*Observers.*
Capt. Sowrey.	—
2nd Lieut. Blayney.	Corpl. Guyat.
,, Kemp.	Lieut. Price.
,, Turnbull.	,, Stedman.
Lieut. Tempest.	2nd-Lieut. Murch.
Capt. Collison.	Lieut. McNaughton.
2nd-Lieut. Kent.	2nd Air Mech. Lem.
,, Lewis.	Lieut. Thompson.

Bombs Dropped.—4 230 lb, 6 112 lb. and 14 20 lb.

Results.—3 230 lb., 3 112 lb. and 14 20 lb. were dropped on objective.

1 230 lb. from 1,500 ft. on the railway track in front of a moving train between WERVICQ and MENIN.

2 112 lb. from 3,000 ft. on a hostile battery in action near LINSELLES.

1 112 lb. dropped from 1,200 ft. on railway track near WEVELGHEM.

100 SQUADRON

Date.—9/10th July, 1917.

Objective. HEULE Aerodrome.

Taking Part:—

Pilots.	Observers.
2nd-Lieut. Carpenter.	Corpl. Hunter.
,, Kent.	Sergt. Doyle.
,, Blayney.	Corpl. Guyat.
,, Boret.	—

Bombs Dropped.—4 230 lb. and 6 20 lb.

Results.—1 230 lb. and 2 20 lb. from 1,000 ft. on WARNETON.
  1 230 lb. and 2 20 lb. from 1,000 ft. on railway track N. of MENIN.
  1 230 lb. and 2 20 lb. from 2,000 ft. on railway junction N.W. of COMINES.
  1 230 lb. from 900 ft. on WERVICQ Station.

FRANKFURT.
RAIDED BY THE SQUADRON.

Date.—10/11th July, 1917.

Objective.—HEULE Aerodrome.

Taking Part:—

Pilots.	Observers.
2nd-Lieut. Kemp.	Lieut. Price.
Capt. Sowrey.	—
2nd-Lieut. Gaynor.	Corpl. Guyat.
Capt. Collison.	Lieut. McNaughton.
2nd-Lieut. Kent.	2nd Air Mech. Lem.
Lieut. Tempest.	2nd-Lieut. Murch.
2nd-Lieut. Turnbull.	Lieut. Stedman.
,, Duncan.	1st Air Mech. Crickmore.
,, Blayney.	Lieut. Godard.

Bombs Dropped.—6 230 lb., 4 112 lb. and 10 20 lb.

Results.—3 230 lb. and 6 20 lb. dropped on target at heights varying from 800 ft. to 1,500 ft.
  1 230 lb. believed to have fallen amongst the 6 large hangars at Eastern end of Aerodrome.
  1 230 lb. and 2 20 lb. dropped from 2,000 ft. on hangars on BISSEGHEN Aerodrome.
  1 230 lb., 4 112 lb. and 2 20 lb. from heights varying from 800 and 2,000 ft. on Railway Station, Sheds and permanent way round MENIN.
  1 230 lb. from 15,000 ft. on railway West of COMINES.

100 SQUADRON

Date.—11/12th July, 1917.

Objective.—RAMEGNIES CHIN Aerodrome and INGELMUNSTER Aerodrome.

Taking Part :—

Pilots.	*Observers.*
Capt. Collison.	Lieut. McNaughton.
2nd-Lieut. Kemp.	,, Price.
,, Carpenter.	Corpl. Hunter.
,, Boret.	—
,, Blayney.	Lieut. Godard.
,, Turnbull.	,, Stedman.
,, Kent.	Sergt. Doyle.
,, Duncan.	—
Capt. Schweitzer.	1st Air Mech. Crickmore.

Bombs Dropped.—7 230 lb., 4 112 lb. and 10 20 lb.

Results.—2 230 lb., 2 112 lb. and 2 20 lb. on RAMEGNIES Aerodrome from 1,200 ft.
3 230 lb., 2 112 lb. and 6 20 lb. on INGELMUNSTER Aerodrome.
2 230 lb. seen to have exploded close to hangars at Western end of Aerodrome, and
1 230 lb. near hangars at Eastern end.
1 230 lb. and 2 20 lb. from 2,000 ft. on MENIN.

Remarks.—Intelligence later state the one shed containing 12 machines completely destroyed at RAMEGNIES CHIN.

Date.—12/13th July, 1917.   *Objective.*—MOORSELE and RECKHEM Aerodrome.

Taking Part :—

Pilots.	*Observers.*
2nd-Lieut. Carpenter.	Corpl. Hunter.
Capt. Sowrey.	—
,, Schweitzer.	Corpl. Guyat.
2nd-Lieut. Turnbull.	Lieut. Stedman.
,, Blayney.	,, Godard.
,, Kemp.	,, Price.
,, Duncan.	2nd Air Mech. Cuss.
Lieut. Tempest.	2nd-Lieut. Murch.
2nd Lieut. Bean.	2nd Air Mech. Lem.
,, Lewis.	Lieut. Thompson.

Bombs Dropped.—7 230 lb., 4 112 lb. and 20 20 lb.

Results.—On MOORSELE, 2 230 lb. and 4 20 lb. dropped from heights varying between 800 and 1,500 ft.
On RECKHAM, 2 112 lb. dropped from 1,000 ft.
2 230 lb. and 2 20 lb. dropped on active hostile battery between WERVICQ and COMINES.
1 230 lb. and 2 20 lb. dropped from 1,500 ft. on HALLUIN.
1 230 lb. and 2 20 lb. dropped from 1,500 ft. on railway track between MOORSELE and LEDEGHEM.
1 230 lb., 2 112 lb. and 10 20 lb. dropped on Railway Tracks and Junctions round MENIN.

100 SQUADRON

Date.—13/14th July, 1917.   *Objective.*—HEULE and CHATEAU DU SART Aerodrome.

Taking Part :—

Pilots.	Observers.
2nd-Lieut. Blayney.	Lieut. Godard.
,, Nock.	—
,, Kent.	Sergt. Doyle.
,, Carpenter.	Corpl. Hunter.
,, Bean.	2nd Air Mech. Lem.
,, Boret.	—
,, Lewis.	Lieut. Thompson.
Capt. Schweitzer.	,, McNaughton.
2nd-Lieut. Duncan.	2nd Air Mech. Cuss.

Bombs Dropped.—9 230 lb. and 18 20 lb.

Results.—3 230 lb. and 6 20 lb. on WERVICQ Station.
  1 230 lb. on sheds alongside.
  3 230 lb. and 6 20 lb. on Station N. of LILLE and just S. of ST. ONORE.
  1 230 lb. and 4 20 lb. from 1,000 ft. on goods sorting station at LA MADELEINE
    Triangle N.E. of LILLE. Small fire started.
  1 230 lb. from 1,500 ft. on sheds alongside Railway Station at HALLUIN.
  1 230 lb. and 2 20 lb. from 1,500 ft. into large rest camp just N. of GHELUVELT,
    on MENIN-YPRES Road.

Date.—15/16th July, 1917.

Objective.—Bombing of Searchlight in 1st and 2nd Armies Area.

Taking Part :—

Pilots.	Observers.
Capt. Schweitzer.	Lieut. McNaughton.
Lieut. Tempest,	2nd-Lieut. Murch.
2nd-Lieut. Boret.	—
,, Kemp.	Lieut. Price.
,, Kent.	Sergt. Doyle.
,, Turnbull.	Lieut. Stedman.
,, Carpenter.	Corpl. Hunter.
,, Duncan.	2nd Air Mech. Cuss.
Capt. Sowrey.	—
Lieut. Nock.	—
2nd-Lieut. Lewis.	Lieut. Thompson.

Bombs Dropped.—2 112 lb. and 74 20 lb.

Results.—2 112 lb. and 68 20 lb. were dropped on and practically all the ammunition was
    fired at active searchlights or batteries in area of the LYS Valley, between
    COMINES and COURTRAI from heights varying between 200 and 2,000 ft.
  2 20 lb. from 1,500 ft. on LA MADELEINE Goods Yard.
  4 20 lb. from 1,500 ft. on transport near COMINES.

100 SQUADRON

Date.—23/24th July, 1917.　　　　　　　　　*Objective.*—MARCKE Aerodrome.

Taking Part :—

Pilots.	Observers.
2nd-Lieut. Kent.	Sergt. Doyle.
,,　　　Turnbull.	2nd-Lieut. Harrington.
,,　　　Lewis.	Lieut. Thompson.
Lieut. Harman.	,,　　Stedman.
2nd-Lieut. Duncan.	2nd Air Mech. Cuss.

Bombs Dropped.—5 230 lb. and 10 20 lb.

Results.—2 230 lb. and 4 20 lb. on a lighted portion of COMINES.
　　　　1 230 lb. and 2 20 lb. on railway S. of HALLUIN.
　　　　1 230 lb. and 2 20 lb. on active battery near ZANDVOORDE.
　　　　1 230 lb. and 2 20 lb. on a lighted camp close to RONCQ-HALLUIN road.　　In no
　　　　case could results be observed owing to intense darkness.

Date.—25/26th July, 1917.　　　　　　　　　*Qbjective.*—MARCKE Aerodrome.

Taking Part :—

Pilots.	Observers.
2nd-Lieut. Bean.	2nd Air Mech. Lem.
Lieut. Nock.	Lieut. Hilton.
2nd-Lieut. Wald.	—
,,　　　Bushe.	2nd Air Mech. Cuss.

Bombs Dropped.—1 230 lb. and 24 20 lb.

Results.—1 230 lb. slightly wide of hangars.
　　　　6 20 lb. on lighted sidings between MENIN and ROULERS, believed LEDEGHEM.
　　　　8 20 lb. on lights in vicinity of HALLUIN Station.
　　　　8 20 lb. on lighted Railway Tracks S.W. of MOUSCRON.
　　　　2 20 lb. on a searchlight near MENIN.

Date.—27/28th July, 1917.　　　　　　　　　*Objective.*—MARCKE Aerodrome.

Taking Part :—

Pilots.	Observers.
2nd-Lieut. Kemp.	Lieut. Price.
,,　　　Carpenter.	Corpl. Hunter.
,,　　　Bushe.	Lieut. McNaughton.
,,　　　Prosser.	Sergt. Doyle.
,,　　　Kent.	2nd Air Mech. Lem.
Capt. Schweitzer.	—

Bombs Dropped.—4 230 lb., 2 112 lb. and 8 20 lb.

Results.—1 230 lb. and 2 20lb. near hangars.
　　　　1 230 lb. and 2 20 lb. on large group of hutments outside GHELUWE, near YPRES-
　　　　MENIN Road.
　　　　1 230 lb. on CHATEAU DU SART Aerodrome from 1,200 ft.
　　　　2 112 lb. on what appeared to be hangars in vicinity of COURTRAI.
　　　　2 20 lb. on Transport lights N.E. of LILLE.

100 SQUADRON

Date.—28/29th July, 1917.

Objective.—MARCKE Aerodrome and Chateau. LEDEGHEM Station and MENIN Station.

Taking Part :—

Pilots.	*Observers.*
Capt. Sowrey.	—
,, Schweitzer.	—
2nd-Lieut. Kent.	Sergt. Doyle.
,, Bean	2nd Air Mech. Lem.
,, Blayney.	Lieut. Godard.
,, Prosser.	Sur. Homer.
,, Kemp.	Lieut. Price.
,, Duncan.	,, Edwards.
,, Turnbull.	,, Duncan, S.M.
Lieut. Harman.	Lieut. Stedman.
2nd-Lieut. Wald.	—
,, Lewis.	Lieut. Thompson.

Bombs Dropped.—11 230 lb., 2 112 lb. and 36 20 lb.

Results.—1 230 lb. on hangars from 1,000 ft.
   6 20 lb. near hangars from 1,000 ft.
   1 230 lb. on Chateau from 1,000 ft.
   1 230 lb. and 4 20 lb. on COURTRAI Station Sidings. Direct hits from 1,200 ft.
   5 230 lb. and 12 20 lb. on MENIN Station and Sidings.
   2 230 lb. and 12 20 lb. on LEDEGHEM Station, of which 1 230 lb. and 8 20 lb. believed hit target.
   2 112 lb. on the Ammunition and Petrol Dump alongside Sidings S. of LEDEGHEM Station from 800 ft. Large fire started.
   2 20 lb. on an Active Battery S.W. of HOUTHEM.

Date.—8/9th August, 1917.   *Objective.*—Enemy Aerodrome in the LYS Valley.

Taking Part :—

Pilots.	*Observers.*
Capt. Schweitzer.	
Lieut. Blayney.	Lieut. Godard.
,, H. E. Duncan.	,, Edwards.

Bombs Dropped.—2 230 lb., 2 112 lb. and 6 20 lb.

Results.—1 230 lb. and 4 20 lb. on the Village of DADIZEELE. Direct hit.
   1 230 lb. on hutments at MORSELE. Direct hit.
   2 112 lb. on hutments near GHELUWE. Fire started.

Date.—9/10th August, 1917.   *Objective.*—Enemy Aerodrome in LYS Valley.

Taking Part :—

Pilots.	*Observers.*
Lieut. Harman.	Lieut. Stedman.
2nd-Lieut. Turnbull.	,, Duncan, S.M.
,, Bean.	2nd-Lieut. Harper.
,, Bushe.	Lieut. McNaughton.
Lieut. Tempest.	2nd Lieut. Greenslade.
,, Nock.	Lieut. Hilton.
2nd-Lieut. Carpenter.	Corpl. Hunter.
,, Kent.	Sergt. Doyle.
,, Boret.	—
,, Kemp.	Lieut. Price.
,, Lewis.	,, Thompson.

100 SQUADRON

Bombs Dropped.—12 230 lb. and 52 20 lb.

Results.—4 230 lb. and 20 20 lb. on HEULE Aerodrome.   Several direct hits.   A fire started.
    4 230 lb. and 20 20 lb. on BISSEGHEM.   All in close vicinity of hangars.
    3 230 lb. and 12 20 lb. on MARCKE.   Four direct hits on hangars claimed.

Casualties—1 machine missing.   2nd-Lieut. Fulton, pilot; and 2nd Air Mech. Hawkins, observer.

Date.—10/11th August, 1917.

Objective.—1st raid : Trains and suitable targets in LYS Valley.   2nd raid : MOUVEAUX Aerodrome.

Taking Part :—

1st Raid.	2nd Raid.
Pilots.	*Pilots.*
2nd-Lieut. Carpenter.	2nd-Lieut. Bean.
,, Turnbull.	,, Kent.
Lieut. Harman.	,, Boret.
2nd-Lieut. Blayney.	,, Carpenter.
Lieut. H. E. Duncan.	Lieut. Harman.
2nd-Lieut. Wald.	2nd-Lieut. Bushe.
Lieut. Tempest.	,, Blayney.
,, Nock.	,, Kemp.
Capt. Schweitzer.	,, H. E. Duncan.
2nd-Lieut. Lewis.	,, Wald.
,, Bean.	Capt. Schweitzer.
,, Kent.	2nd-Lieut. Nock.
,, Boret.	,, Lewis.
Observers.	*Observers.*
Corpl. Hunter.	Lieut. Harper.
Lieut. Duncan, S.M.	Sergt. Doyle.
,, Stedman.	
,, Godard.	Corpl. Hunter.
,, Edwards.	Lieut. Stedman.
—	,, McNaughton.
Lieut. Greenslade.	,, Godard.
,, Hilton.	,, Price.
—	,, Edwards.
Lieut. Thompson.	—
,, Harper.	
Sergt. Doyle.	,, Hilton.
—	,, Thompson.

Bombs Dropped.—24 230 lb., 3 112 lb. and 112 25 lb.

Results.—8 230 lb., 2 112 lb. and 31 25 lb. on hangars and sheds at MOUVEAUX Aerodrome. Several believed direct hits.   Fire started.
    5 230 lb. and 10 25 lb. on WERVICQ Town, Dumps and vicinity of Station.   All hits, one caused rather heavy explosion.
    1 230 lb. and 17 25 lb. on COMINES.   All hits.
    2 230 lb., 1 112 lb. and 6 25 lb. on MENIN Town.
    2 230 lb. and 10 25 lb. on LINSELLES and Factory.   Hits observed.
    1 230 lb. and 6 25 lb. on LEDEGHEM Station.   Small fire started.
    2 230 lb. and 10 25 lb. on GHELUVE Village.   Some direct hits.
    2 230 lb. and 18 25 lb. on Railway Traffic near WESQUEHAL.
    1 230 lb. and 10 25 lb. on factory N. of TOURCOING.   Direct hit with 230 lb.

100 SQUADRON

Date.—12/13th August, 1917.　　　　*Objective.*—Trains and suitable targets in Lys Valley.

Taking Part :—

Pilots.	*Observers.*
2nd-Lieut. Carpenter	Corpl. Hunter.
,,　　Boret.	—
,,　　Wald.	—
,,　　Bean.	Lieut. S. M. Duncan.
,,　　Kemp.	,,　　Price.
,,　　Bushe.	,,　　McNaughton.
,,　　Nock.	,,　　Hilton.

Bombs Dropped.—7 230 lb. and 28 25 lb.

Results.—5 230 lb. and 18 25 lb. on WERVICQ.
　　　　2 230 lb. and 10 20 lb on Active Battery near COMINES.

Date.—13/14th August, 1917.

Objective.—1st raid : Trains and suitable targets in Lys Valley.　　2nd raid : Ascq Station and LEZENNES Aerodrome.

Taking Part :—

1st Raid.

Pilots.	*Observers.*
Capt. Schweitzer.	Corpl. Guyat.
2nd-Lieut. Wald.	—
Lieut. Duncan.	Lieut. Edwards.
2nd-Lieut. Kent.	Sergt. Doyle.
,,　　Alexander.	—
,,　　Carpenter.	Corpl. Hunter.
,,　　Lewis.	Lieut. Thompson.
,,　　Blayney.	,,　　Godard.

2nd Raid.

Pilots.	*Observers.*
Capt. Schweitzer.	Corpl. Guyat.
2nd-Lieut. Kent.	Sergt. Doyle.
Lieut. Tempest.	Lieut. Greenslade.
2nd-Lieut. Blayney .	,,　　Godard.
,,　　Lewis.	,,　　Thompson.
,,　　H. E. Duncan.	,,　　Edwards.
,,　　Kemp.	,,　　Price.
,,　　Bushe.	,,　　McNaughton.
,,　　Bean.	,,　　S. M. Duncan.
,,　　Carpenter.	Corpl. Hunter.
,,　　Nock.	,,　　Hilton.

Bombs Dropped.—19 230 lb. and 89 25 lb.

Results.—2 230 lb. and 10 25 lb. on ASCQ Station.　1 230 lb. direct hit.
　　　　6 230 lb. and 30 25 lb. on lights East of LILLE.
　　　　2 230 lb. and 10 25 lb. on lights West of LILLE.
　　　　1 230 lb. and 6 25 lb. on Railway Line near LEZENNES.
　　　　8 230 lb. and 33 25 lb. on lighted targets in Lys Valley.

100 SQUADRON

Date.—14/15th August, 1917.

Objective.—Trains and suitable targets in Lys Valley, Ascq Sidings, and Lezennes Aerodrome.

Taking Part:—

Pilots.	Observers.
Lieut. Nock.	Lieut. Hilton.

Bombs Dropped.—8 25 lb.

Results.—8 25 lb. on the Engine Workshops at Hellennes.

Date.—15/16th August, 1917.   *Objective.*—Roulers Station and Dump.

Taking Part:—

Pilots.	Observers.
Major Christie.	
2nd-Lieut. Kemp.	Lieut. Price.
,, H. E. Duncan.	,, Edwards.
,, Lewis.	,, Thompson.
,, Boret.	—
Capt. Schweitzer.	—
2nd-Lieut. Bushe.	Corpl. Guyat.
,, Alexander.	—
Lieut. Harman.	Lieut. Reece.
2nd-Lieut. Bean.	,, Harper.
,, Kent.	Sergt. Doyle.
,, Carpenter.	Corpl. Hunter.
Lieut. Tempest.	Lieut. Greenslade.

Bombs Dropped.—8 230 lb., 4 112 lb. and 58 25 lb.

Results.—1 230 lb. and 8 25 lb. on train entering Roulers Station.
  2 230 lb. and 7 25 lb. on Roulers Station.
  1 230 lb. and 5 25 lb. on Licherbelde Town.
  2 230 lb. and 7 25 lb. on Railway Line S. of Roulers.
  1 230 lb. and 13 25 lb. on Wervicq.
  8 25 lb. on Rest Billet at Houth.
  8 25 lb. on Hostile Batteries S.E. of Ypres.
  2 112 lb. on Roulers.

Date.—16/17th August, 1917.   *Objective.*—Courtrai Station. Three Raids.

Taking Part:—

Pilots.	Observers.
Capt. Schweitzer (3).	—
2nd-Lieut. Bean (3).	Lieut. Wallace (2).
Lieut. Harman (3).	,, Duncan, S. M. (3).
2nd-Lieut. Kemp (2).	,, Price, (2).
,, Carpenter (2).	2nd-Lieut. Reece (3).
,, Kent (2).	,, Harper (2).
,, Bushe (3).	Lieut. Godard (2).
,, Duncan, H. E. (3).	,, Edwards (2).
Capt. Tempest (3).	,, Greenslade (3).
2nd-Lieut. Boret (2).	—
,, Lewis (2).	,, Thompson (2).
Capt. Blayney (2).	,, Colbert (2).
2nd-Lieut. Nock (2).	2nd-Lieut. Allan.

88

100 SQUADRON

Bombs Dropped.—21 230 lb., 6 112 lb. and 152 25 lb.

Results.—1 230 lb., 4 112 lb. and 5 25 lb. on LEDEGHEM.
2 230 lb. and 18 25 lb. on MENIN Town. Large explosions seen.
3 230 lb. and 30 25 lb. on WERVICQ. Direct hits in Town.
5 239 lb., 2 112 lb. and 27 25 lb. on COURTRAI Station. Large fire started.
1 230 lb. and 13 25 lb. on COMINES.
1 230 lb. and 7 25 lb. on LILLE. Direct hit in centre of Town.
1 230 lb. and 13 25 lb. on MOORSLEDE Town.
8 230 lb. on DADIZELE.
2 230 lb. and 7 25 lb. on ROULERS.
1 230 lb. and 5 25 lb. on road between MENIN and YPRES.
1 230 lb. on 5 25 lb. on BECELAERE Road.
3 230 lb. and 22 25 lb. on GHELUVELT.

Date.—20/21st August, 1917.   *Objective.*—LEZENNES AERODROME. Two Raids.

Taking Part :—

Pilots.	Observers.
Capt. Blayney.	Lieut. Godard.
2nd-Lieut. Bean (2).	,, Wallace (2).
Lieut. Harman.	,, Duncan, S.M.
2nd-Lieut. Wells (2).	Corpl. Hunter (2).
,, Carpenter.	Lieut. Reece.
,, Kent.	,, Harper.
,, Duncan, H. E.	,, Edwards.
,, Bushe.	,, Colbert.
,, Boret.	—
,, Kemp.	,, Lunghi.
,, Lewis.	,, Hewitt.
,, Wald (2).	,, Thompson (2).
,, Alexander.	—
Capt. Schweitzer.	,, Hilton.

Bombs Dropped.—11 230 lb. and 70 25 lb.

Results.—11 230 lb. and 38 25 lb. on LEZENNES Aerodrome.
32 25 lb. on MENIN.

Date.—21/22nd, August, 1917.

Objective.—TURCOING Station, Factory and LEZENNES Aerodrome.

Taking Part :—

Pilots.	Observers.
2nd-Lieut. Wald.	Lieut. Matthews.
,, Boret.	
,, Lewis.	,, Lunghi.
,, Kemp.	,, Price.
Lieut. Harman.	Capt. Barry.
2nd-Lieut. Alexander.	—
,, Kent.	Lieut. Greenslade.
,, Carpenter.	,, Reece.
,, Wells.	Corpl. Hunter.
,, Nock.	Lieut. Hilton.
,, Bean.	,, Wallace.
,, Blayney.	,, Godard.
,, Bushe.	2nd-Lieut. Colbert.

Bombs Dropped.—10 lb. and 61 25lb.

Results.—3 230 lb. and 22 25 lb. on GARE DE FRANCE.
3 230 lb. and 16 25 lb. on LEZENNES Aerodrome. Several direct hits.
4 230 lb. and 23 25 lb. on Factory.

100 SQUADRON

Date.—22/23rd August, 1917.　　*Objective.*—COURTRAI Railway Sidings and LEDEGHEM.

Taking Part :—

Pilots.	Observers.
2nd-Lieut. Alexander.	—
,,　　　Boret.	—
,,　　　Duncan, H. E.	Lieut. Edwards.
,,　　　Kent.	,,　　Price.
,,　　　Wells.	,,　　Harper.
,,　　　Bean.	,,　　Wallace.
Capt. Schweitzer.	,,　　Hewitt.
Lieut. Harman.	Capt. Barry.
2nd-Lieut. Nock.	Lieut. Hilton.
,,　　　Lewis.	,,　　Thompson.
,,　　　Wald.	,,　　Matthews.
Capt. Blayney.	—

Bombs Dropped.—9 230 lb. 52 25 lb.

Results.—3 230 lb. and 12 25 lb. on LEDEGHEM.
　　　5 230 lb. 36 25 lb. on COURTRAI Sidings. Small fire caused.
　　　1 230 lb. and 4 25 lb. on hostile battery north of YPRES ; believed direct hit.

Date.—25/26th August, 1917.

Objective.—FROYEUNES CHATEAU, LEZENNES and MOUVEAUX Aerodrome.

Taking Part :—

Pilots.	Observers.
2nd-Lieut. Wells.	2nd Air Mech. Lem.
,,　　　Lewis.	Lieut. Thompson.
Lieut. Nock.	Capt. Scudamore.
2nd-Lieut. Duncan, H. E.	Lieut. Edwards.
Capt. Blayney.	,,　　Godard.
2nd-Lieut. Wald.	,,　　Hilton.
Capt. Schweitzer.	—
Lieut. Harman.	Capt. Barry.
2nd-Lieut. Bean.	Lieut. Wallace.
,,　　　Alexander.	—
,,　　　Kent.	,,　　Harper.
,,　　　Carpenter.	,,　　Reece.
,,　　　Bushe.	,,　　Colbert.
,,　　　Kemp.	—
,,　　　Boret.	—

Bombs Dropped.—5 230 lb., 6 112 lb. and 66 25 lb.

Results.—3 230 lb., 2 112 lb., and 32 25 lb. on MOUVEAUX Aerodrome.
　　　1 230 lb. and 22 25 lb. on LEZENNES Aerodrome.
　　　4 112 lb. on FROYEUNES Chateau. 1 112 lb. direct hit.
　　　1 230 lb. and 4 20 lb. on ASCQ Sidings. Direct hits with 4 20 lb.
　　　8 25 lb. on moving train, LILLE-COURTRAI.

100 SQUADRON

Date.—31st August—1st September, 1917.

Objective.—HUELE and LEZENNES Aerodromes.

Taking Part :—

1st Raid.

Pilots.	*Observers.*
Lieut. Harman.	Lieut. Reece.
2nd-Lieut. Wells.	2nd-Lieut. Boyle.
Capt. Tempest.	Capt. Barry.
2nd-Lieut. Wald.	Lieut. Matthews.
,, Nock.	,, Hilton.
,, Bean.	,, Wallace.
Capt. Sowrey.	—
2nd-Lieut. Alexander.	—
,, Turnbull.	,, Duncan, S. M.
2nd-Lieut. Duncan, H. E.	,, Edwards.
,, Bushe.	2nd-Lieut. Colbert.
,, Boret.	—

2nd Raid.

Pilots.	*Observers.*
2nd-Lieut. Alexander.	—
Lieut. Harman.	Lieut. Reece.
Capt. Tempest.	Capt. Barry.
2nd-Lieut. Wells.	2nd-Lieut. Boyle.
,, Nock.	Lieut. Hilton.
,, Bean.	,, Wallace.
,, Duncan, H. E.	,, Edwards.
,, Wald.	,, Matthews.
,, Turnbull.	,, Duncan, S. M.
,, Bushe.	,, Colbert.

Bombs Dropped.—21 230 lb., 2 112 lb. and 89 25 lb.

Results.--9 230 lb. and 36 25 lb. on LEZENNES Aerodrome. Several direct hits on hangars and workshops claimed.

    2 230 lb. and 5 25 lb. on HUELE Aerodrome. One direct hit on hangars with a 230 lb. claimed.

    1 230 lb. on MOUVEAU Aerodrome.

    1 230 lb. and 5 25 lb. on MOORSELE Aerodrome. Bombs exploded close to hangars.

    1 230 lb. and 3 25 lb. on ASCQ Aerodrome. One direct hit claimed.

    1 230 lb. on SECLIN Station. Direct hit.

    1 230 lb. and 3 25 lb. on ASCQ Station Sidings. Direct hits.

    2 112 lb. on TOURNAI Station. Direct hit on rolling stock, and fire started.

    1 230 lb. and 5 25 lb. on lighted factory north of COURTRAI.

    1 230 lb. and 2 25 lb. on railway junction west of MENIN Station.

    1 230 lb. and 2 25 lb. on Engine Repair Shops at HELLEMMES. One hit large shed, remainder fell on sidings.

    1 230 lb. and 3 25 lb. on Junction south-east of LILLE.

    1 230 lb. on WARVIN Station.

    12 25 lb. on trains around LILLE. In two cases, trains pulled up dead.

    12 25 lb. on lights and searchlights around LILLE.

100 SQUADRON

Date.—1/2nd September, 1917.　　　　　*Objective.*—Mouveaux Aerodrome.

Taking Part :—

Pilots.	Observers.
Capt. Schweitzer.	—
2nd-Lieut. Turnbull.	Lieut. Duncan.
,,　Duncan, H. E.	,,　Edwards.
,,　Nock.	,,　Hilton.
,,　Wald.	,,　Matthews.
,,　Kent.	,,　Harper.
,,　Bean.	,,　Wallace.
,,　Wells.	,,　McNaughton.
,,　Bushe.	,,　Colbert.

Bombs Dropped.—2 112 lb. and 64 25 lb.

Results.—2 112 lb. and 50 25 lb. on sheds and buildings at Mouveaux Aerodrome ; results mainly unknown, but several direct hits claimed.
4 25 lb. on Quesnoy Station Sidings.
2 25 lb. on St. Andre Station Sidings.
8 25 lb. on La Madeleine Triangular Junction.

Date.—2/3rd September, 1917.　　　　　*Objective.*—Ramegnies Chin.

Taking Part :—

1st Raid.

Pilots.	Observers.
Lieut. Duncan.	Lieut. Edwards.
,,　Harman.	,,　Stedman.
2nd-Lieut. Kent.	,,　Harper.
,.　Kemp.	,,　Lunghi.
,,　Bean.	,,　Wallace.
Capt. Tempest.	Lieut. Colbert.
2nd-Lieut. Bushe.	Capt. Barry.
,,　Nock.	,,　Hilton.
Capt. Schweitzer.	,,　McNaughton
2nd-Lieut. Kent.	,,　Harper.
,,　Wald.	Capt. Scudamore.
,,　Boret.	—
,,　Alexander.	—

2nd Raid.

Pilots.	Observers.
Capt. Schweitzer.	Lieut. McNaughton.
Lieut. Harman.	Lieut. Stedman.
2nd-Lieut. Turnbull.	,,　Duncan.
,,　Nock.	,,　Hilton.
.,　Kemp.	,,　Lunghi.
Bushe.	,,　Colbert.
Capt. Sowrey.	—
Capt. Tempest.	Capt. Barry.

Results.—13 230 lb. and 24 25 lb. on workshops and hangars at Ramegnies Chin. Several direct hits recorded.

Bombs Dropped.—22 230 lb. and 40 25 lb.
4 230 lb. and 108 25 lb. on hangars at Chateau du Sart.
2 230 lb. and 2 25 lb. on Lezennes Aerodrome. Believed direct hits with 2 230 lb.
1 230 lb. and 2 25 lb. on lighted flares at Ascq Aerodrome.
1 230 lb. and 2 25 lb. on lighted Aerodrome near Menin.
1 230 lb. and 2 25 lb. on Fort Carnot, near Lille. Direct hit.

100 SQUADRON

MUSEUM TRIER (TREVES) DESTROYED.

Date.—3/4th September, 1917.

Objective.—FAMARS, HEULE and LEZENNES Aerodromes, ASCQ Sidings.

Taking Part:—

Pilots.	Observers.
2nd-Lieut. Kent.	Lieut. Harper.
,, Bean.	,, Wallace.
Lieut. Harman.	,, Stedman.
Capt. Tempest.	Capt. Barry.
2nd-Lieut. Duncan, H. E.	Lieut. Edwards.
,, Wald.	,, Hilton.
,, Turnbull.	,, Duncan, S. M.
Capt. Schweitzer.	,, McNaughton.
2nd-Lieut. Bushe.	,, Colbert.
Capt. Tempest.	Capt. Barry.
2nd-Lieut. Kemp.	Lieut. Lunghi.

Bombs Dropped.—11 230 lb. and 54 25 lb.

Results.—1 230 lb. and 5 25 lb. on hangar at FAMARS. Direct hits.
     1 230 lb. and 2 25 lb. on LEZENNES Aerodrome. Direct hit with 230 lb.
     3 25 lb. on moving trains outside ASCQ Sidings.
     3 25 lb. on moving trains outside Ascq Sidings. Direct hits from 700 ft.
     1 230 lb. and 19 25 lb. on hangars at HUELE.
     1 230 lb. and 5 25 lb. on Camp between LILLE and WAMBRECAIES.

100 SQUADRON

Date.—4/5th September, 1917.

Objective.—Famars Aerodrome, Aerodromes South of Lys Valley and Somain Sidings.

Taking Part :—

Pilots.	Observers.
2nd-Lieut. Boret.	—
Capt. Schweitzer.	Lieut. Hyde.
2nd-Lieut. Kemp.	,, Lunghi.
Capt. Tempest.	Capt. Barry.
2nd-Lieut. Kent.	Lieut. Harper.
,, Turnbull.	,, Duncan, S. M.
,, Bushe.	,, Colbert.
,, Bean.	,, Wallace.
,, Wald.	,, Hilton.
,, Duncan, H. E.	,, Edwards.
Lieut. Harman.	,, Stedman.

Bombs Dropped.—9 230lb., 4 112 lb. and 39 25 lb.

Results.—4 112 lb. on hangars at Famars.
2 230 lb. and 10 25 lb. on hangars at Ramegines Chin.
2 230 lb. and 10 25 lb. on Somain Junction Sidings and Dump, the large bombs exploded direct on sidings.
1 230 lb. and 5 25 lb. on Mouveaux hangars.
2 230 lb. and 9 25 lb. on Lezennes hangars.
1 230 lb. and 5 25 lb. on sidings and junction between Douai-Somain.

Date.—5/6th September, 1917.

Objective.—Lighted Aerodromes in Areas Lys Valley and Lille-Tourcoing.

Taking Part :—

Pilots.	Observers.
2nd-Lieut. Wells.	Lieut. Carroll.
,, Turnbull.	,, Duncan.
,, Boret.	—
,, Bean.	,, Wallace.
,, Kent.	,, Harper.
,, Kemp.	,, Lunghi.

Bombs Dropped.—44 25 lb.

Results.—8 25 lb. on hangars at Lezennes.
8 25 lb. on lights (Aerodrome or Dump near Moorsele).
8 25 lb. on lights at Bisseciiem Aerodrome.
12 25 lb. on goods traffic in La Madeleine Triangle. A considerable fire started.
8 25 lb. on Comines Station.

Date.—9/10th September, 1917.

Objective.—Aerodromes in and to south of Lys Valley.

Taking Part :—

Pilots.	Observers.
2nd-Lieut. Bushe.	Lieut. Colbert.
Capt. Schweitzer.	—
2nd-Lieut. Boret.	—

Bombs Dropped.—19 25 lb.

Results.—8 25 lb. on Aerodrome in vicinity of Ascq.
8 25 lb. on searchlights west of Roubaix.
3 25 lb. on flares of Mouveaux Aerodrome.

94

100 SQUADRON

Date.—10/11th September, 1917.   *Objective.*—Aerodromes in and South of Lys Valley.

Taking Part :—

Pilots.	Observers.
2nd-Lieut. Kent.	Lieut. Harper.
,, Wells.	,, Pitman.
,, Duncan, H. E.	,, Edwards.
,, Kemp.	—
,, 'Bean.	,, Wallace.
Capt. Harman.	,, Stedman.
2nd-Lieut. Turnbull.	,, Duncan.
,, Alexander.	—

Bombs Dropped.—58 25 lb.

Results.—2 25 lb. on lighted Aerodrome in vicinity of COURTRAI, believed MARCKE.
36 25 lb. on Searchlights in the vicinity of COURTRAI.
12 25 lb. on Searchlights N.E. of LILLE.
8 25 lb. on active enemy battery near QUESNOY.

Date.—11/12th September, 1917.

Objective.—BISSEGHEM Dump and Lighted Stations and Trains S. of LYS Valley.

Taking Part :—

Pilots.	Observers.
2nd-Lieut. Turnbull.	Lieut. Duncan.
Capt. Harman.	,, Stedman.
2nd-Lieut. Boret.	—
,, Wald.	Capt. Scudamore.
,, Kent.	Lieut. Harper.
,, Duncan, H. E.	,, Edwards.
,, Bushe.	,, Colbert.
,, Bean.	,, Wallace.
,, Wells.	,, Pitman.
,, Kemp.	,, Lunghi.
,, Bushe, L. A.	—
Capt. Schweitzer.	—
2nd-Lieut. Morley.	—

Bombs Dropped.—3 320 lb., 6 112 lb., 4 40 lb. and 60 25 lb.

Results.—6 112 lb., 4 40 lb. and 24 25 lb. on BISSEGHEM Dump. Many hits, but no visible destruction.
3 320 lb. and 7 25 lb. on ASQC Sidings. All believed direct hits, but no fire seen to result.
5 25 lb. on moving train on LILLE-TOURNAI line near ASQC. Hits claimed, bombs appeared to burst right on the line.
8 25 lb. on railway track LILLE-TOURNAI near ASCQ.
8 25 lb. on Aerodrome in LYS Valley, showing red and white lights believed MARCKE or BISSEGHEM.
8 25 lb. on active battery near LEMPRETT.

100 SQUADRON

Date.—12/13th September, 1917.   *Objective.*—BISSEGHEM DUMP.

Taking Part :—

Pilots.	Observers.
2nd-Lieut. Turnbull.	Lieut. Duncan, S. M.
,, Alexander.	—
,, Kent.	,, Harper.
,, Wald.	Capt. Scudamore.
,, Bushe, L. A.	—
,, Wells.	Lieut. Pitman.

Bombs Dropped.—2 230 lb., 2 112 lb., 2 40 lb. and 28 25 lb.

Results.—2 112 lb., 2 40 lb. and 16 25 lb. on Searchlights and A.A. Batteries in the LYS VALLEY.
2 230 lb., 12 25 lb. on large active hostile batteries near GHELUVELT or BECELAERE.

Date.—19/20th September, 1917.   *Objective.*—Enemy's Billets at RUMBEKE and HOOGLEDE.

Taking Part :—

Pilots.	Observers.
Capt. Tempest.	Capt. Barry.
2nd-Lieut. Alexander.	—
,, Carpenter.	Lieut. Reece.
,, Lewis.	,, Lunghi.
,, Wells.	,, Pitman.
,, Kemp.	Capt. Scudamore.

Bombs Dropped.—5 230 lb. and 21 25 lb.

Results.—4 230 lb. and 11 25 lb. on RUMBEKE Village. Several direct hits.
1 230 lb. and 10 25 lb. on HOOGLEDE Village. Several direct hits.

Date.—20/21st September, 1917.   *Objective.*—MENIN Road and Transport on same.

Taking Part :—

Pilots.	Observers.
2nd-Lieut. Duncan, H. E.	2nd-Lieut. Boyle.
,, Wald.	Lieut. Hilton.
,, Bean.	2nd-Lieut. Wallace.
Lieut. Windsor.	—
,, Harman.	Lieut. Stedman.
,, Turnbull.	,, Duncan, S. M.
2nd-Lieut. Bushe, J. F.	2nd-Lieut. Colbert.
,, Bushe, L. A.	Lieut. Hyde.
,, Morley.	—
,, Carpenter.	2nd-Lieut. Reece.
,, Boret.	—
,, Wells.	Lieut. Pitman.
,, Lewis.	,, Thompson.
,, Cudemore.	,, Greenslade.

Bombs Dropped.—6 230 lb., 8 112 lb. and 42 25 lb.

Results.—5 230 lb., 6 112 lb. and 16 25 lb. on MENIN. Several direct hits in town, fires caused.
2 112 lb. on GHELUWE.
1 230 lb and 18 25 lb. on WERVICQ.
8 25 lb. on LEDEGHEM.

100 SQUADRON

Date.—21/22nd September, 1917.   *Objective.*—MENIN Station.

Two Raids.

Taking Part:—

Pilots.	Observers.
2nd-Lieut. Bean (2).	Lieut. Wallace (2).
,, Wald (2).	,, Hilton (2).
,, Lewis (2).	2nd-Lieut. Lunghi.
,, McCreath (2).	—
,, Carpenter (2).	,, Reece.
,, Turnbull (2).	Lieut. Duncan, S. M. (2).
,, Bushe, J. F. (2).	2nd-Lieut. Colbert (2).
,, Bushe, L. A. (2).	Lieut. Hyde (2).
,, Aryton.	2nd-Lieut. Boyle.
,, Archibald.	—
,, Cudemore.	Lieut. Greenslade.
Lieut. Windsor (2).	—
,, Kemp (2).	Capt. Scudamore (2).
,, 2nd-Lieut. Wells (2).	Lieut. Pitman (2.
Lieut. Tempest.	Capt. Barry.
2nd-Lieut. Morley (2).	
,, Boret (2).	—
Lieut. Harman (2).	Lieut. Stedman (2).

Bombs Dropped.—30 230 lb., 2 112 lb., 1 40 lb. and 115 25 lb.

Results.—20 230 lb., 2 112 lb., 1 40 lb. and 75 25 lb. on and around MENIN Station. Several fires caused.

10 230 lb. and 50 25 lb. on WERVICQ. Large fires caused in town.

Date.—22/23rd September, 1917.

Objective.—MENIN Station, WERVICQ Station and following Roads :—GHELUVELT-MENIN, GHELUVELT-WERVICQ.

Taking Part:—

Pilots.	Observers.
2nd-Lieut. Morley.	—
,, McCreath.	—
,, Duncan, H. E.	Lieut. Price.
,, Archibald.	—
Lieut. Windsor,	—
2nd-Lieut. Aryton.	2nd-Lieut. Boyle.
Capt. Tempest.	Capt. Barry.
2nd-Lieut. Wald.	Lieut. Hilton.
,, Bushe, J. F.	,, Colbert.
,, Bushe, L. A.	,, Hyde.
,, Wells.	,, Pitman.
,, Kemp.	Capt. Scudamore.
,, Turnbull.	Lieut. Duncan, S. M.
,, Bean.	,, Wallace.
,, Carpenter.	,, Reece.

Bombs Dropped.—14 230 lb., 8 40 lb. and 41 25 lb.

Results.—7 230 lb. and 6 40 lb. on WERVICQ Town and Station. Small fire caused.

6 230 lb. and 13 25 lb. on MENIN Town and Station.

1 230 lb. and 25 25 lb. on main cross roads GHELUVELT-MENIN and GHELUVELT-WERVICQ.

G

100 SQUADRON

Date.—25/26th September, 1917.

Objecive.—MENIN, WERVICQ and Transport and Troops on and Billets alongside of the roads between MENIN-GHELUVELT, WERVICQ-GHELUVELT, and WERVICQ-ZANDVOORDE.

Two Raids.

Taking Part:—

Pilots.	Observers.
Capt. Tempest (2).	Capt. Barry (2).
2nd-Lieut. Boret.	—
,, Wald (2).	Lieut. Hilton (2).
,, Bean (2).	,, Wallace (2).
,, Duncan, H. E. (2)	—
,, Turnbull (2).	,, Duncan, S.M. (2).
,, Wells (2).	,, Pitman (2).
,, Morley.	—
,, Lewis.	,, Thompson.
Capt. Harman (2).	,, Stedman (2).
Lieut. Windsor (2).	,, Price.
2nd-Lieut. Carpenter (2).	,, Reece (2).
,, Aryton.	2nd-Lieut. Boyle.
,, Bushe, L. A. (2).	Lieut. Hyde (2).
,, Kemp.	Capt. Scudamore.
,, McCreath.	—
,, Archibald.	

Bombs Dropped.—23 230 lb., 4 112 lb. and 140 25 lb.

Resuls.—8 230 lb. and 25 25 lb. on WERVICQ Town and Station. All direct hits.
    6 230 lb., 2 112 lb. and 32 25 lb. on MENIN Town and Station. All direct hits. Fire started in Station.
    1 230 lb. and 3 25 lb. on GHELUVELT Village. Direct hits.
    6 25 lb. on MENIN-GHELUVELT Road.
    3 25 lb. on BECELACRE Village. Direct hit.
    8 230 lb., 2 112 lb. and 70 25 lb. on WERVICQ-GHELUVELT Road, WERVICQ-ZANDVOORDE Road.

Date.—26/17th September, 1917.   *Objective.*—WERVICQ Station.

Taking Part:—

Pilots.	Observers.
2nd-Lieut. Boret.	—
,, Wald.	Lieut. Hilton.
,, Morley.	—

Bombs Dropped.—3 230 lb. and 7 25 lb.

Results.—3 230 lb. and 7 25 lb. on WERVICQ Town and Station. Direct hits.

100 SQUADRON

Date.—27/28th September, 1917.

Objective.—MENIN Station, WEVELGHEM Station and LEDEGHEM Station.

Two Raids.

Taking Part :—

Pilots.	Observers.
Capt. Harman (2).	Lieut. Stedman (2).
2nd-Lieut. Kemp.	Capt. Scudamore.
Capt. Tempest.	,, Barry.
2nd-Lieut. Lewis (2).	Lieut. Thompson (2).
,, McCreath.	—
,, Wald (2).	,, Hilton (2).
,, Carpenter (2).	,, Reece (2).
,, Bean.	,, Wallace.
,, Bushe, J. F.	,, Colbert.
,, Turnbull (2).	,, Duncan, S. M. (2).
,, Duncan, H. E. (2).	—
,, Aryton (2).	,, Samson (2).
,, Boret.	—
Lieut. Windsor.	Capt. Scudamore.
2nd-Lieut. Wells.	Lieut. Pitman.
,, Morley.	
,, Archibald.	

Bombs Dropped.—18 230 lb., 8 112 lb. and 105 25 lb.

Results.—8 230 lb., 6 112 lb. and 42 25 lb. on LEDEGHEM. Practically all of which hit the Station or Buildings in vicinity of same.

6 230 lb., 2 112 lb. and 37 25 lb. on MENIN. Practically all of which hit the Station or Buildings and Sidings alongside same.

4 230 lb. and 18 25 lb. on WEVELGHEM. All fell on Station or near to same in village.

6 25 lb. on RONCQ.

2 25 lb. on DADIZELLE Village. Direct hits.

Date.—28/29th September, 1917. *Objective.*—GONTRODE Airship Shed.

Taking Part :—

Pilots.	Observers.
2nd-Lieut. Bushe, J. F.	Lieut. Colbert.
Lieut. Windsor.	Capt. Scudamore.
2nd-Lieut. Lewis.	Lieut. Thompson.
,, Turnbull.	,, Duncan, S. M.
,, Wells.	,, Pitman.
,, Barnes.	2nd-Lieut. Boyle.
,, Aryton.	Lieut. Samson.
,, McCreath.	—
,, Morley.	—
,, Carpenter.	Lieut. Reece.
,, Bean.	,, Wallace.
,, Cudemore.	,, Greenslade.

Bombs Dropped.—11 230 lb., 2 40 lb., 2 112 lb. and 33 25 lb.

Results.—7 230 lb., 1 40 lb. and 33 25 lb. on GONTRODE.

4 230 lb. and 1 40 lb. on ST. DENIS WESTREM.

100 SQUADRON

Date.—29/30th September, 1917.   *Objective.*—GONTRODE Airship Shed.

Taking Part :—

Pilots.	Observers.
2nd-Lieut. Carpenter.	Lieut. Reece.
,, Turnbull.	,, Duncan, S. M.
Capt. Harman.	,, Stedman.
,, Schweitzer.	—
2nd-Lieut. Wald.	,, Hilton.
,, . Bean.	,, Wallace.
,, Morley.	—
Lieut. Windsor.	Capt. Scudamore.
2nd-Lieut. Boret.	—
,, Kent.	Lieut. Harper.
,, Barnes.	2nd-Lieut. Boyle.
,, Archibald.	—
.. ,, McCreath.	—

Bombs Dropped.—10 230 lb., 6 112 lb., 2 40 lb. (phos.) and 23 25 lb.

Results.—4 230 lb., 4 112 lb., 2 40 lb. and 4 25 lb. on GONTRODE.   Results unknown.
 5 230 lb. and 13 25 lb. on COURTRAI Station. Small fire started.
 1 230 lb. and 6 25 lb. on Hutments at HALLUIN. All direct hits.
 2 112 lb. on MENIN Station. Bombs fell close.

Date.—30th September/1st October, 1917.

Objective.—GONTRODE Airship Shed, COURTRAI Station, Sidings and Trains in vicinity.

Taking Part :—

Pilots.	Observers.
2nd-Lieut. Carpenter.	Lieut. Reece.
Lieut. Windsor.	Capt. Scudamore.
Capt. Schweitzer.	—
2nd-Lieut. Wells.	Lieut. Pitman.
,, Boret.	—
,, Barnes.	2nd-Lieut. Boyle.
,, Wald.	Lieut. Hilton.
,, Bean.	,, Wallace.
Capt. Tempest.	,, Samson.
2nd-Lieut. Kent.	,, Harper.
. ,, Archibald.	—

Bombs Dropped.—9 230 lb., 2 112 lb., 2 40 lb. and 28 25 lb.

Results.—2 230 lb., 2 112 lb., 2 40 lb. and 2 25 lb. on GRONTRODE.... Several direct hits
 claimed.
 5 230 lb. and 8 25 lb. on COURTRAI Station. Large fire started amongst the traffic
 in the Goods Station.
 12 25 lb. on BISSEGHEM Dump.
 1 230 lb. and 2 25 lb. N. of WERVICQ.
 4 25 lb. on train W. of COURTRAI.

Casualties.—One machine, pilot, 2nd-Lieut. Bushe and Lieut. Colbert, observer, missing.
 One pilot wounded. 2nd-Lieut. Bean was hit in leg by bullet.

100 SQUADRON

Date.—24/25th October, 1917,

Objective.—Trains, Junctions, Stations and Goods Sidings on Railway line between FALKEN-BERG and SAARBRUCKEN.

Taking Part :—

Pilots.	Observers.
2nd-Lieut. Morley.	Lieut. Price.
,, Wald.	Capt. Barry.
,, Carpenter.	Lieut. Reece.
Lieut. Barnes.	2nd-Lieut. Boyle.
2nd-Lieut. Drummond.	Lieut. Wallace.
,, Kent.	,, Harper.
,, Parnell.	,, Samson.
Lieut. Windsor.	,, Lunghi.
2nd-Lieut. Wells.	,, Pitman.
,, Jackson.	2nd Air Mech. Guyat.
,, Duncan, H. E.	Lieut. Edwards.
,, Reed.	,, Duncan.

Bombs Dropped.—12 230 lb. and 23 25 lb.

Results.—1 230 lb. and 2 25 lb. on Railway Junction W. of SAARBRUCKEN.
   1 230 lb. and 2 25 lb. on buildings on the town side of SAARBRUCKEN Station.
   5 230 lb. and 10 25 lb. on MERLENBACH Junction. Several direct hits.
   2 230 lb. and 3 25 lb. on FALKENBERG Station. Believed direct hits.
   1 230 lb. and 2 25 lb. on train near WALLERSBERG Junction. 230 burst on train.
   1 230 lb. and 2 25 lb. on Station at ST. AVOLD.
   1 230 lb. and 2 25 lb. on train in HOMBERG Station.

Casualties.—Two machines missing. Pilots, Lieut. Jones and Lieut. Archibald. Observers, Lieut. Greenslade and Lieut. Godard.

Date.—29/30th October, 1917.

Objective.—Trains, Junctions, Stations, and Goods Sidings on Railway line between FALKEN-BERG and SAARBRUCKEN.

Taking Part :—

Pilots.	Observers.
2nd-Lieut. Turnbull.	Lieut. Duncan, S.M.
,, Lewis.	,, Thompson.
,, Duncan, H. E.	,, Edwards.

Bombs Dropped.—3 230 lb. and 9 25 lb.

Results.—1 230 lb. and 3 25 lb. on train S. of ST. AVOLD Station. Results unknown.
   1 230 lb. and 3 25 lb. on train near FALKENBERG.
   1 230 lb. and 3 25 lb. on SAARBRUCKEN.

100 SQUADRON

Date.—30/31st October, 1917.　　　　　*Objective.*—Volkingen Steel Works.

Taking Part :—

Pilots.	Observers.
2nd-Lieut. Kemp.	Capt. Scudamore.
„ Wells.	Lieut. Pitman.
Lieut. Barnes.	2nd-Lieut. Boyle.
2nd-Lieut. Rawlinson.	Lieut. Duncan, S. M.
„ Drummond.	„ Wallace.
„ Jackson.	2nd Air Mech. Guyat.
„ Reed.	Capt. Barry.
„ Boret.	Lieut. Price.
„ Taylor.	„ Howard.
Lieut. Windsor.	„ Lunghi.

Bombs Dropped.—10 230 lb. and 31 25 lb.

Results.—All bombs were dropped on or near the furnaces. Several direct hits claimed, but actual damage could not be seen.

German Report :—

30/31/10/17 Voelklingen.
　　7.40. p.m. 6 bombs dropped, 2 fell on Construction Workshops, also on truck loaded up with iron. 2 fell near the Office Camp near the railway, one on Rolling Mills, one on the shed turning machinery. Damage, 47,646 marks.

Date.—3/4th January, 1918.　　　　　*Objective.*—Mazieres Steel Works.

Taking Part :—

Pilots.	Observers.
2nd-Lieut. Kent.	Lieut. Reid.
„ McCreath.	„ Curry.
„ Parnell.	„ Tatham.
„ Wells.	„ Lunghi.
Capt. Windsor.	—

Bombs Dropped.—4 230 lb. and 20 25 lb.

Results.—2 230 lb. and 8 25 lb. on Mazieres. Large explosion caused.
　　1 230 lb. and 6 25 lb. on Station, believed to be Woippy.
　　1 230 lb. and 6 25 lb. on Railway Junction S. of Metz.

Date.—4/5th January, 1918.　　　　　*Objective.*—Mazieres Blast Furnaces.

Taking Part :—

Pilots.	Observers.
2nd-Lieut. McCreath.	Lieut. Curry.
„ Chambers, H. C.	2nd-Lieut. Boyle.
„ Parnell.	Lieut. Tatham.
„ Kent.	Capt. Lindsay.
„ Wells.	2nd-Lieut. Lunghi.
Lieut. Rutherford.	Lieut. Lucas.
„ Henry.	„ Foster.
2nd-Lieut. Morley.	2nd-Lieut. Fielding-Clarke.
„ Wald.	„ Pollard.

Bombs Dropped.—8 230 lb., 2 40 lb. and 44 25 lb.

Results.—7 230 lb., 2 40 lb. and 38 25 lb. on Mazieres Blast Furnaces.
　　1 230 lb. and 6 230 lb. on Courcelles Junction. Results unknown owing to bad visibility.

100 SQUADRON

Date.—5/6th January, 1918.

Objective,—CONFLANS Railway Station and Siding

Taking Part :—

Pilots.	Observers.
2nd-Lieut. McCreath.	Lieut. Curry.
Lieut. Windsor.	Capt. Scudamore.
2nd-Lieut. Wells.	,, Reid.
,, Chambers, H. C.	2nd-Lieut. Rogers.
,, Taylor.	Lieut. Price.
Lieut. Martin.	,, Foster.

Bombs Dropped.—6 230 lb., 2 40 lb. and 32 25lb.

Results.—5 230 lb., 2 40 lb. and 26 25 lb. on and around CONFLANS Station. Good bursts observed and large explosion caused.
1 230 lb. and 6 25 lb. on MARS-LES-PONS Station. Results unobserved.

Date.—14/15th January, 1918.

Objective.—DIEDENHOFEN Steel Works.

Taking Part :—

Pilots.	Observers.
Lieut. Barnes.	2nd-Lieut. Boyle.
2nd-Lieut. Parnell.	,, Tatham.
,, Wald.	,, Duncan, S. M.

Bombs Dropped.—3 230 lb. and 16 25 lb.

Results.—1 230 lb. and 6 25 lb. on DIEDENHOFEN. All burst in centre of town.
1 230 lb. and 6 25 lb. on UCKINGEN Station. Results unknown.
1 230 lb. and 4 25 lb. on Anti-Aircraft Battery just South of DIEDENHOFEN. Battery ceased fire.

German Report :—

14/15/1/18—THIONVILLE (DIEDENHOFEN).

Track No. 4 rendered unserviceable until 11.0 a.m. 16/1/18. Damage 500 marks.

Date.—16/17th January, 1918.

Objective.—DIEDENHOFEN Steel Works.

Taking Part :—

Pilots.	Observers.
Lieut. Rutherford.	Lieut. Lucas.
2nd-Lieut. Box.	2nd-Lieut. Boyle.

Bombs Dropped.—2 230 lb. and 4 25 lb.

Results.—1 230 lb. and 2 25 lb. on Railway Sidings presumed BERNSDORF.
1 230 lb. and 2 25 lb. on lights at ORNEY. Results unknown.

100 SQUADRON

Date.—21/22nd January, 1918.

Objective.—DIEDENHOFEN Steel Works and BERNSDORF Railway Sidings.

Taking Part :—

Pilots.	Observers.
Capt. Windsor.	2nd-Lieut. Edwardes-Evans.
,, Chambers.	,, Pollard.
2nd-Lieut. McCreath.	,, Sawyer.
Lieut. Barnes.	,, Boyle.
,, Martin.	Lieut. Foster.
,, Rutherford.	,, Lucas.
2nd-Lieut. Parnell.	,, Tatham.
Lieut. Albu.	Capt. Lindsay.
2nd-Lieut. Taylor.	2nd-Lieut. Le Fevre.
,, Box.	Lieut. Nunn.
,, Jackson.	2nd Air Mech. Guyat.
,, Peile.	Lieut. Reid.

Bombs Dropped.—11 230 lb., 2 40 lb. and 36 25 lb.

Results.—5 230 lb., 1 40 lb. and 16 25 lb. on DIEDENHOFEN Steel Works. Several direct hits claimed.

6 230 lb., 1 40 lb. and 24 25 lb. on BERNSDORF Railway Sidings. Results unobserved.

Casualties.—One machine missing. Pilot, 2nd-Lieut. Piele and Lieut. Reid, observer.

Date.—24/25th January, 1918.   *Objective.*—TRIER Barracks and Railway Station.

Taking Part :—

Pilots.	Observers.
2nd-Lieut. Parnell.	2nd-Lieut. Rogers.
Capt. Albu.	Capt. Lindsay.
2nd-Lieut. Box.	2nd-Lieut. Nunn.
Lieut. Rutherford.	Lieut. Lunghi.
2nd-Lieut. Chambers.	2nd-Lieut. Pollard.
,, Wells.	Lieut. Edwards.
,, Henry.	2nd-Lieut. Edwardes-Evans.
Capt. Windsor.	Capt. Scudamore .
Lieut. Martin.	2nd-Lieut. Sawyer.
,, Barnes.	,, Boyle.

Bombs Dropped.—8 230 lb., 22 112 lb., 2 40 lb. and 18 25 lb.

Results.—4 230 lb., 2 40 lb. and 6 25 lb. on TRIER. All bombs dropped in Town.

4 230 lb., 2 112 lb. and 12 25 lb. on DIEDENHOTEN Steel Works. All bombs dropped in factory, but actual results unobserved.

Casualties.—One machine missing. Pilot, 2nd-Lieut. Taylor and Lieut. Le Fevre, observer.

100 SQUADRON

Date.—9/10th February, 1918. *Objective.*—Courcelles Railway Station and Junction.

Taking Part :—

Pilots.	Observers.
Capt. Schweitzer.	—
2nd-Lieut. Miles.	Lieut. Lucas.
,, Swart.	2nd-Lieut. Fielding-Clarke.
,, Kingsford.	,, Edwardes-Evans.

Bombs Dropped.—6 112 lb., 1 40 lb. and 10 25 lb.

Results.—6 112 lb., 1 40 lb. and 10 25 lb. on Courcelles Railway Station and Junction. Results could not be observed on account of darkness.

Casualties.—One machine missing. Pilot, 2nd-Lieut. Stewart ; observer, 2nd-Lieut. Fielding-Clarke.

Date.—16/17th February, 1918. *Objective.*—Conflans Station and Sidings.

Taking Part :—

Pilots.	Observers.
2nd-Lieut. McCreath.	Lieut. Price.
,, Kingsford.	2nd-Lieut. Edwardes-Evans.
,, Miles.	Lieut. Samson.
Lieut. Martin.	,, Foster.
,, Bright.	,, Rogers.

Bombs Dropped.—4 230 lb., 4 112 lb., 1 40 lb. and 12 25 lb.

Results.—4 230 lb., 4 112 lb. 1 40 lb. and 12 25 lb. on Conflans Stations and Sidings. Actual results could not be observed on account of the darkness.

Date.—17/18th February, 1918. *Objective.*—Conflans Railway Station and Sidings.

Taking Part :—

Pilots.	Observers.
2nd-Lieut. Miles.	Lieut. Lunghi.
,, Henry.	2nd-Lieut. Edwardes-Evans.
,, Harker.	Lieut. Harper.
Capt. Schweitzer.	—
2nd-Lieut. Jackson.	2nd Air Mech. Guyat.
Lieut. Bright.	2nd-Lieut. Rogers.
2nd-Lieut. Chambers.	Capt. Lindsay.
Lieut. Martin.	Lieut. Foster.
2nd-Lieut. Miles.	,, Samson.
Lieut. Barnes.	2nd-Lieut. Boyle.
2nd-Lieut. McCreath.	Lieut. Price.
,, Henry.	2nd-Lieut. Edwardes-Evans.

Bombs Dropped.—3 230 lb., 6 112 lb., 2 40 lb. and 30 25 lb.

Results.—3 320 lbs., 6 112 lb., 2 40 lb. and 30 25 lb. on Conflans Station and Sidings. A large fire started.

105

100 SQUADRON

Date.—18/19th February, 1918.

Objective.—TRIER Barracks and Railway Station.   THIONVILLE Railway Communications and Steel Works.

Taking Part :—

Pilots.	Observers.
2nd-Lieut. Chambers.	Capt. Lindsay.
Lieut. Martin.	Lieut. Foster.
2nd-Lieut. Miles.	,, Samson.
Lieut. Barnes.	2nd-Lieut. Boyle.
2nd-Lieut. McCreath.	Lieut. Price.
,, Henry.	2nd-Lieut. Edwardes-Evans.
,, Wald.	Lieut. Duncan, S. M.
,, Jackson.	2nd Air Mech. Guyat.
2nd-Leut. Kingsford.	Lieut. Lunghi.
2nd-Lieut. Harker.	,, Harper.

Bombs Dropped.—6 230 lb., 8 112 lb., 2 40 lb. and 20 25 lb.

Results.—4 230 lb., 8 112 lb., 1 40 lb. and 14 25 lb. on TRIER Barracks and Railway Station.   Large fire started in station.

  2 230 lb., 1 40 lb. and 6 25 lb. on THIONVILLE Sidings.   A large fire caused.

Casualties.—One machine missing.   Pilot, 2nd-Lieut. Jackson ; observer, 2nd Air Mech. Guyat.

German Report :—

18/19/2/18—TREVES.

Two on track in Railway Station, 1 in front of Railway Station, 2 incendiary bombs hit main building of Station, Stationmaster's Dwelling considerably damaged. 1 bomb fell in the market, another fell in a house where the local Chancery Court was wont to be held, building destroyed, no casualties. On this raid one machine flew very low just missing the tops of the houses and dropped two bombs near the Station.

NOTE.—(This machine was piloted by Lieut. A. Wald, with Lieut. S. M. Duncan, observer).—ED.

Date.—26/27th February, 1918.   *Objective.*—FRESCATY Aerodrome.

Taking Part :—

Pilots.	Observers.
2nd-Lieut. Johnson.	Lieut. Naylor.
,, Chambers.	2nd-Lieut. Pollard.
,, Crofts.	Capt. Scudamore.

Bombs Dropped.—1 230 lb., 4 112 lb., 3 40 lb. and 10 25 lb.

Results.—1 230 lb., 4 112 lb., 3 40 lb. and 10 25 lb. on FRESCATY Aerodrome.   Results unobserved, owing to mist.

100 SQUADRON

Date.—6/7 March, 1918   *Objective.*—FRESCATY Aerodrome.

Taking Part :—

Pilot.	*Observer.*
Lieut. Bright.	Lieut. Roe.

Bombs Dropped.—1 230 lb., 1 40 lb. and 5 25 lb.

Results.—1 230 lb., 1 40 lb. and 5 25 lb. on FRESCATY Aerodrome. Results unknown.

German Report :—

6/7/3/18—FRESCATY.
One shed completely burnt out, all machines destroyed. Considerable damage.

FRESCATY. SHOWING SITE OF SHED (SIMILAR TO THAT IN THE LEFT-HAND CORNER) CONTAINING MACHINES WHICH WAS BURNT DOWN ON NIGHT OF 6/7TH MARCH, 1918. ZEPPELIN SHED CAN BE SEEN IN BACKGROUND.

Date.—23/24th March, 1918.   *Objective.*—FRESCATY Aerodrome.

Taking Part :—

Pilots.	*Observers.*
Lieut. Rutherford.	—
2nd-Lieut. Miles.	Capt. Wilson.
Lieut. Kirk.	Lieut. Naylor.
2nd-Lieut. Harker.	,, Ford.
,, Box.	,, Inches.
,, Wald.	2nd-Lieut. Keely.
,, Henry.	,, Edwardes-Evans.
Lieut. Darby.	2nd-Lieut. Boyle.
2nd-Lieut. Crofts.	,, Pascoe.
Capt. Windsor.	Lieut. Bourne.
Lieut. Martin.	,, Foster.

Bombs Dropped.—4 230 lb., 9 112 lb., 9 40 lb. and 32 25 lb.

Results.—All bombs were dropped on objective with very good results.

Remarks.—One pilot saw sixteen enemy machines waiting to take off and dropped his bombs on same.

100. SQUADRON

(1.) BEFORE THE RAID. THE WORKS CAN BE SEEN IN FULL SWING.

Date.—24/25th March, 1918.

Objective.—THIONVILLE and METZ Communications.

Two Raids.

Taking Part :—

Pilots.	Observers.
Lieut. Kirk.	Lieut. Naylor.
2nd-Lieut. Wald.	2nd-Lieut. Keely.
Lieut. Darby.	„ Boyle.
„ Martin (2).	Lieut. Foster (2).
„ Rutherford (2).	—
2nd-Lieut. Parnell.	Capt. Lindsay.
Capt. Savory.	2nd-Lieut. Rogers.
2nd-Lieut. Anderson (2).	Lieut. Lucas (2).
„ Miles (2).	Capt. Wilson (2).
„ Box (2).	Lieut. Inches. (2).
„ Harker.	„ Ford.
„ Crofts.	2nd-Lieut. Pascoe.
„ Henry (2).	„ Edwardes-Evans (2).

Bombs Dropped.—8 230 lb., 9 112 lb. and 61 25 lb.

Results.—7 230 lb., 7 112 lb. and 55 25 lb. on METZ Triangle. Large fire started.
1 230 lb., 2 112 lb. and 6 25 lb. on THIONVILLE. Results unobserved.

German Report :—

24/25/3/18—METZ-SABLONS.

Last night from 8.55 p.m. onwards, hostile aircraft appeared over METZ. The fall of bombs was as follows :—Several bombs fell on the main No. 6 track in the station. 15

100 SQUADRON

trucks caught fire and seven munition wagons amongst them exploded, tracks No. 6 and 16 were very extensively damaged and others also suffered (20 in all).

The whole train exploded, blew up and burnt itself out. Seven houses were very seriously damaged. The Northerly gasometer in the triangle was struck and damaged. The force of the explosion was so great that the building South of the gasometer had its roof blown off and exploding shells damaged the machinery. Traffic was held up for hours. Only 6 men killed and 2 wounded.

Date.—12/13th April, 1918. *Objective.*—JUNIVILLE Station and Sidings.

Taking Part :—

Pilots.	Observers.
2nd-Lieut. Kingsford.	Lieut. Bourne.
,, Miles.	Capt. Wilson.
,, Henry.	2nd-Lieut. Edwardes-Evans.
,, Harker	,, Fearnside.
Capt. Windsor.	,, Sawyer.
Lieut. Bright.	,, Rogers.

Bombs Dropped.—12 112 lb.

Results.—12 112 lb. on JUNIVILLE Sidings. Results unobserved owing to mist and darkness.

(2.) AFTER THE RAID. SHOWING COMPLETE CESSATION OF WORK.

100 SQUADRON

Date.—19/20th April, 1918.   Objective.—JUNIVILLE Station and Sidings.

Taking Part :—

Pilots.	Observers.
2nd-Lieut. Henry.	2nd-Lieut. Edwardes-Evans.
Capt. Savory.	,, Keely.
2nd-Lieut. Johnson.	Lieut. Naylor.
Lieut. Martin.	,, Ross.
,, Bright.	2nd-Lieut. Rogers.
Capt. Chambers.	,, Pollard.

Bombs Dropped.—14 112 lb.

Results.—14 112 lb. on JUNIVILLE Station and Sidings.   Results unobserved.

Date.—20/21st April, 1918.   Objective.—Railway Station South of CHAULNES.

Taking Part :—

Pilots.	Observers.
Lieut. Darby.	2nd-Lieut. Keely.
2nd-Lieut. Brown.	Capt. Wilson.
,, Johnson.	Lieut. Naylor.
,, Box.	,, Inches.
,, Dickens.	Corpl. O'Donoghue.
,, Miles.	2nd-Lieut. Boyle.
Capt. Savory.	Capt. Lindsay.

Bombs Dropped.—19 112 lb.

Results.—7 112 lb. on CHAULNES Railway Station.   Large fire started.
    3 112 lb. on NESTLE Railway Station.   Results unobserved.
    3 112 lb. on Railway Junction at ROLE.   Direct hit on track with 1 112 lb.
    3 112 lb. on HAM Railway Station.   Missed Station but hit track.
    3 112 lb. on Railway Track at MARCHELEPOT.   All direct hits.

Date.—21/22nd April, 1918.   Objective.—JUNIVILLE Railway Station and Sidings.

Taking Part :—

Pilots.	Observers.
2nd-Lieut. Henry.	2nd-Lieut. Edwardes-Evans.
,, Chambers.	,, Pollard.
,, Siddaway.	,, Sawyer.
Lieut. Kirk.	,, Dyson.
2nd-Lieut. Williamson.	Lieut. Bourne.
,, Crofts.	2nd-Lieut. Pascoe.
Lieut. Bright.	,, Rogers.
2nd-Lieut. Anderson.	,, Lucas.
Lieut. Martin.	,, Ross.

Bombs Dropped.—24 112 lb.

Results.—22 112 lb. on JUNIVILLE Station and Sidings.   Several direct hits on Sidings and Tracks.   Large explosion caused.
    2 112 lb. on WARMERVILLE Station.   Results unknown.

100 SQUADRON

Date.—2/3rd May, 1918.   Objective.—Mohon Railway Station.

Taking Part :—

Pilots.	Observers.
Lieut. Martin.	Lieut. Foster.
Capt. Windsor.	2nd-Lieut. Sawyer.
Lieut. Bright.	,, Rogers.
2nd-Lieut. Williamson.	,, Penruddocke.
,, Sawyer.	,, Chainey.
,, . Anderson.	Lieut. Lucas.
,, Box.	,, Inches.
,, Johnson.	,, Pitman.
Lieut. Darby.	2nd-Lieut. Keely.

Bombs Dropped.—18 112 lb.

Results.—2 112 lb. on Railway Station at AMAGUE-LUCQUY. Believed O.K.
14 112 lb. on Railway Station at JUNIVILLE. Results unobserved owing to mist.
2 112 lb. on Railway line near WARNEVILLE. Results unobserved.

Date.—3/4th May, 1918.   Objective.—Mohon Railway Station.

Taking Part :—

Pilots.	Observers.
2nd-Lieut. Blakemore.	2nd-Lieut. Boyle.
,, Chambers.	,, Pollard.
Lieut. Kirk.	,, Richards.
2nd-Lieut. Anderson.	Lieut. Lucas.
Lieut. Darby.	2nd-Lieut. Keely.
2nd-Lieut. Bright.	Lieut. Rogers.
,, Williamson.	2nd-Lieut. Penruddocke.
,, Miles.	Lieut. Naylor.
,, Brown.	Capt. Wilson.

Bombs Dropped.—18 112 lb.

Results.—12 112 lb. on Railway lines near JUNIVILLE. Results unobserved.
4 112 lb. on ASFELD Sidings. Very large explosions caused.
2 112 lb. on Railway lines near AMAGNE-LUCQUY. Results unknown.

Date.—17/18th May, 1918.   Objective.—THIONVILLE Railway Station.

Taking Part :—

Pilots.	Observers.
2nd-Lieut. Blakemore.	Lieut. Lucas.
,, Siddaway.	,, Ross.
,, Kingsford.	,, Bourne.
Capt. Savory.	Capt. Lindsay.
Lieut. Bright.	—
2nd-Lieut. Johnson.	Lieut. Naylor.
,, Box.	2nd-Lieut. Dyson.
Lieut. Darby.	,, Keely.
,, Kirk.	,, Richards.
2nd-Lieut. Brown.	Capt. Wilson.

Bombs Dropped.—20 112 lb.

Results.—14 112 lb. on THIONVILLE Railway Station and Works. Fire caused in works, several direct hits on Station.
6 112 lb. on METZ Stations.

Casualties.—One machine missing. Pilot, 2nd-Lieut. Williamson ; observer, Lieut. Penruddocke.

100 SQUADRON

Date.—20/21st May, 1918.   *Objective.*—Railway Station at THIONVILLE.

Taking Part :—

Pilots.	Observers.
2nd-Lieut. Blakemore.	Lieut. Lucas.
Lieut. Darby.	2nd-Lieut. Keely.
2nd-Lieut. Henry.	,, Edwardes-Evans.
,, Brown.	Lieut. Pitman.
,, Siddaway.	,, Ross.
,, Sawyer.	,, Rogers.
Lieut. Kirk.	2nd-Lieut. Richards.
,, Bright.	—
2nd-Lieut. Dickens.	Corpl. O'Donoghue.
,, Box.	Lieut. Inches.
,, Johnson.	2nd-Lieut. Dyson.

Bombs Dropped.—22 112 lb.

Results.—8 112 lb. on THIONVILLE. South Station. Good bursts.
     14 112 lb. on METZ Railway. Several direct hits.

German Report :—

20/21/5/19—THIONVILLE.
     11.40 p.m.—3.15 a.m. Several bombs dropped. Some rails near the unloading platforms seriously damaged.

Date.—21/22nd May, 1918.

Objective.—SAARBRUCKEN Railway Station and Sidings and Railway Stations THIONVILLE.

Taking Part :—

Pilots.	Observers.
Lieut. Kirk.	2nd-Lieut. Richards.
2nd-Lieut. Miles.	Lieut. Naylor.
,, Kingsford.	,, Bourne.
,, Johnson.	,, Pitman.
Capt. Savory.	Capt. Lindsay.
2nd-Lieut. Dickens.	Corpl. O'Donoghue.
Capt. Chambers.	Lieut. Inches.
2nd-Lieut. Siddaway.	,, Ross.
Lieut. Henry.	2nd-Lieut. Edwardes-Evans.
,, Bright.	—
2nd-Lieut. Blakemoer.	Lieut. Lucas.
,, Brown.	2nd-Lieut. Dyson.
Lieut. Darby.	,, Keely.
2nd-Lieut. Box.	2nd Air Mech. Johnson.

Bombs Dropped.—29 112 lb

Results.—20 112 lb. on SAARBRUCKEN. Good bursts observed all over town.
     9 112 lb on THIONVILLE Stations and Sidings. Fire caused on Sidings.

German Report :—

21/22/5/18—SAARBRUCKEN.

1.35 p.m.—4.20 a.m. On Railway installations. Attacks repulsed. 10 bombs dropped in DILLINGEN, of which 3 fell in the factory. 2 bombs fell in SAARLOUIS Barracks. 3 killed and 20 wounded.

100 SQUADRON

Date.—22/23rd May, 1918.   *Objective.*—KREUZWALD Power Station.

Taking Part :—

Pilots.	*Observers.*
Lieut. Kirk.	2nd-Lieut. Richards.
,, Darby.	,, Keely.
2nd-Lieut. Miles.	,, Lamieson.
, Brown.	Lieut. Naylor.
,, Blakemore.	,, Lucas.
Lieut. Bright.	—
2nd-Lieut. Box.	,, Inches.
,, Siddaway.	,, Ross.
,, Harker.	2nd-Lieut. Dyson.
,, Chambers, J. A.	Lieut. Pitman.
,, Dickens.	Corpl. O'Donoghue.

Bombs Dropped.—29 112 lb. and 4 40 lb.

Results.—26 112 lb. and 4 40 lb. on KREUZWALD Power Station. A large fire started.
3 112 lb. on SPETTEL. Results unknown.

Date.—27/28th May, 1918.   *Objective.*—KREUZWALD Power Station.

Taking Part :—

Pilots.	*Observers.*
Capt. Savory.	Capt. Lindsay.
Lieut. Bright.	—
2nd-Lieut. Johnson.	Lieut. Pitman.
,, Dickens.	,, Sherwood.
Lieut. Henry.	2nd-Lieut. Pascoe.
2nd-Lieut. Kingsford.	,, Sawyer.
,, Harker.	,, Dyson.
,, Siddaway.	Lieut. Ross.
,, Box.	,, Inches.
Lieut. Darby.	2nd-Lieut. Keely.
2nd-Lieut. Sawyer.	,, Chainey.
,, Blakemore.	Lieut. Lucas.

Bombs Dropped.—27 112 lb. and 10 40 lb.

Results.—21 112 lb. on KREUZWALD Power Station. Very large explosions caused.
6 112 lb. and 10 40 lb. on METZ Railway Station.

NOTE.—Photographs showed : Two direct hits on a large square building, probably the Power House.

Date.—28/29th May, 1918.   *Objective.*—METZ Railway Stations.

Taking Part :—

Pilots.	*Observers.*
2nd-Lieut. Crofts.	2nd-Lieut. Pascoe.
,, Chambers, J. A.	,, Fearnside.
,, Siddaway.	Lieut. Ross.

Bombs Dropped.—7 112 lb. and 2 40 lb.

Results. —7 112 lb. and 2 40 lb. on METZ South Railway Station. Fire started in Station.

Casualties.—One machine missing. Pilot, 2nd-Lieut. Brown ; observer, Pte. 2nd Class Johnson.

H

100 SQUADRON

Date.—30/31st May, 1918.   *Objective.*—METZ Railway Station.

Taking Part :—

Pilots.	Observers.
2nd-Lieut. Siddaway.	Lieut. Ross.
Lieut. Coombs.	2nd-Lieut. Rogers.
,, Bright.	Lieut. Pitman.
2nd-Lieut. Kingsford.	2nd-Lieut. Sawyer.
,, Dickens.	,, Sherwood.
,, Crofts.	,, Pascoe.

METZ-SABLON. SHOWING PORTION OF DAMAGE DONE ON NIGHT OF 24/25 MARCH, 1918.
IN LEFT-HAND CORNER CAN BE SEEN DAMAGE TO BUILDING AND RIGHT-HAND CORNER
DAMAGE TO GASOMETER.

bombs Dropped.—14 112 lb. and 4 40 lb.

Results.—4 112 lb. and 4 40 lb. on METZ Station South. Results unknown.

German Report :—

30/31/5/18—METZ.

Between 10.35 p.m. and 11.0 p.m., 4 bombs dropped on METZ-SABLONS sidings. Cement and wood trucks and points damaged.

114

100 SQUADRON

Date.—31st May/1st June, 1918.   Objective.—THIONVILLE Railway Junction and Station.

Taking Part :—

Pilots.	Observers.
Lieut. Coombs.	2nd-Lieut. Rogers.
,, Bright.	Lieut. Pitman.
2nd-Lieut. Sawyer.	2nd-Lieut. Chainey.
,, Blakemore.	Lieut. Lucas.
,, Crofts.	2nd-Lieut. Pascoe.
,, Dickens.	,, Sherwood.
Capt. Savery.	Capt. Lindsay.
2nd-Lieut. Miles.	2nd-Lieut. Dyson.
,, Johnson.	,, Jamieson.
,, Chambers, J. A.	,, Fearnside.

Bombs Dropped.—22 112 lb. and 6 40 lb.

Results.—14 112 lb. and 6 40 lb. on THIONVILLE Railway Station.   Results unobserved
owing to darkness and mist.

8 112 lb. on METZ Station South.   Results unobserved.

German Report :—

31/1/6/18.—METZ.

Between 10.5—11.20 p.m.   One bomb hit private house, penetrated three storeys and exploded, much damage.   One bomb on METZ-SABLONS (E.).

Date.—3/4th June, 1918.   Objective.—THIONVILLE Railway Station and Junction.

Taking Part :—

Pilots.	Observers.
2nd-Lieut. Blakemore.	Lieut. Lucas.
,, Bright.	,, Pitman.

Bombs Dropped.—1 230 lb. and 2 112 lb.

Results.—1 230 lb. and 2 112 lb. on Railway South of METZ.   Results unobserved.

Date.—5/6th June, 1918.   Objective.—Triangle of Railways at METZ-SABLON.

Taking Part :—

Pilots.	Observers.
2nd-Lieut. Kingsford.	2nd-Lieut. Sawyer.
,, Box.	Lieut. Inches.
Capt. Savery.	Capt. Lindsay.
Lieut. Hewett.	2nd-Lieut. Pollard.
,, Martin.	,, Wilkins.
Capt. Chambers, H. C.	,, Fearnside.
Lieut. Coombs.	Lieut. Ross.

Bombs Dropped.—3 230 lb., 7 112 lb. and 3 25 lb.

Results.—3 230 lb. 7 113 lb. and 3 25 lb. on METZ Station South.   Results unknown.

100 SQUADRON

Date.—6/7th June, 1918.   *Objective.*—MAIZIERES Blast Furnaces.

Taking Part :—

Pilots.	Observers.
Lieut. Miles.	2nd-Lieut. Jamieson.
2nd-Lieut. Chambers, J. A.	,, Fearnside.
Lieut. Sawyer.	,, Chainey.
,, Hewett.	, Pollard.
Capt. Chambers.	,, Wilkins.
Lieut. Henry.	,, Edwardes-Evans.
,, Blakemore.	Lieut. Lucas.
,, Coombs.	2nd-Lieut. Keely.
Lieut. Box.	Lieut. Inches.
,, Siddaway.	,, Ross.

Bombs Dropped.—5 230 lb., 10 112 lb. and 1 25 lb.

Results.—1 230 lb. and 2 112 lb. on MAIZIERES.

    2 112 lb. on METZ Railway. Good bursts on track.

    4 230 lb., 6 112 lb. and 1 25 lb. on THIONVILLE Station. Good bursts on Station. Fire caused.

Date.—23/24th June, 1918.   *Objective.*—METZ-SABLON Triangle.

Taking Part :—

Pilots.	Observers.
Lieut. Darby.	2nd-Lieut. Keely.
,, Hewett.	,, Pollard.
,, Sawyer.	,, Chainey.
,, Middleton.	,, Fearnside.
Capt. Savery.	,, Wilkins.
Lieut. Johnson.	Jamieson.
,, Bright.	Capt. Wilson.
,, Miles.	Lieut. Naylor.
Capt. Chambers.	2nd-Lieut. Sawyer.
Lieut. Kingsford.	Lieut. Bourne.
,, Siddaway.	,, Ross.
,, Dickens.	Sergt. O'Donoghue.

Bombs Dropped.—4 230 lb., 19 112 lb., 1 40 lb. and 34 25 lb.

Results.—3 230 lb., 6 112 lb. and 11 25 lb. on METZ-SABLON Triangle.

    3 112 lb. and 1 25 lb. on Trains entering Triangle. Results unobserved owing to bad visibility.

    1 230 lb., 10 112 lb., 1 40 lb. and 22 25 lb. in METZ.

German Report :—

23/24/6/18.—METZ.

At 8.45 p.m., 5 bombs dropped at SABLONS, track No. 86 destroyed, several lines rendered unserviceable. Several trucks seriously damaged. No stoppage of traffic. At 1.30 a.m., 5 bombs dropped on Workshops. Only slight damage to buildings. 500 marks damage.

100 SQUADRON

Date.—25/26th June, 1918.   *Objective.*—BOULAY Aerodrome.

Taking Part :—

Pilots.	*Observers.*
Lieut. Chambers, J. A.	2nd-Lieut. Fearnside.
Capt. Savery.	Lieut. Lucas, .
Lieut. Miles.	,, Naylor.
,, Darby.	2nd-Lieut. Keely.
Capt. Chambers, H. C.	2nd-Lieut. Sawyer.
Lieut. Bright.	Capt. Wilson.
,, Martin.	2nd-Lieut. Wilkins.
,, Kingsford.	Lieut. Bourne.
,, Johnson.	2nd-Lieut. Dyson.
,, Dickens.	Sergt. O'Donoghue.
,, Siddaway.	Lieut. Ross.
,, Crofts.	2nd-Lieut. Pascoe.
,, Coombs.	,, Pollard.
,, Proctor.	,, Sherwood.
,, Hobson.	,, Jamieson.

Bombs Dropped.—26 112 lb., 4 40 lb. and 67 25 lb.

Results.—21 112 lb., 56 25 lb. and 4 40 lb. on and around BOULAY.

   2 112 lb. on Railway Junction S.E. of REMILLY Junction.   1 direct hit on line remainder unobserved.

German Report :—

25/26/6/18.—BOULAY.

   Civilians stated considerable damage done. 4 hangars East end of Aerodrome burnt out.

They contained stores. All 4 hangars had to be rebuilt.

Date.—26/27th June, 1918.   *Objective.*—BOULAY Aerodrome.

Taking Part :—

Pilots.	*Observers.*
Lieut. Johnson.	2nd-Lieut. Dyson.
Capt. Savery.	Capt. Lindsay.
2nd-Lieut. Chambers, J. A.	2nd-Lieut. Fearnside.
Lieut. Bright.	Capt. Wilson.
,, Darby.	2nd-Lieut. Keely.
,, Miles.	Lieut. Naylor.

Bombs Dropped.—10 112 lb., 6 40 lb. (Phos.) and 20 25 lb.

Results.—10 112 lb. 6 40 lb. and 20 25 lb. on BOULAY Aerodrome.

   Of these 2 112 lb. and 4 25 lb. were dropped on 2 Gothas with a group of men round them. 3 112 lb. and 1 40 lb. on a Gotha landing in Flare Path Machine set on fire.

Casualties.—2nd-Lieut. Chambers, J. A., wounded.

100 SQUADRON

Date.—27/28th June, 1918.   *Objective.*—BOULAY Aerodrome.

Taking Part :—

Pilots.	*Observers.*
Lieut. Reed.	2nd-Lieut. Fearnside.
,, Miles	,, Sherwood.
Capt. Savery.	Lieut. Naylor.
Lieut. Bright.	Capt. Wilson.
,, Johnson.	2nd-Lieut. Dyson.

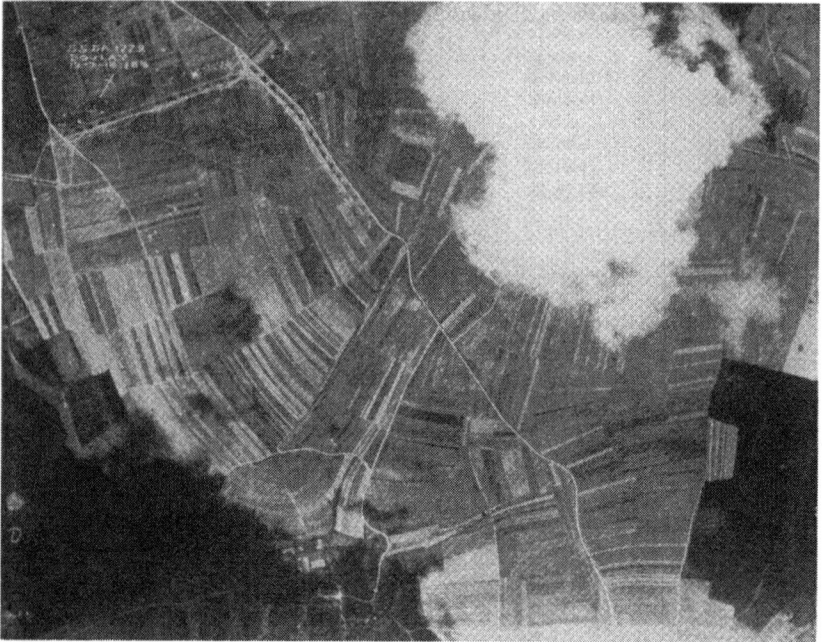

AERIAL PHOTOGRAPH OF THE HOSTILE AERODROME AT BOULAY.

Bombs Dropped.—9 112 lb., 6 40 lb. (Phos.) and 12 25 lb.

Results.—5 112 lb., 4 40 lb. and 10 25 lb. on and around hangars. Two hangars set on
fire.
2 112 lb. and 2 40 lb. on Railway East of CONTILON. Results unobserved.
2 112 lb. and 2 25 lb. on METZ-SABLON Triangle.

Date.—29/30th June, 1918.   *Objective.*—FRESCATY Aerodrome.

Taking Part :—

Pilots.	*Observers.*
Lieut. Sawyer.	2nd-Lieut. Chainey.
,, Hobson.	,, Jamieson.

118

100 SQUADRON

,,	Johnson	,,	Dyson.
Capt.	Savery.	,,	Richards.
Lieut.	Coombs.	Lieut.	Naylor.
,,	Martin.	2nd-Lieut.	Wilkins.
,,	Kingsford.	Lieut.	Bourne.
,,	Siddaway.	,,	Ross.
,,	Darby.	2nd-Lieut.	Keely.
,,	Dickens.	Lieut.	Lucas.
,,	Bright.	Capt.	Wilson.
,,	Hewett.	2nd-Lieut.	Pollard.

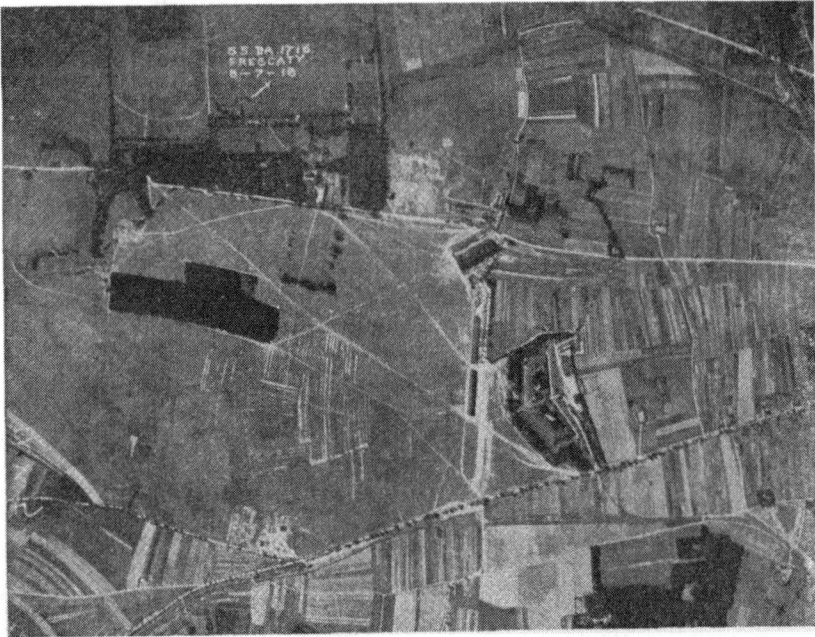

AN AERIAL PHOTOGRAPH OF THE HOSTILE AERODROME AT FRESCATY (SOUTH OF METZ).

Bombs Dropped.—5 230 lb., 12 112 lb., 4 40 lb (Phos.) and 46 25 lb.

Results.—4 230 lb., 9 112 lb., 2 40 lb. and 31 25 lb. on and around hangars on FRESCATY Aerodrome.

    1 230 lb. and 2 40 lb. on BOULAY Aerodrome.

    2 112 lb. and 4 25 lb. on large shed S.E. of MEZIERES.

    1 112 lb. on train proceeding in direction of METZ.

    4 25 lb. on train in BAYONVILLE Station.

    7 25 lb. on Searchlights.

100 SQUADRON

Date.—30th June/1st July, 1918.   *Objective.*—BOULAY Aerodrome.

Taking Part :—

Pilots.	Observers.
Lieut. Box.	Lieut. Inches.
,, Bright.	Capt. Wilson.
,, Crofts.	2nd-Lieut. Pascoe.
,, Dickens.	Lieut. Lucas.
,, Martin.	,, Siddaway.
,, Kingsford.	,, Bourne.
,, Proctor.	2nd-Lieut. Sherwood
,, Hobson.	Lieut. Naylor.
,, Hewett.	,, Pollard.
,, Middleton.	2nd-Lieut. Jamieson.
,, Sawyer.	,, Chainey.
,, Reed.	,, Fearnside.
,, Darby.	,, Keely.
,, Coombs.	,, Dyson.

Bombs Dropped.—2 230 lb., 17 112 lb., 2 40 lb. and 60 25 lb.

Results.—2 230 lb., 15 112 lb. 2 40 lb. and 34 25 lb. on BOULAY Aerodrome.
  8 25 lb. on train.
  2 25 lb. on Convoy.
  2 25 lb. on THIONVILLE.
  8 25 lb. on Anti Aircraft Batteries
  4 25 lb. on Searchlights.
  2 112 lb. and 2 25 lb. on Railway Junction S.W. of REMILLY Forest.

Date.—1/2nd July, 1918.   *Objective.*—BOULAY Aerodrome.

Taking Part :—

Pilots.	Observers.
Lieut. Miles.	2nd-Lieut. Sherwood.
,, Johnson.	,, Jamieson.
,, Crofts.	,, Pascoe.
,, Dickens.	Corpl. O'Donoghue.
,, Siddaway.	Lieut. Ross.
,, Martin.	2nd-Lieut. Wilkins.
,, Kingsford.	Lieut. Bourne.
Capt. Savery.	2nd-Lieut. Shillinglaw.
Lieut. Reed.	,, Fearnside.
,, Darby.	,, Keely.
,, Hewett.	,, Pollard.
,, Middleton.	,, Chainey.
,, Bright.	Capt. Wilson.
,, Box.	Lieut. Inches.

Bombs Dropped.—4 230 lb., 16 112 lb., 2 40 lb. (Phos.) and 48 25 lb.

Results.—4 230 lb., 13 112 lb., 2 40 lb. and 34 25 lb. on and around hangars on BOULAY Aerodrome.
  3 112 lb. and 8 25 lb. on Group of Buildings between BOULAY and the Aerodrome.
  4 25 lb. on Searchlights.
  2 25 lb. on FALKENBERG Station.

100 SQUADRON

Date.—6/7th July, 1918.

Objective.—SAARBURG Railway Junction.

Taking Part :—

Pilots.	*Observers.*
Capt. Savery.	Lieut. Gilson.
Lieut. Proctor.	2nd-Lieut. Dyson.
,, Crofts.	Lieut. Ross.
,, Reed.	2nd-Lieut. Fearnside.
,, Coombs.	Lieut. Bourne.
,, Hewett.	2nd-Lieut. Pollard.
,, Johnson.	,, Jamieson.
,, Bright.	Capt. Wilson.
,, Box.	Lieut. Inches.

Bombs Dropped.—2 230 lb., 9 112 lb. and 40 25 lb.

Results.—2 230 lb., 9 112 lb. and 40 25 lb. on SAARBURG Railway Junction.

BOULAY.—DESTROYED MACHINE AND HANGAR.

Date.—8/9th July, 1918.

Objective.—BOULAY Aerodrome.

Taking Part :—

Pilots.	*Observers.*
Lieut. Bright.	Capt. Wilson.
,, Box.	Lieut. Inches.
,, Miles.	2nd-Lieut. Sherwood.
,, Sawyer.	,, Chainey.
,, Johnson.	,, Jamieson.
,, Darby.	,, Keely.
,, Coombs.	Lieut. Bourne.
,, Martin.	2nd-Lieut. Wilkins.
,, Hewett.	,, Pollard.
,, Proctor.	,, Dyson.
,, Reed.	,, Fearnside.

Bombs Dropped.—3 230 lb., 11 112 lb., 6 40 lb. (Phos.) and 36 25 lb.

Results.—3 320 lb., 11 112 lb., 6 40 lb. (Phos.) and 28 25 lb. on and around hangars on BOULAY Aerodrome.
8 25 lb. on Trains in FALKENBERG Station.

100 SQUADRON

Date.—11/12th July, 1918.   *Objective.*—BOULAY Aerodrome.

Taking Part :—

Pilots.	*Observers.*
Capt. Bright.	Capt. Wilson.
Lieut. Box.	Lieut. Inches.
,, Miles.	2nd-Lieut. Sherwood.
,, Proctor.	,, Dyson.
,, Middleton.	,, Shillinglaw.
,, Coombs.	Lieut. Bourne.
,, Darby.	,, Gilson.
,, Reed.	2nd-Lieut. Fearnside.
,, Johnson.	,, Jamieson.
,, Crofts.	,, Wilkins.

Bombs Dropped.—2 230 lb., 10 112 lb., 4 40 lb. (Phos.) and 31 25 lb.

Results.—2 230 lb., 8 112 lb., 4 40 lb. and 27 25 lb. on and around hangars on BOULAY Aerodrome.

2 112 lb. and 4 25 lb. on Aerodrome in vicinity of STANOLD.

Date.—16/17th July, 1918.   *Objective.*—HAGENDINGEN Blast Furnaces.

Taking Part :—

Pilots.	*Observers.*
Lieut. Middleton.	2nd-Lieut. Shillinglaw.
,, Taylor.	,, Naylor.
,, Crofts.	,, Conover.
,, Darby.	,, Gilson.
,, Martin.	2nd-Lieut. Wilkins.
,, Proctor.	Corpl. O'Donoghue.
,, Blakemore.	Lieut. King.
,, Johnson.	2nd-Lieut. Jamieson.
,, Miles.	,, Sherwood.
,, Reed.	,, Warneford.
Capt. Bright.	Capt. Wilson.
Lieut. Box.	Lieut. Inches.

Bombs Dropped.—2 230 lb., 12 112 lb., 4 40 lb. (Phots.) and 44 25 lb.

Results.—2 230 lb., 11 112 lb., 4 40 lb. and 36 25 lb. on HAGENDINGEN Blast Furnaces.

1 112 lb. and 8 25 lb. on HAM Railway Junction.

German Report :—

16/17/7/18.—HAGONDANGE.

8 bombs dropped. 8 killed and 14 injured.

Date.—21/22nd July, 1918.

Objective.—BOULAY, FRIESDORF and MORHANGE Aerodromes.

Two Raids.

Taking Part :—

Pilots.	*Observers.*
Lieut. Taylor.	2nd-Lieut. Sherwood.
,, Reed (2).	,, Pollard (2).
,, Van Schaack.	Lieut. Bourne.
,, Darby.	,, Gilson.
,, Erwin.	Corpl. O'Donoghue.
,, Coombs.	2nd-Lieut. Sawyer.
,, Middleton.	,, Shillinglaw.
,, Hobson.	Lieut. Naylor.
,, Crofts.	2nd-Lieut. Pascoe.
,, Blakemore.	Lieut. Conover.
,, Proctor.	Lieut. Lucas.
,, Martin.	2nd-Lieut. Wilkins.
,, Siddaway.	,, Warneford.
,, Ebrey.	,, Jamieson.
,, Box.	Lieut. Inches.
,, Miles.	Capt. Wilson.

100 SQUADRON

Bombs Dropped.—1 230 lb., 20 112 lb. and 104 25 lb

Results.—1 230 lb., 3 112 lb. and 6 25 lb. on BOULAY.   Two hangars hit and bursts observed alongside machines near wood.
6 112 lb. and 32 25 lb. on FREESDORF. Good bursts near hangars.   One direct hit.
7 112 lb. and 42 25 lb. on Trains. Five trains hit and brought to a standstill.
2 112 lb. and 16 25 lb. on MORHANGE. Direct hits observed on hangars.
1 112 lb. and 6 26 lb. on REMILLY Railway Junction. 3 direct hits.
1 112 lb. on Station at BRULANGE.
2 25 lb. on Searchlight at REMILLY FOREST.

BOULAY—DESTROYED HANGARS.

Date.—22/23rd July, 1918.   *Objective.*—BOULAY Aerodrome.

Two Raids.

Taking Part :—

Pilots.	Observers.
Lieut. Darby.	Lieut. Gilson.
,, Coombs.	2nd-Lieut. Sawyer.
,, Proctor.	,, Sherwood.
,, Blakemore.	Lieut. Conover.
,, Siddaway.	,, King.
,, Crofts.	,, Pascoe.
,, Martin.	2nd-Lieut. Wilkins.
,, Hobson.	Lieut. Naylor.
,, Middleton.	2nd-Lieut. Shillinglaw.
,, Reed.	,, Warneford.
,, Taylor.	,, Jamieson.
,, Miles (2).	Capt. Wilson (2).
,, Box (2).	Lieut. Inches (2).

Bombs Dropped.—16 112 lb., 14 40 lb. (Phos.) and 42 25 lb.

Results.—8 112 lb. and 22 25 lb. on and between hangars.
4 112 lb., 8 40 lb. and 8 25 lb. Hits observed and fire caused with phos. bombs.
2 112 lb. and 4 25 lb. on Chateau North of BOULAY Aerodrome.
6 40 lb. and 2 25 lb. Western end of woods South of BOULAY Aerodrome.
2 25 lb. on Railway at LESSE.

100 SQUADRON

Date.—25/26th July, 1918.   *Objective.*—BOULAY, FRIESDORF and MORHANGE Aerodrome.

Two Raids.

Taking Part :—

Pilots.	Observers.
Lieut. Darby.	Lieut. Gilson.
,, Erwin.	2nd-Lieut. Sawyer.
,, Blakemore.	Lieut. Conover.
Capt. Coombs.	2nd-Lieut. Pollard.
Lieut. Reed (2).	,, Fearnside (2).
,, Middleton (2).	,, Shillinglaw (2).
,, Hobson.	Lieut. Naylor.
,, Crofts.	2nd-Lieut. Pascoe.
,, Ebrey.	,, Jamieson.
,, Martin.	,, Wilkins.
,, Dickens.	Sergt. O'Donoghue.
,, Kingsford (2).	Lieut. Bourne.
,, Miles.	Capt. Wilson.
,, Box.	Lieut. Inches.

Bombs Dropped.—14 112 lb. and 128 25 lb.

Results.—7 112 lb. and 64 25 lb. on BOULAY Aerodrome. Direct hits on hangars. Bombs also fell close to a group of machines on the ground.
    4 112 lb. and 38 25 lb. on FRIESDORF.
    1 112 lb. and 8 25 lb. on MORHANGE.
    1 112 lb. and 10 25 lb. at 3 Trains, bringing trains to a standstill, but no direct hits claimed.
    1 112 lb. and 8 25 lb. on Battery of Guns in action.

Date.—29/30th July, 1918.   *Objective.*—BOULAY and FRIESDORF Aerodromes.

Taking Part :—

Pilots.	Observers.
Lieut. Dickens.	2nd-Lieut. Warneford.
Capt. Savery.	Lieut. Gilson.
Lieut. Taylor.	,, Lucas.
,, Crofts.	2nd-Lieut. Pascoe.
,, Kingsford.	Lieut. King.
,, Ebrey.	2nd-Lieut. Jamieson.
,, Reed.	,, Fearnside.
,, Box.	Lieut. Inches.
,, Proctor.	2nd-Lieut. Sherwood.

Bombs Dropped.—1 230 lb., 8 112 lb. and 60 25 lb.

Results.—7 112 lb. and 35 25 lb. on BOULAY. Results unobserved.
    1 112 lb. and 8 25 lb. on MORHANGE. Results unobserved.
    1 230 lb. and 4 25 lb. on REMILLY Station. Results unobserved.
    2 25 lb. on HERLINGEN Station. Results unobserved.
    2 25 lb. on HAM Station. Results unobserved.
    8 25 lb. on lights on road between COURCELLES and REMILLY.
    1 25 lb. on Searchlights. Results unobserved.

100 SQUADRON

Date.—30/31st July, 1918.   *Objective.*—KREUZWALD Power Station.

Taking Part :—

Pilots.	*Observers.*
Lieut. Van Schaack.	2nd-Lieut. Pascoe.
Capt. Savery.	Lieut. Gilson.
Lieut. Middleton.	2nd-Lieut. Shillinglaw.
,, Hobson.	Lieut. Naylor.
,, Kingsford.	,, Bourne.
,, Taylor.	,, Lucas.
,, Darby.	2nd-Lieut. Keely.
,, Ebrey.	,, Jamieson.
,, Erwin.	,, Wilkins.
,, Box.	Lieut. Inches.
,, Proctor.	2nd-Lieut. Sherwood.

Bombs Dropped.—3 230 lb., 12 112 lb., 2 40 lb. and 46 25 lb.

Results.—2 230 lb., 10 112 lb., 2 40 lb. and 42 25 lb. on MORHANGE.
  2 112 lb. and 2 25 lb. on BOULAY. Results unknown.
  1 230 lb. and 2 25 lb. on REMILLY Junction. Results unobserved.

Date.—11/12th August, 1918.   *Objective.*—MORHANGE Aerodrome.

Taking Part :—

Pilots.	*Observers.*
Lieut. Proctor.	2nd-Lieut. Dyson.
,, Johnson.	Capt. Wilson.

Bombs Dropped.—2 112 lb. and 16 25 lb.

Results.—2 112 lb. and 16 25 lb. on MORHANGE. Results unobserved owing to bad visibility.

Date.—12/13th August, 1918.   *Objective.*—MORHANGE Aerodrome.

Taking Part :—

Pilots.	*Observers.*
Lieut. Erwin.	Lieut. Conover.
,, Blakemore.	2nd-Lieut. Warneford.
,, Van Schaack.	Lieut. King.
Capt. Darby.	2nd-Lieut. Keely.
Lieut. Taylor.	,, Pascoe.
,, Box.	Lieut. Inches.
,, Hobson.	,, Naylor.
,, Ebrey.	2nd-Lieut. Sherwood.
Capt. Savery.	Lieut. Gilson.
Lieut. Johnson.	Capt. Wilson.
,, Dickens.	,, Ross.

Bombs Dropped.—11 112 lb., 4 40 lb. and 70 25 lb.

Results.—8 112 lb., 4 40 lb. and 46 25 lb. on MORHANGE. Results unknown.
  1 112 lb. and 8 25 lb. on Anti-Aircraft Battery at S.W. of DIEUZE.
  1 112 lb. and 8 25 lb. on train at FALKENBURG.
  1 112 lb. and 8 25 lb. on Railway S.W. of DIEUZE.

100 SQUADRON

Date.—13/14th August, 1918.   *Objective.*—BUHL Aerodrome.

Taking Part :—

Pilots.	*Observers.*
Lieut. Erwin.	Lieut. Conover.
,, Van Schaack.	,, King.
,, Hobson.	,, Naylor.
,, Crofts.	2nd-Lieut. Pascoe.
,, Siddaway.	Lieut. Ross.
,, Box.	,, Inches.
Capt. Savery.	,, Gilson.
Lieut. Proctor.	2nd-Lieut. Dyson.
,, Johnson.	Capt. Wilson.

Bombs Dropped.—7 112 lb., 4 40 lb. and 58 25 lb.

Results.—4 112 lb., 2 40 lb. and 28 25 lb. on BUHL. Results unobserved.
     3 112 lb., 2 40 lb. and 14 25 lb. on SAARBURG Railway Junction.
     8 25 lb. on MORHANGE Aerodrome. Results unobserved.
     1 25 lb. on a Car.
     7 25 lb. on Furnaces West of FREIMENGES.

Date.—14/15th August, 1918.   *Objective.*—BUHL Aerodrome.

Taking Part :—

Pilots.	*Observers.*
Lieut. Van Schaack.	Lieut. King.
,, Johnson.	Capt. Wilson.
,, Erwin.	Lieut. Conover.
,, Siddaway.	Lieut. Ross.
,, Proctor.	2nd-Lieut. Dyson.
,, Ebrey.	,, Sherwood.
,, Hobson.	Lieut. Naylor.
,, Taylor.	2nd-Lieut. Warneford.
,, Crofts.	,, Pascoe.
,, Middleton.	,, Shillinglaw.
Capt. Savery.	Lieut. Gilson.
Lieut. Box.	,, Inches.

Bombs Dropped.—11 112 lb., 2 40 lb. and 86 25 lb.

Results.—11 112 lb., 2 40 lb. and 86 25 lb. on BUHL. Results unknown owing to bad
visibility.

Date.—15/16th August, 1918.   *Objective.*—BOULAY, FRIESDORF and BUHL Aerodromes.

Taking Part :—

Pilots.	*Observers.*
Lieut. Potter.	2nd-Lieut. Shillinglaw.
,, Gower.	,, Chainey.
,, Siddaway.	Lieut. Ross.
,, Ebrey.	2nd-Lieut. Sherwood.
,, Proctor.	,, Dyson.
,, Van Schaack.	Lieut. King.
,, Middleton.	2nd-Lieut. Segnor.
,, Box.	Lieut. Inches.
,, Erwin.	,, Conover.
,, Johnson.	Capt. Wilson.

Bombs Dropped.—10 112 lb. and 80 25 lb.

100 SQUADRON

Results.—5 112 lb. and 40 25 lb. on BOULAY. Results unknown.
  2 112 lb. and 16 25 lb. on BUHL. Results unknown.
  2 112 lb. and 16 25 lb. on FRIESDORF. Results unknown,
  1 112 lb. and 8 25 lb. on train going East at MAILWEILER.

Remarks.—Lieut. Johnson, Pilot ; and Capt. Wilson, Observer, on their way back from
  FRIESDORF saw a twin engine machine below them. Lieut. Johnson dived on
  to this machine, Capt. Wilson opening fire, and after a burst of about 45
  rounds, the machine crashed alongside the flare path, the searchlight on the
  ground immediately put its beam on to this machine which was observed to be
  a total wreck.

Date.—16/17th August, 1918.   *Objective.*—Active Aerodromes.

Taking Part :—

Pilots.	Observers.
Lieut. Blakemore.	2nd-Lieut. Warneford.
,, Middleton.	,, Shillinglaw.
,, Taylor.	Lieut. Ross.
,, Gower.	2nd-Lieut. Chainey.
,, Box.	Lieut. Inches.
,, Johnson.	Capt. Wilson.

Bombs Dropped.—7 112 lb. and 63 25 lb.

Results.—1 112 lb. and 8 25 lb. on BUHL Aerodrome. Results unknown owing to mist.
  1 112 lb. and 8 25 lb. on MORHANGE Aerodrome.   Results unknown, owing to
    mist.
  4 112 lb. and 39 25 lb. on BOULAY Aerodrome. Results unknown, owing to mist.
  1 112 lb. and 8 25 lb. on REMILLY Junction. Results unknown, owing to mist.

  German Report :—

16/17/8/18.—MORHANGE.

  The long hangar to the North of the Aerodrome was hit and burnt to the ground, other
bombs destroyed two other hangars containing machines. A third hangar rendered unserviceable and machines were riddled.

Date.—17/18th August, 1918.   *Objective.*—Active Aerodromes.

Taking Part :—

Pilots.	Observers.
Lieut. Erwin.	Lieut. Conover.
,, Van Schaack.	Lieut. King.
,, Ebrey.	2nd-Lieut. Sherwood.
,, Middleton.	,, Shillinglaw.
,, Hobson.	,, Segner.
,, Siddaway.	Lieut. Hobson.
,, Taylor.	2nd-Lieut. Pascoe.
,, Gower.	,, Chainey.

Bombs Dropped.—9 112 lb. and 72 25 lb.

Results.—3 112 lb. and 23 25 lb. on MORHANGE. Direct hits on two hangars.
  3 112 lb. and 12 25 lb. on FRIESDORF. Results unknown.
  1 112 lb. and 14 25 lb. on BOULAY. Direct hit on one hangar.
  2 112 lb. and 23 25 lb. on Landing Ground at BUSCHDORF.

Casualties.—One machine missing. Pilot Lieut. Van Schaack ; Observer, Lieut. King.

100 SQUADRON

BOULAY—DESTROYED HANGARS.

Date.—18/19th August, 1918.   *Objective.*—Active Aerodromes.

Taking Part :—

Pilots.	Observers.
Lieut. Blakemore.	2nd-Lieut. Warneford.
,, Hobson.	,, Segner.
,, Taylor.	,, Pascoe.
,, Gower.	,, Chainey.
,, Siddaway.	Lieut. Ross.
,, Middleton.	2nd-Lieut. Shillinglaw.
,, Dickens.	Sergt. O'Donoghue.

Bombs Dropped.—7 112 lb. and 56 25 lb.

Results.—1 112 lb. and 8 25 lb. on Railway at HAMPONT. Results unknown.
    1 112 lb. and 8 25 lb. on MANY. Results unknown.
    4 112 lb. and 28 25 lb. on BOULAY Aerodrome. Results unknown.
    1 112 lb. and 14 25 lb. on MORHANGE Aerodrome. Results unknown.

Date.—19/20th August, 1918.   *Objective.*—BOULAY Aerodrome.

Two Raids.
Taking Part :—

Pilots.	Observers.
Lieut. Ebrey.	2nd-Lieut. Shillinglaw.
,, Siddaway.	Lieut. Ross.
,, Hobson.	2nd-Lieut. Segner.
,, Blakemore.	,, Warneford.
,, Dickens (2).	Sergt. O'Donoghue (2).
,, Gower.	2nd-Lieut. Chainey.
,, Taylor.	,, Pascoe.
,, Erwin.	Lieut. Conover.

100 SQUADRON

Bombs Dropped.—9 112 lb. and 72 25 lb.

Results.—3 112 lb. and 48 25 lb. on BOULAY Aerodrome. Several direct hits claimed.
2 112 lb. and 14 25 lb. on Trains. These were brought to a standstill.
1 112 lb. and 8 25 lb. on Railway Triangle N.E. of AVRICOURT.
2 25 lb. on MORHANGE Aerodrome. Results unknown.

Date.—20/21st August, 1918.　　　　　*Objective.*—BOULAY and Active Aerodromes.

Taking Part :—

Pilots.	Observers.
Lieut. Erwin.	Lieut. Conover.
,, Dickens.	Sergt. O'Donoghue.
,, Blakemore.	2nd-Lieut. Warneford.
,, Middleton.	,, Shillinglaw.
,, Ebrey.	,, Segner.
,, Taylor.	,, Pascoe.
,, Siddaway.	Lieut. Ross.

Bombs Dropped.—7 112 lb. and 56 25 lb.

Results.—6 112 lb. and 51 25 lb. on BOULAY Aerodrome. Results unknown.
1 25 lb. on MANY. Results unknown.
1 112 lb. and 4 25 lb. on machine landing on MORHANGE. Results unknown.

Date.—21/22nd August, 1918.　　　　　*Objective.*—MORHANGE Aerodrome.

Taking Part :—

Pilots.	Observers.
Lieut. Blakemore.	2nd-Lieut. Warneford.
,, Hobson.	,, Segner.
,, Box.	Lieut. Inches.
,, Miles.	2nd-Lieut. Pascoe.
,, Dickens.	Sergt. O'Donoghue.
,, Gower.	2nd-Lieut. Chainey.

Bombs Dropped.—6 112 lb. and 48 25 lb.

Results.—1 112 lb. and 8 25 lb. on BUHL. Bursts alongside machine landing.
5 112 lb. and 40 25 lb. on MORHANGE. Several direct hits.

MORHANGE. THREE HANGARS, SIMILAR TO THE ONES SHOWN, AND WHICH CONTAINED MACHINES, WERE DESTROYED DURING A RAID BY THE SQUADRON.

129

J

100 SQUADRON

Date.—22/23rd August, 1918. *Objective.*—FOLPESWEILIER Aircraft Park.

Taking Part :—

Pilots.	*Observers.*
Lieut. Miles.	2nd-Lieut. Keely.
,, Dickens.	Sergt. O'Donoghue.
,, Blakemore.	2nd-Lieut. Warneford.
,, Hobson.	,, Segner.
,, Gower.	,, Pascoe.
,, Box.	Lieut. Inches.

Bombs Dropped.—6 112 lb. and 48 25 lb.

Results.—4 112 lb. and 32 25 lb. on FOLPESWEILIER.   Very good shooting.   A large fire
was started in Store Hangar.
1 112 lb. and 8 25 lb. on Factory at SAARALBEN.   Direct hits on Factory.   Several explosions seen and large fire started.
1 112 lb. and 8 25 lb. on Railway Triangle N.E. of AVRICOURT.
    (*a*)   Photographs of SAARALBEN taken 23rd August, show :—
        (1) A building of the Chemical Factory has been severely damaged.
        (2) Two buildings east of the Quarry considerably damaged.
    (*b*)   Intelligence reports " Works damaged and 100 containers destroyed."
    (SAARALBE works were attacked by Lieut. Miles (p.) and Lieut Keely (o.).

Date.—23/24th August, 1918. *Objective.*—BOULAY Aerodrome.

Taking Part :—

Pilots.	*Observers.*
Lieut. Siddaway.	Lieut. Ross.
,, Gower.	2nd-Lieut. Pascoe.
Capt. Darby.	,, Keely.

Bombs Dropped.—16 112 lb. and 16 25 lb.

Results.—16 112 lb. and 16 25 lb. on line of hangars at BOULAY.   Results unknown.

Date.—30/31st August, 1918. *Objective.*—BOULAY Aerodrome.

Taking Part :—

Pilots.	*Observers.*
Lieut. Johnson.	2nd-Lieut. Chainey and 2nd-Lieut. Jamieson.
Capt. Savery.	Lieut. Gilson and Sergt. O'Donoghue.
Lieut. Taylor.	2nd-Lieut. Dyson.
,, Siddaway.	Lieut. Ross.
,, Ebrey.	2nd-Lieut. Shillinglaw.

Bombs Dropped.—31 112 lb. and 24 25 lb.

Results—31 112 lb. and 24 25 lb. on BOULAY Aerodrome.   Four small fires started.

100 SQUADRON

Date.—2/3rd September 1918.   *Objective.*—DOULAY Aerodrome.

Taking Part :—

Pilots.   *Observers.*

Lieut. Johnson.   2nd-Lieut. Chainey and 2nd-Lieut. Jamieson.
Capt. Savery.   Lieut. Gilson and Sergt. O'Donoghue.

Bombs Dropped.—27 112 lb.

Results.—27 112 lb. on hangars running North and South and East and West.   Results unknown.

Date.—3/4th September, 1918.   *Objective.*—MORHANGE Aerodrome.

Taking Part :—

Pilots.   *Observers.*

Lieut. Johnson.   2nd-Lieut. Segner and 2nd-Lieut. Jamieson.
" Gower.   2nd-Lieut. Shillinglaw and 2nd-Lieut. Warneford.
" Matthews.   Sergt. O'Donoghue and 2nd.-Lieut. Pascoe.

Bombs Dropped.—42 112 lb.

Results.—42 112 lb. on MORHANGE. A fire started at South-east corner.

Date.—6/7 September, 1918.   *Objective.*—LORQUIN Aerodrome.

Taking Part :—

Pilot.   *Observers.*

Lieut. Matthews.   2nd-Lieut. Pascoe and Sergt. O'Donoghue.

Bombs Dropped.—13 112 lb.

Results.—13 112 lb. on LORQUIN. A fire started in large Building.

Date.—12/13 September, 1918.   *Objective.*—METZ-SABLON Railway.

Taking Part :—

Pilot.   *Observers.*

Lieut. Johnson.   2nd-Lieut. Chainey and Lieut. Blakemore.

Bombs Dropped.—16 112 lb.

Results.—16 112 lb. on and near Railway.

German Report :—

12/13/9/18.—METZ.
   1.30 a.m. 4 bombs dropped. METZ Local Goods Station hit.   Tracks 19 and 20 put out of action. 3 trucks very badly damaged. Telephone wires broken.

100 SQUADRON

Date.—13/14 September, 1918.

Objective.—COURCELLES Railway Junction, BUHL and BOULAY Aerodromes.

Taking Part :—

Pilots.	*Observer.*
Capt. Savery.	2nd-Lieut. Wilkins and 2nd-Lieut. Rennie.
2nd-Lieut. Gower.	2nd-Lieut. Shillinglaw and 2nd-Lieut. Warneford.

Bombs Dropped.—10 112 lb.

Results.—10 112 lb. on Railway line S.E. of COURCELLES Junction.

Date.—14/15th September, 1918.

Objective.—METZ-SABLON Triangle and BOULAY Aerodrome.

Taking Part :—

Pilots.	*Observers.*
Lieut. Matthews.	2nd-Lieut. Pascoe and Lieut. Potter.
,, Miles.	Lieut. Ross and 2nd-Lieut. Mason.
,, Matthews.	2nd-Lieut. Pascoe and Lieut. Potter.

Bombs Dropped.—47 112 lb.

Results.—4 112 lb. on Railway Junction East of METZ.
27 112 lb. inside METZ Triangle.
16 112 lb. on BOULAY Aerodrome.

German Report :—

14/15/9/18.—METZ.
12.45 a.m.—3.0 a.m., 14 bombs dropped on METZ-SABLONS. A large number of tracks rendered unserviceable. Electric light circuits SABLONS West serious damage. A number of locomotives and trucks very seriously damaged. Considerable damage to buildings, stoppage of traffic for 24 hours.

Date.—15/16th September, 1918.   *Objective.*—LORQUIN Aerodrome.

Taking Part :—

Pilot.	*Observers.*
Capt. Coombs.	2nd-Lieut. Wilkins and 2nd-Lieut. Mason.

Bombs Dropped.—40 112 lb., 6 Cases of B.I.

Results.—24 112 lb. and 6 cases B.L. on LORQUIN. Small fire started.
8 112 lb. on BUHL.
8 112 lb. on Transport. Direct hits observed.

100 SQUADRON

Date.—16/17th September, 1918.   *Objective.*—FERSCATY Aerodrome and FRANKFURT

Taking Part :—

Pilot.	Observers.
Capt. Miles.	2nd-Lieut. Jamieson and 2nd-Lieut. Segner.

Bombs Dropped.—24 112 lb. and 7 Cases of B.I.

Results.—24 112 lb. and 7 Cases of B.I. on Zeppelin Shed, which was set on fire.

Casualties.—One machine missing, Lieut. Johnson; Observers, Lieut. Pitman and 2nd Lieut. Chainey. (All prisoners of war).

A PORTION OF LUDWIGSHAFEN AND MANNHEIM. THE BADISCHE ANILINE WORKS CAN BE SEEN IN THE LEFT-HAND BOTTOM CORNER.

Date.—20/21st September, 1918.

Objective.—LANZ Works, MANNHEIM, Gas Works, KARLSRUHE and BURBACH Works.

Taking Part :—

Pilots.	Observers.
Capt. Coombs.	2nd-Lieut. Wilkins and 2nd-Lieut. Mason.
Lieut. Gower.	Lieut. Ross and 2nd-Lieut. Wood.

Bombs Dropped.—42 112 lb.

Results.—14 112 lb. on KARLSRUHE. Several direct hits on Wharves.
     14 112 lb. on MANNHEIM. Results unobserved.
     14 112 lb. on BURBACH Works. Three distinct hits on Blast Furnaces.

133

100 SQUADRON

Date.—21/22nd September, 1918.   *Objective.*—FRESCATY Aerodrome.

Taking Part :—

Pilots.	*Observers.*
Lieut. Gower.	2nd-Lieut. Ross and 2nd-Lieut. Rennie.
Capt. Miles.	2nd-Lieut. Jamieson and 2nd-Lieut. Wood.
,, Savery.	2nd-Lieut. Shillinglaw and 2nd-Lieut. O'Sullivan.

Bombs Dropped.—48 112 lb.

Results.—48 112 lb. on FRESCATY. 9 direct hits on hangars and sheds.
4 direct hits on buildings West of sheds. 6 direct on Railway Junction East of
FRESCATY.

Date.—26/27th September, 1918.   *Objective.*—MEZIERES Junctions.

Taking Part :—

Pilots.	*Observers.*
Lieut. Gower.	Capt. Lewis and Lieut. Ross.
Capt. Coombs.	2nd-Lieut. Wilkins.

Bombs Dropped.—1 550 lb. and 24 112 lb.

Results.—1 550 lb. and 8 112 lb. on THIONVILLE Railway Junction. Bursts with 112 lb. observed on Station.
16 112 lb. on Triangle of railway at METZ-SABLON. Direct hits observed.

German Report :—

26/27/9/18.—METZ.

17 bombs dropped, water main, six locomotives, a number of passenger and goods trucks
seriously damaged, also tracks seriously damaged. Considerable interruption of traffic for
24 hours.

Date.—30th September/1st October, 1918.   *Objective.*—BURBACH Works.

Taking Part :—

Pilot.	*Observers.*
Capt. Coombs.	2nd-Lieut. Wilkins and 2nd-Lieut. Cooper.

Bombs Dropped.—1 550 lb. and 8 112 lb.

Results.—1 550 lb. and 8 112 lb. on BURBACH Works. All bombs burst in and around
furnaces.

Date.—3/4th October, 1918. *Objective.*—BURBACH Works and MEZIERES Railway Junctions..

Taking Part :—

Pilots.	*Observers.*
Capt. Coombs.	2nd-Lieut. Wilkins and 2nd-Lieut. Lister.
Lieut. Gower.	Lieut. Ross and 2nd-Lieut. Greaves.

Bombs Dropped.—2 550 lb. and 16 112 lb.

Results.—1 550 lb and 8 112 lb. on MORHANGE. Results unobserved.
1 550 lb. and 8 112 lb. on METZ-SABLON. Results unobserved.

100 SQUADRON

Date.—5/6 October, 1918.

Objective.—Burbach Works and Mezieres Railway Junctions.

Taking Part :—

Pilots.	Observers.
2nd-Lieut. Hall.	2nd-Lieut. Segner and 2nd-Lieut. Wood.
,, Rattle.	2nd-Lieut. Jamieson and 2nd-Lieut. Rennie.
Capt. Coombs.	2nd-Lieut. Wilkins and 2nd-Lieut. Lister.
Lieut. Gower.	Lieut. Ross and 2nd-Lieut. Greaves.

Bombs Dropped.—2 550 lb. and 48 112 lb.

Results.—32 112 lb. on Morhange. Bursts along row of hangars.
  1 550 lb. and 8 112 lb. on Burbach Works. Bursts observed in Factory.
  1 550 lb. and 8 112 lb. on Mezieres. Bursts observed in Triangle.

Date.—9/10th October, 1918.   *Objective.*—Mezieres Railway Junctions.

Taking Part :—

Pilots.	Observers.
Lieut. Gower.	Lieut. Conover and 2nd-Lieut. Mason.
Capt. Coombs.	2nd-Lieut. Wilkins and 2nd-Lieut. Cooper.

Bombs Dropped.—2 550 lb. and 16 112 lb.

Results.—2 550 lb. and 16 112 lb. on Mezieres Railway Junction. All bombs burst in and
  around Triangle. Very good shooting observed.

Date.—10/11th October, 1918.   *Objective.*—Thionville Railway Junctions.

Taking Part :—

Pilot.	Observers.
2nd-Lieut. Hall.	2nd-Lieut. Segner and 2nd-Lieut. Birch.

Bombs Dropped.—16 112 lb.

Results.—16 112 lb. on Thionville. Good bursts in vicinity of Railways.

Date.—18/19th October, 1918.   *Objective.*—Metz-Sablon Triangle.

Taking Part :—

Pilot.	Observers.
Capt. Coombs.	2nd-Lieut. Wilkins and Sergt. Crutchett.

Bombs Dropped.—16 112 lb.

Results.—16 112 lb. on Saarburg Railway Junction. Results unobserved.

100 SQUADRON

Date.—21/22nd October, 1918.

Objective.—KAISERELAUTERN and MEZIERES Railway Junctions.

Taking Part :—

Pilots.	Observers.
Lieut. Gower.	2nd-Lieut. Cooper and Capt. Lewis.
Proctor.	2nd-Lieut. Sherwood and 2nd-Lieut. Wood.
Middleton.	2nd-Lieut. Shillinglaw and 2nd-Lieut. O'Sullivan.

KAISERLAUTERN. EFFECTS OF 1,600 LB. BOMB DROPPED NIGHT OF 21/22 SEPTEMBER, 1918.

Bombs Dropped.—1 1,600 lb. 16 112 lb. and 14 Cases of B.I.

Results.—1 1,600 lb. and 14 Cases of B.I. on KAISERSLAUTERN. B.I. started 3 small fires. 1,600 lb. in North-East corner.
16 112 lb. on MEZIERES. All direct hits in Triangle.

German Report :—

21/22/10/18.—KAISERSLAUTERN.

About 9.25 p.m. on the 21/22/10/18 a machine dropped a very large bomb in the N.E. corner of the town. The result was terrific. Several houses were very badly hit by pieces from this bomb which burst in a field 50—100 yards away from the houses. Several families are left homeless. The whole quarter is extensively damaged.

100 SQUADRON

Date.—23/24th October, 1918,

Objective.—MANNHEIM, MEZIERES, FRANKFURT and COLOGNE.

Taking Part :—

Pilots.	Observers.
Lieut. Gower.	2nd-Lieut. Cooper and 2nd-Lieut. King.
,, Taylor.	Capt. Lewis and 2nd-Lieut. Greaves.
,, Proctor.	2nd-Lieut. Sherwood and Sergt. Adair.
Capt. Coombs.	2nd-Lieut. Wilkins and Sergt. Crutchett.

KAISERLAUTERN. EFFECTS OF 1,600 LB. BOMB DROPPED ON NIGHT OF 21/22 SEPTEMBER, 1918.

Bombs Dropped.—1 1,600 lb., 1 550 lb. and 40 112 lb.

Results.— 1 1,600 lb., 1 550 lb. and 8 112 lb. on SAARBRUCKEN. Direct hits on Railway Station.
16 112 lb. on METZ. Results unknown.
16 112 lb. on BURBACH Works. Large explosion caused.

Date.—28/29th October, 1918.　　　　　　*Objective.*—LONGUYON Railway Junction.

Taking Part :—

Pilot.	Observers.
Lieut. Taylor.	2nd-Lieut. Shillinglaw and 2nd-Lieut. Birch.

Bombs Dropped.—1 550 lb. and 8 112 lb.

Results.—1 550 lb. and 8 112 lb. on LONGUYON Railway Junction. A large fire started.

100 SQUADRON

Date.—29/30th October, 1918.   Objective.—MANNHEIM.

Taking Part :—

Pilots.   *Observers.*

Lieut. Taylor.   2nd-Lieut. Shillinglaw and 2nd-Lieut. Birch.
2nd-Lieut. Hall.   2nd-Lieut. Cooper and 2nd-Lieut. Loftus.

Bombs Dropped.—1 550 lb. and 24 112 lb.

Results.—1 550 lb. and 24 112 lb. on OFFENBURG.   Results unobserved.

Date.—30/31st October, 1918.   Objective.—KARLSRUHE and BURBACH Works.

Taking Part :—

Pilots.   *Observers.*

Lieut. A. F. Evans.   Lieut. McKenzie and 2nd-Lieut. Warneford.
2nd-Lieut. Hall.   2nd-Lieut. Cooper and 2nd-Lieut. Loftus.

Bombs Dropped.—2 550 lb. and 16 112 lb.

Results.—1 550 lb. and 8 112 lb. on KARLSRUHE.   Railway Workshops.
1 550 lb. and 8 112 lb. on BURBACH Works.   Results unobserved.

Date.—5/6th November, 1918.   Objective.—LILLINGEN Aerodrome.

Taking Part :—

Pilot.   *Observers.*

Lieut. Taylor.   2nd-Lieut. Shillinglaw and 2nd-Lieut. Greaves.

Bombs Dropped.—14 Cases of B.I.

Results.—14 Cases of B.I. on LILLINGEN.   Results unobserved.

Date.—10/11th November, 1918.   Objective.—LILLINGEN and FRESCATY Aerodromes.

Taking Part :—

Pilots.   *Observers.*

Lieut. Crocker.   2nd-Lieut. Greaves and 2nd-Lieut. Best.
  ,,   White.   2nd-Lieut. Loftus and 2nd-Lieut. Gwyther.

Bombs Dropped.—8 112 lb. and 12 Cases of B.I.

Results.—8 112 lb. on LILLINGEN.   Results unobserved.
12 Cases of B.I. on FRESCATY.   A large fire started.

CHAPTER VII

CAPTURE. 24th January, 1918

By Lieut. Louis G. Taylor.

FIVE o'clock in the evening, and dusk is turning to darkness. The Pilots and Observers of 100 Squadron are all standing by their machines waiting for the start out. This show is to be the longest yet accomplished by a night flying Squadron. The target is Trier (Tréves) in Germany, and the return journey will be about 200 miles.

The order came, and my Observer (Lieut. Le Fevre) and I climbed into our machine, and away we went. The lights of Trier were extinguished on our approach, and a very heavy A.A. barrage was put up around the Central Station, which was the objective. After successfully dropping our bombs we were unfortunate enough to be hit by anti-aircraft, which put our rudder controls out of action. I looked towards my observer, who was leaning over the side and pouring a stream of machine gun fire into the City, and seemed to be thoroughly enjoying himself, although he looked like the Devil framed in a curtain of flickering shrapnel bursts from the A.A. guns. I tried to get the machine flying south, but failed, and finally by putting on a slight bank I got a straight course in a S. Westerly direction, but was slowly losing height. We travelled about 30 miles in this crippled condition. It was a maddening feeling to hear the roar of a perfect running engine and to be constantly losing height, but I kept on my course. I could at least fly as far as possible towards the lines and then, if opportunity offered we could try to escape from the country without being captured.

Ahead of us I saw the town of Esche in Luxemburg, and hearing a shout from my observer, I followed his pointing arm and saw that the town was defended by a balloon barrage (which is a steel net held up by balloons at intervals of about 50 yards). The balloons were at a height of about 4,000 feet, and it was impossible to get over them in our crippled condition, and to try to get round was worse than useless, so trusting to good luck I kept straight on, hoping to pass through the barrage without hitting a wire. My Observer immediately opened fire on the balloon above and straight in front of us, in the vain hope of setting it on fire, and dropping the net, but nothing happened. We were now passing underneath the balloons and for a moment I had the elated feeling that we must have missed the wires, but suddenly the machine gave a violent lurch, and was thrown backwards; I immediately put the nose down, but the speed indicator dial only registered 30 miles per hour, and then I knew that I was caught. I wondered why the machine did not stall and plunge to the ground. The aileron controls went out of order immediately we struck the net, and now the only control left was the elevator. Then followed a sickening five minutes, during which I tried to get down to the ground dragging the balloon and net round and round with me, and, thanks to a perfect engine we finally got close to the ground, which was heavily wooded. My Observer placed his machine gun to one side, and sat down to await the inevitable crash as calmly as possible, shouting a few encouraging words over his shoulder. We were only a few feet from the ground, the engine roaring, when I saw directly ahead a small quarry surmounted by a wood, while we were making direct for it. I frantically pulled back the control lever, the machine leapt into the air, hovering over the wood for a second, coming down with a crash in a small field just beyond. We fell on one wing which crumpled up beneath the weight: I saw the Observer leave the machine, when something struck my head and I lost consciousness. I could not have been unconscious for more than a few seconds when I came to my senses and found myself hanging out of the machine, while the wing which was sticking straight up into the air seemed to my dizzy brain to be toppling over on to me bringing the heavy engine with it. I tried to extricate myself from the wreck, and get away from the machine, but was too weak to do so. Eventually a voice roared into my ear, " All right, old thing, out you come," and a strong pair of arms went about me, when I was dragged clear. I staggered to my feet a few moments later to be met by a flash of rifle fire at about 20 yards distance by about 10 or more Huns, who were running and shouting like maniacs. I felt my Observer grab me by the shoulder and I was flung down on my face, he dropping beside me. The bullets were whistling by and it's a great wonder neither of us was hit. We were immediately

DAWN.
" THE LAST HOME."

surrounded by the Huns and taken prisoners in no gentle manner. They marched us to a guard house, gibbering to each other and to us all the while, we were thrown inside and a guard placed over us.

After waiting for about an hour the door opened and a German officer swaggered in, followed by several gaudily dressed officials, one of whom was an interpreter, and the usual questioning started :

Where did you come from?
The other side of the lines.
Yes, we know that, but whereabouts?
We can't tell you.
You must.
We refuse.

After a short conversation amongst themselves they changed their tactics, the Interpreter produced some paper and pen and the questioning was resumed :—

Which of you is the Pilot?
I am.
Your name?
Lieut. ———
Age?
28.
Address?
Air Board, England.
What type of machine are you flying?
Cannot answer.
Where have you been to-night?
Cannot say.
You might as well answer, because your machine was followed all the way from Trier by the telephones.
Well, if you know, why ask?
How long were you in the air?
I suppose another question will be what speed does your machine travel, in other words, you're trying to find how far it is from here to my aerodrome.
Do you refuse to answer?
Certainly.
What bombs were you carrying?
Cannot answer.
How much petrol does your machine carry?
Cannot answer.
You mean you refuse to answer these questions?
Certainly, but you can take this down :—My name is Lieut. —
My age is 28 years.. My address is Air Board, England. You can save yourself the trouble of asking further questions, because I refuse to answer.
Hum, now the Observer. Will you answer any questions?

Certainly, you can have my name, rank, age, and Army address.

Good, what is your Army address?

Air Board, England.

Where did you come from?

My name is Lieut. ——, age ——. I answer nothing more.

Well, I suppose you gentlemen know your own business best, but you are foolish, and you will be sorry. The Commandant of

ONE OF THE M.G. EMPLACEMENTS FOR REPELLING AIRCRAFT ATTACKS.

Luxembourg will interview you to-morrow, and then you will answer questions. Now you can come with me.

Our examination over, we were met at the door by another officer with a bloodhound, which was allowed to give us a good sniff, and then we were put in a large Staff Motor-car, with three German Officers and the bloodhound, and driven through Esche. It was now about 9.30 p.m., and as we were entering the main part of the town I heard the cheerful sound of one of our machines, homeward bound. Our car then glided out from under the railway bridge under which it had gone for safety, and we finally drew up outside the civilian jail of Esche, where we were searched and placed in separate cells for the night.

Next morning the staff car with its complement of officers and bloodhound called for us, and we were driven back to the field on which we were captured and allowed to stroll about within a short radius of the guard room.   It was a beautiful sunny morning, and it seemed as if the whole of the civil population of Esche had turned up to see us and our crashed machine, and they seemed to be in sympathy with us and had to be kept away by the Hun guards with fixed bayonets, who repeatedly threatened to shoot them if they did not keep their distance.   (These people were natives of Luxemburg, and this perhaps accounts for their sympathy towards us.)   I had a chat in broken English and French with a German Sergt-Major, who seemed to be quite a decent chap, and did not seem to care how far we wandered so long as the sentries could keep us in view, but we could not go as far as the civilian crowds.

From the guard house the balloon barrage was regulated electrically, and I was sitting on the large winding drum outside talking to the Sergt-Major, when there arrived our questioner of the previous night, followed by a very important looking person with a bulgy bull-like neck and glittering buttons.   He had the look of a typical Hun as cartooned in England, and a fierce moustache, and we both immediately took a violent dislike to him and looked ahead for trouble.   We were taken inside the Guard room, and after returning salutes with the Commandant the questioning again started on exactly the same lines as on the previous night, but with no better results for them.   There was a short conversation held between the Interpreter and the Commandant and then the former turned to me and said :—"The Commandant asks me to tell you that until you tell us where you came from there will be no food for you, so you might as well tell us now instead of having to give in later."   This information made me furious, and I told him to tell the Commandant that I expected he knew a Britisher well enough by now to know that that kind of threat would not help him, and to carry on and execute it.   After hearing this the Commandant got furiously angry, I thought he would have a fit, his face got so red, but he finally calmed down, and we all went over to the wretched machine.   When I saw it I could have cried, it was such a mess.   The planes and nacelle were riddled with shrapnel holes, and one of the tail booms was almost cut in two near the main planes. The nose was driven into the ground and one wing was crumpled up underneath the engine. The other wing was sticking straight up in the air, and I saw the balloon wire which had been our final undoing. It had just missed the nacelle by about two feet, and had entered both top and bottom planes of the upper wings just in front of the bomb rack. It had sawed its way anglewise towards the propeller from this point, and had cut the aileron balance wires through, passed through the steel bomb rack and was finally held up by the Michelin flare rack which was fairly heavy steel, but it had completely worked its way through about three-quarters of the distance from leading to trailing edges of both top and bottom planes. This accounted for the loss of my aileron controls on the previous night. The undercarriage was gone and the tail broken off at the end of the booms. The rudder wires on one side were cut clean by Archie and there was practically no fabric left on the rudder. The cockpit was a mess of accumulators. I picked up the loaded Very's pistol and was looking for a place to fire it at the petrol soaked planes, when it was knocked out of my hand by one of the German officers, but it didn't matter, for the machine was a total wreck.

We were then photographed standing by the wreck by the Staff photographer. Then followed a very clever questioning by a German aviator, who walked round the machine with me. He was speaking in a very friendly tone, in perfect English. "This was a good machine, wasn't it?" "Yes."

" You must feel rotten to see its finish in this way?"

" Yes, I do."

" Well, I'm sorry for you, really I am, but if you had our latest bomber to fly, this wouldn't have happened."

" Why?"

" Well, because it has so many advantages over this machine, let me demonstrate; our machine travels at 80 miles per hour, how fast does yours go?"

" Oh, about the same (altho' I knew it would only go 65)."

" Hum, I wouldn't have thought it, but our Gotha can stay up so much longer than yours, you see we carry more petrol, does this machine carry much?"

"Oh, quite a fair amount."

"How much petrol does your machine use in an hour?"

"Why don't you ask me right out where I came from instead of making calculations on my answers if I give any?"

"Well, you see, I personally am not interested in where you came from, so I'm sure you won't mind answering me for my own personal information."

"I'm very sorry, you seem to wish to be friendly, but I cannot answer any such questions, I'm sure you will excuse me."

Then followed other ruses to induce me to talk. Two of their flying officers started picking up different things, and after holding an argument amongst themselves they would finally turn to me to settle the argument, but it was all quite apparent to me that they were only after information. When they finally returned to the Guard house thoroughly beaten, we were placed in a motor lorry with a guard of five soldiers with rifles and bayonets and driven away.

It was a long drive through the country, by the sun I judged we were going direct south towards the lines and was only hoping for a chance later of giving our guards the slip, but the chance did not come. After driving for about two hours we arrived at the town Diedenhoffen. More questioning followed here; we were then taken away, and if it had not been for our guard, who had great trouble with the civil population, we should have been mobbed and torn to bits. We finally arrived at a civilian jail, and were unceremoniously searched by a brute of a Hun, then thrown into dirty concrete cells. There was absolutely no light in these cells, and the only furniture consisted of a dirty wooden pallet to lie on, but I was so tired that I was glad to fall on to it, and immediately fell asleep. A little while later I was awakened by the heavy bolts and locks being undone. Thinking I was in for more questioning I jumped up to be greeted by the jailor with a bowl of liquid and some bread. "Coffee and Bread," he informed me, and as I was almost famished I made a dive for it, and tried to eat, but the dirty greasy black bread stuck in my throat and would not go down. I tried to wash it down with the lukewarm coffee, but found to my disgust that the liquid was a concoction of what I afterwards discovered was acorn water.

I awoke next morning almost frozen. The night had been bitterly cold and my limbs were all cramped up; I could hardly move. My hunger was awful, but still I could not eat the filth I had been given the previous night. At about 9 o'clock we were taken out of our cells and under a new guard of two young soldiers we

A GROUP OF PILOTS AND OBSERVERS.

were marched to the station. There I sat down on one of the platform benches and we were immediately surrounded by a gaping crowd of Hun soldiers and subjected to jeering remarks, such as "L'Allemagne ober England," "King George Kaput," and other such compliments as "Schweinerei Engländer"; at last I saw our guard losing his temper and he ordered them all back, but with no effect. Just then a German officer swaggered by and keeping our seats we took no notice of him. He immediately turned on us, shouting "England Schweinerei, get up when I pass," but still we took no notice of him and working himself into a fury he screamed "Get up," advancing on us meanwhile with his hand on his revolver holster. But one thing was certain, I would not get up for this bully. I got angry, and pulling my flying kit on one side I exposed the stars on my shoulder, and shouted something back at him. This seemed to set him thinking, for he suddenly stopped short, stammered and finally slunk away like a whipped puppy. I was smiling to myself when the voice of my young guard whispered in my ear, " You beat that beast, Engländer." I was so surprised that you could have knocked me down with a feather, but just then our train pulled in and we got aboard, just we two and our guard in a carriage. The guard told me we were going to Flying Corps Headquarters at Jarny, and would stop for two hours at noon in Metz.

Metz is quite a large town with a beautiful station building, and we were immediately taken by our guards into a huge waiting and refreshment room to sit and wait for our train. I felt very hungry, watching the Germans come in and order a meal, so I asked the guard if he could obtain us something to eat. He asked me if I had any money, I replied I had English money. "Give it me," he replied, "I will see what can be done." I handed it over and he went away leaving us in charge of his comrade. When he came back a few minutes later, he told me he had ordered dinner and he handed me 40 marks for the £2 which was fair exchange. I thought that it was very good of him after the kind of treatment we had been getting, and when the meal finally came along I asked them both to order something for themselves; by the way they tucked in I thought they appeared more hungry than I was. Next I asked for a shave, which I greatly needed, and was taken to the station barber. It was now time to catch the train.

We travelled from Metz to Conflans without anything exciting, and I found that although our guards were kind to us, they did not take any chances; which made escape impossible.

There was a large car waiting for us at Conflans, and after getting in we were run to a Flying Headquarters, where we were left in a room to await events. First the Observer was called away, so while I was waiting for him I busied myself in looking at the photos which the German Flying Corps had taken from the air. I walked round the room looking first at one Aerodrome I knew and then another and finally came to a beautiful photo of our own Aerodrome, but I paid no special attention to it and passed along to another which I studied closely for the benefit of anyone who might be

watching.   When I was finally called away I passed the Observer
in the corridor and whispered to him to take no notice of the photos
on the walls of the waiting room.

I was taken upstairs to a comfortably furnished sitting room in
which were three officers of the German Flying Corps.   They were
all young fellows, very smart, and at once set themselves the task
of being amiable.   On the small side table was a tray containing
a bottle of some kind of liqueur, and four liqueur glasses, after
asking me if I cared for a drink they filled the four glasses and passed
them round.   The conversation started on the present weather rela-
tive to flying, what a nice time they were having in the Flying
Corps, and about the Americans who they thought were not coming
to France at all, and several other things, but never a question until
they thought I had had sufficient drink to make me talkative.   They
started their conversation with sarcasm, expecting me to get indig-
nant; boasts about their machines, an attempt to get me to draw com-
parisons having failed, they asked me a straight question.   Now this
was just what I was waiting for and it gave me a chance to test the
sportsmanlike instincts of these young airmen, so I said :—'' Now
that you fellows have perhaps finished attempting to get me drunk
on liqueurs (I may say you chose the wrong class of a drink to do it
with), and you have given up all mean attempts to gain information
you come out on top with a straight honest question.   Now let's
change places, suppose yourselves to be prisoners on my side of the
lines and being questioned to death by our Intelligence Department.
How much would you tell them?''   They all three looked at me for
a full minute, and then one of them who was a German American
and spoke English perfectly said, '' I guess you're right, we won't
bother you any more, but I'm disappointed, your Observer was like
an image, and wouldn't open his mouth either.''   '' Well, if you
gentlemen have really finished with me, maybe I can retire,'' with
this retort I went back to the Observer.   We were then placed in the
car again and driven to Jarny, which was only about two miles from
Conflans, and here we were taken to the Commandant of the Flying
Corps Office and further questioning ensued, but this time of a more
simple character, confined to Name, Rank, Address, etc., and so we
had no trouble.   We were then invited to his billets for dinner that

night and on arrival found quite a passable meal, beer to take
with it.   This Commandant had undoubtedly been told by telephone
that I had been drinking liqueurs, so was going to attempt to get me
talkative by the quickest and shortest method, that of mixing our
drinks.   He was very wise, this man, and when I refused to drink

A CHEERY PICNIC AT OCHEY.

he did not object.   He could not speak good English, so he spoke
in disjointed French, which I had no trouble in understanding, as I
could speak French fairly well.

"You speak good French," he remarked.

"Yes, fairly well," I answered.

"Where did you learn it? "

I thought over this question for a while, and replied, "At
school, of course."

"Not in France? "

"No."

"Perhaps you had no chance of learning French there when
you were constantly working with Englishmen?"

"Perhaps not."

"Is there much snow on your side of the lines? "

"Whereabouts? "

"Where your Squadron is?"

"I cannot answer that question."

"Why not, you don't for a moment think that we don't know your Aerodrome, do you?"

A FLIGHT READY FOR OPERATIONS.

"I shouldn't be surprised at anything."

"Just wait a moment, and we will see."

He went to a desk and after a moment he returned with a large photo stuck on foolscap paper in his hand, and underneath the photo was some writing in English. He handed it to me, and stood watching me out of the corner of his eyes, and pretending not to notice me. I looked at the photo and would have started if it wasn't for the fact that I was prepared for it; what I saw was the photograph of our Aerodrome with all our machines in line, as also the Handley Pages. Underneath was printed "Ochez Aerodrome." Squadron of Naval No. 1 A. Handley Pages, under the command of Major— and Squadron 100 R.F.C. F.E.2B. Night Bombers commanded by Major ———. It was a perfect photograph taken from about 18,000 feet, but I paid very little attention to it and handed it back to him. He then handed it to the Observer, but got no satisfaction.

"Well," said the German, "Wouldn't you like us to drop a letter over the lines to tell your people you are alive and well?"

"Yes, I would, will you do it?"

"Certainly, we will, here's paper and pen. You write it and let me have it."

I addressed a letter home, sealed it up, and handed it to him.

"Whereabouts shall we drop it? I dropped one personally the other day for a prisoner at Izel-le-Hameau, behind Arras."

"You can drop it anywhere behind the lines, I will take chances on it getting home."

"We cannot do that, it would never get home."

"All right, tear it up then. My people can wait until I can let them know in the usual way."

"But that will take two months, and this way will only take about a week to get to England."

I could see the devilish cunning in his method of playing on the feelings of your people at home, but it didn't work this time.

Finally, they tired of this useless battle of wits, and we were sent under guard to Conflans for the night.

On the next day, January 27th (the Kaiser's birthday) we witnessed through the window a large ceremonial parade. Several bands played the German National Anthem, and the troops goose stepped past the flag.

Then arrived a meal of saurkraut, potatoes, meat, bread, and soup, we being told that even prisoners were well fed on the Kaiser's birthday.

That evening we were sent back to Jarny, and there put in a hut on the outskirts of the village. We stayed in this bitterly cold hole for three days and nights, being only allowed out of our hut to walk in the cage for half an hour a day, consequently we were stiff with cold.

During the three days we were in this cage at Jarny nothing of any importance happened, and when on the fourth morning we were escorted from the place we were very thankful. Under the escort of a Prussian Sergeant-Major we walked to Conflans where we entrained, not knowing our destination.

After travelling for about two hours we changed trains, necessitating a wait of two hours. We were taken into the refreshment room, where our presence was objected to by some young German Officers, so we were moved to the Guard Room.

Entraining again, we travelled to our destination, which was Montmedy, where we were imprisoned in an old castle. We were put into separate cells and after being served with some black bread I was told by a Hun that my friend was in a room on the other side of the corridor and that I could go and see him. I went across immediately and knocked on the door, which to my surprise was opened by a young French aviator. He immediately saluted, stated his name and Squadron, and invited me into the room. Having been previously warned at my Squadron Headquarters against German impersonators, I was immediately on my guard, but this man could apparently speak no English and also no German, so I pretended not to know much French with the idea of forcing him to attempt explanations for his sentences in order to ascertain if I could connect him in any way with the Germans.

He immediately began telling me about his aerial flights against Huns and the awful treatment he had been subjected to as a prisoner, and when I pretended not to understand some of his words, his explanations more than confirmed my suspicions, so I refused to return his frankness. I left him and returned to my room, where I was locked in. Shortly afterwards I heard someone coming downstairs whistling, knowing it to be my Observer I called his name softly through the door, warning him against the French aviator. Sure enough the two were thrown together, but I afterwards learnt from my Observer that the only satisfaction the bogus Frenchman received was to be told to his face that he spoke French with a German accent. After an unpleasant night on the floor, and a few rats for company, I was taken to a small house, with barred windows, which stood inside the Castle walls. Shortly I was visited by a German Officer to whom I complained of the unnecessary separation of myself and Observer, and had the satisfaction of getting the Observer sent to me.

The meals in this place were worse than anything we had yet endured, consisting as they did of nothing more than three slices of black bread per day.

Four days later, in a half-starved and very unclean condition, we were taken to Montmedy Station, where we entrained for Karlsruhe, Germany. Arriving there about one o'clock in the morning we were taken to a large prisoners' hotel and shown into a room containing four beds, two of which were occupied by young Italian Officers. The place was clean and beds were covered with blankets and sheets. So feeling thoroughly tired we went to bed. Not being able to trust any strangers we refused to talk while in the room with the two Italians. About noon we were ordered to strip in order that our clothes could be fumigated. We were presented with bath robes and were taken to baths. On returning we were not allowed into our own room, but were shown to another. There were two officers inside the room whom I immediately recognised as Pilot and Observer from 100 Squadron, who had gone missing two days before myself and were believed killed. There was no recognition shown between us, although we knew each other perfectly well, until the watching Hun at the door had departed. This was probably a ruse to find out if we were from the same Squadron. We were subjected to another individual cross-examination in this hotel with no results.

In the evening we were put in a large room containing six beds, occupied by the four of us from 100 Squadron, and two English Infantry Officers. About an hour after one of these Infantry Officers drew our attention to a small disc of light shining through the wall paper near the ceiling, so climbing on to a bed I tore away the wallpaper and discovered a microphone behind. This was destroyed. We had always been on the alert for similar appliances having been previously warned before capture. The next morning we were moved to the regular internment camp for Officers at Karlsruhe, which contained about 250 Allied Officers, French, English and Italian, where we met many old acquaintances, two of whom were from 100 Squadron, and we were left in peace.

We spent two pleasant weeks at Karlsruhe Camp, at least, they seemed pleasant after our sojourns since capture, and to be left alone was something worth having. Here all our flying kit was taken from us, except the high sheepskin boots, this being the only footwear we possessed. Life was now intolerable and the Armistice, bringing along with it " release," came none too soon.

CHAPTER VIII

MAJOR-GENERAL TRENCHARD'S DISPATCH

AIR MINISTRY, Jan. 1st.

T HE Secretary of State for the Royal Air Force has received the following dispatch from Maj-Gen. Sir H. M. Trenchard, K.C.B., D.S.O., commanding the Independent Force, Royal Air Force :—

My Lord,—I have the honour to submit the following report 'on the work of the Independent Air Force from June 5th to the signing of the Armistice on Nov. 11th, 1918.

I have also mentioned in the early part of this report the work done in the attack on Germany by the squadrons from a base south-east of Nancy before the establishment of the Independent Air Force.

In May, 1918, you informed me that you considered it advisable to constitute an Independent Force to undertake the bombing of the industrial centres of Germany.

You further intimated to me that you intended to place the whole of the British effort in attacking Germany from the air under my command, and that it would be probable that squadrons would be available to carry out this work from England, as well as from the eastern area of France.

On May 20th, 1918, I proceeded to the Nancy area, where the 8th Brigade, R.A.F., under the local command of Brig.-Gen. C. L. N. Newall, consisting of :—

No. 55 Squadron, De Hav. 4, 275 h.p. Rolls-Royce ;
No. 99 Squadron, De Hav. 9, 200 h.p. B.H.P. ;
No. 100 Squadron, F.E. 2b, 160 h.p. Beardmore ;
No. 216 Squadron, Handley Page, 375 h.p. Rolls-Royce ;

was already established under Field-Marshal Sir Douglas Haig.

With the exception of No. 99 Squadn., this Force had been in this area since Oct. 11th, 1917.

I took over from Field-Marshal Sir Douglas Haig the tactical command of this Force on June 5th, and the administrative and complete control on June 15th, 1918.

From Oct. 11th, 1917, to June 5th, 1918, this small Force had, in spite of a very severe winter, carried out no less than 142 raids. Fifty-seven of these raids were made in Germany, and included night and day attacks on Cologne, Stuttgart, Mannheim, Mainz, and Coblenz. Long-distance raids had also been carried out against Namur, Charleroi, and Liège, in order to help in attacking the enemy's communications to the Western Front.

155

It should be remembered that No. 216 Sqdn. (at that time R.N.A.S.) was hastily formed, and was not equipped until October, 1917. No. 100 Sqdn. was only equipped with short-distance machines, and No. 99 Sqdn. only joined in May, 1918.

. . . .

The work during last winter called for exceptional efforts of endurance and perseverance on the part of the commanders, pilots, and observers.

. . . .

I take this opportunity of mentioning that the Independent Force was operating throughout in the zone of the group of the French Armies of the East under the command of Gen. de Castlenau, to whom I am indebted for the very valuable assistance which he and his staff gave me and for advice which helped me over the many difficulties inseparable from an organisation of such a kind. In fact, without his assistance it would have been almost impossible to have made an efficient organisation.

. . . .

My first work was to at once push on and arrange for the accommodation of a Force in the neighbourhood of 60 squadrons. This was a much larger task than may appear at first sight.

The country is throughout hilly and woody, and where there are any level places they consist of deep ridge and furrow, there being as much as 3 ft. 6 ins. between furrow and ridge.

The aerodromes had to carry heavy machines and heavy bomb loads; in order to enable this to be done, draining work on a large scale had to be very carefully carried out, and arrangements had to be made for a large installation of electrical power for workshops and lighting and petrol in order to save transport.

This work was practically completed by Nov. 1st, 1918.

It will be within your recollection that in the past I had referred to the necessity for equipping the British Expeditionary Force on the Western Front with sufficient aircraft to hold and beat the German aerial forces on the Western Front; that the bombing of Germany was a luxury till this had been accomplished, but that, once this had been accomplished, it became a necessity. That is to say, it became necessary to attack what I may call the German Army in Germany, and to strike at its most vital point—its sources of supply; and the Independent Force was formed with this object.

The question I had to decide was how to use this Force in order to achieve the object—*i.e.,* the breakdown of the German Army in Germany, its Government, and the crippling of its sources of supply.

The two main alternative schemes were :—

1. A sustained and continuous attack on one large centre after another until each centre was destroyed, and the industrial population largely dispersed to other towns, or

2. To attack as many of the large industrial centres as it was possible to reach with the machines at my disposal.

I decided on the latter plan, for the following reasons :—

(i.) It was not possible with the Forces at my disposal to do sufficient material damage so as to completely destroy the industrial centres in question.

156

(ii.) It must be remembered that, even had the Force been still larger, it would not have been practical to carry this out unless the war had lasted for at least another four or five years, owing to the limitations imposed on long-range bombing by the weather.

The weather during June, July, and August, was extremely favourable for long-distance bombing, but during September, October, and the first 10 days of November, it could hardly have been worse for this particular work. Day after day attempts were made to try to reach the long-distance targets, but the wind was generally too strong; or, if here was no wind, heavy rain and fog prevailed by day and dense mist by night, which lasted often until ten or eleven o'clock the next morning. Often the nights were perfect, but dense white mist completely obliterated the ground, making it impossible for machines to ascend.

Besides this, there are always a large number of technical difficulties to overcome which still further interfere with the continuity of long-range bombing.

By attacking as many centres as could be reached, the moral effect was first of all very much greater, as no town felt safe, and it necessitated continued and thorough defensive measures on the part of the enemy to protect the many different localities over which my Force was operating.

At present the moral effect of bombing stands undoubtedly to the material effect in a proportion of 20 to 1, and therefore it was necessary to create the greatest moral effect possible.

I also recommended, as you will recollect, the proportion of day bombing squadrons in the Force should be slightly larger than that of night bombing squadrons, as I considered that, although day bombing squadrons suffer higher casualties than night bombing squadrons, at the same time, if day bombing is excluded, at least four-fifths of the value of night-bombing must necessarily be wasted, owing to the fact that the enemy can then make his arrangements to work by day and live at a distance by night, and take many other similar defensive steps.

Also, if the bombing had been carried out exclusively by night it would not have caused the enemy to make such a large use of his men and material in defensive measures, and therefore it would not have affected the Western Front to such an extent as it did.

Though night bombing is the safer, many mistakes are made at night in reaching the locality it has been decided to bomb.

My Intelligence Department provided me with the most thorough information on all targets such as gas factories, aeroplane factories, engine factories, poison-gas factories, etc., each target having a complete detailed and illustrated plan, and maps were prepared of every target that was within reach. These were supplemented in a large way by the aerial photographs taken by reconnaissance machines.

Before it was possible to attack Germany successfully it was necessary to attack the enemy's aerodromes heavily in order to prevent his attacking our aerodromes by night, and by destroying his machines to render his attacks by day less efficacious. I considered that it was probable during the spring and early summer of 1919 that at least half my Force would be attacking the enemy's aerodromes, whilst the other half carried out attacks on long-distance targets in Germany.

It was also necessary several times during the period the Force operated to carry out attacks in conjunction with the Armies on the enemy's communications.

I also had to decide, when it was impossible for squadrons to reach their objectives well in the interior of Germany, what alternative objective should be attacked, and which attacks would have the greatest effect in hastening the end of hostilities. I decided that railways were first in order of importance, and next in importance the blast furnaces.

The reason of my decision was that the Germans were extremely short of rolling stock, and also some of the main railways feeding the German Army in the West passed close to our front, and it was hoped that these communications could be seriously interefered with, and the rolling stock and trains carrying reinforcements or reliefs or munitions destroyed. They were also fairly easy to find at night.

I chose the blast furnaces for the second alternative targets, as they were also easy to find at night, although it was difficult to do any really serious damage to them owing to the smallness of the vital part of the works.

On my arrival in the Nancy area the 8th Brigade consisted of those squadrons shown above. Additional squadrons arrived on the dates as shown :—

No. 104 Squadron, De Hav. 9, B.H.P., May 23rd.
No. 97 Squadron, Handley Page, Rolls Royce, Aug. 9th.
No. 215 Squadron, Handley Page, Rolls-Royce, Aug. 19th.
No. 115 Squadron, Handley Page, Rolls-Royce, Aug. 31st.
No. 110 Squadron, De Hav. 10, Liberty, Aug. 31st.
No. 45 Squadron, Sopwith Camel, Sept. 22nd.

During August No. 100 Squadron, which was armed with F.E. 2b short-distance machines, commenced re-equipping with Handley Pages. While it was being re-equipped—which process took nearly the whole month—scarcely any work could be carried out by the squadron.

Below are a few interesting figures :—

The total weight of bombs dropped between June 6th and Nov. 10th was 550 tons, of which 160 tons were dropped by day and 390 tons by night. Of this amount no less than 220¼ tons were dropped on aerodromes. This large percentage was due to the necessity of preventing the enemy's bombing machines attacking our aerodromes and in order to destroy large numbers of the enemy's scouts on their aerodromes, and it was impracticable to deal with them on equal terms in the air. I think this large amount of bombing was thoroughly justified when it is taken into consideration that the enemy's attacks on our aerodromes were practically negligible, and not a single machine was destroyed by bombing during the period June 5th to Nov. 11.

Photographs have proved time and again the efficiency of the work of the bombing machines. Captured correspondence testified to the great moral effect of the bombing attacks on Germany.

I would like to state here that the courage and determination shown by the pilots and observers were magnificent. There were cases in which a

100 SQUADRON

squadron lost the greater part of its machines on a raid, but this in no wise damped the other squadron's keenness to avenge their comrades, and to attack the same target again and at once.

It is to this trait in the character of the British pilots that I attribute their success in bombing Germany, as even when a squadron lost the greater part of its machines, the pilots, instead of taking it as a defeat for the Force, at once turned it into a victory by attacking the same targets again with the utmost determination. They were imbued with the feeling that whatever their casualties were, if they could help to shorten the war by one day and thus save many casualties to the Army on the ground, they were only doing their duty. I never saw, even when our losses were heaviest, any wavering in their determination to get well into Germany.

.   .   .   .

On the night of Oct. 21st-22nd machines of Nos. 97 and 100 Squadrons attacked the railways at Kaiserslautern in very bad weather. Several 1,650 lb. bombs were dropped, but bad visibility obscured the results. One very large fire and five smaller ones were observed, and all these fires were seen to be still burning when the town was lost sight of in the mist.

I would like to bring to your notice the work of bombing aerodromes done by No. 100 Squadron, commanded by Major C. G. Burge, when it was equipped with the short-distance F.E.2b machines, and also with Handley Pages. The squadron bombed aerodromes from low heights, and photographs show that a large number of sheds were hit.

The Independent Force, at the request of Marshal Foch, co-operated with the American First Army in its attack on the St. Mihiel salient, and it further co-operated with the Army by attacking important railway junctions behind the French lines in the combined offensive of Sept. 26th.

.   .   .   .

I have the honour to be, my Lord, your obedient Servant,

(Sgd.) H. TRENCHARD, Major--General, Commanding

Independent Force, Royal Air Force.

The Rt. Hon. the Lord Weir of Eastwood, Secretary of State for Air,
Air Ministry, London, W.C.

CHAPTER IX

EXPERIENCES OF PRISONERS OF WAR

A .Sequel to a Forced Landing in Enemy Territory.

THE EXPERIENCES OF LIEUTS. O. B. SWART AND A. FIELDING-CLARKE, AS TOLD BY THE FORMER

ON the evening of the 9th February, 1918, we started on a raid into Germany. My machine did not climb well, and the engine occasionally showed signs of some unpleasantness, but being a new pilot I was ashamed to return. Pride again. Well, we circled round the specified lighthouse, and then followed behind the leading machine when it arrived. We had a fairly quiet passage over the lines, and eventually came to the railway line which we followed up until we came to a junction, and saw a small village next to it. This appeared to be the spot we were looking for, so we pulled off our bombs and my observer fired at targets beneath. I only saw one bomb, a Cooper, go off to the South of the line, and near some houses. I had turned to the North sharply, and came past the station of Courcelles in order to give my observer a better chance of using his gun, and also to see the bombs go off. This was the juncture where my engine failed me, not completely, but as though two or three cylinders had stopped firing. I was hardly at a height of more than 1,900 feet, but I turned her head towards the lines and steered S.W. as the wind was more or less from the West. I also had a look at all my instruments which recorded everything correct, except the revolutions per minute. The pressure was all right, but I tried her on Gravity tank. No better, the vibrations were so bad I tried throttling back, but to no purpose. So we glided gradually nearer to the ground and also nearer to the line, but just when I thought we might do it the engine " cut out " completely. My observer behaved very well, firing at searchlights, and machine gun posts, though he knew what had happened to the engine. I was only a couple of hundred feet up now, and I decided to use my parachute flares, even if I was still in German territory, as it was rather misty, and I wanted to see what I had to land on. The first one did not show me much, but those my observer sent out showed that I was going to land on some small trees beneath. I thereupon lit my wing tip flare, and by its light saw a small clearing to the east, which I turned for, and in five seconds I was sailing down to it, and landed amongst hundreds of hares sitting bolt upright with the gleam of the reflected light shining out of their great big saucy eyes. The machine touched the ground without a jar, and came to a stop within thirty feet. My observer and I were both very thankful for this, and after talking it over we decided that there was just a possibility of having come down just across the line. I, however, had my doubts, and asked him to remain in charge while I went back to the nearest French telephone post, if any, and 'phoned up for assistance. I walked about a hundred yards from the machine and came to a road, and in the obscure distance I saw a cart. Not knowing if it was coming or going, I gave it a " Holloa." I drew nearer, and when only five yards away I spotted the four occupants wearing fur Jerry helmets. You can well imagine how I wished I could sink into the earth. I was absolutely flabbergasted, and stood frozen to the spot. The Hun in charge gazed at me, and noticing my R.F.C. cap which I always carried with me, and which I had already donned, he put two and two together and made five, with the result that he asked " Sind Sie ein Franzosischer Flieger? " (" Are you a French Flyer? ") Fortunately I had learnt a little German at school in S. Africa, and so I summoned up my courage and answered him to the best of my ability in German, " No, do you not know who I am? " and then asked, " Have you seen my automobile? " This puzzled them immensely, and I did not wait to be found out, especially as the four of them were already half out of the cart, and each had a rifle, but I turned on my heel and walked into the darkness. Why they didn't shoot at me I know not. I had started off in the wrong direction to put them off the lie of the machine, but doubled back to the machine when out of their sight. My observer was showing a light from his torch, so I told him hurriedly to put it out, and it went out like lightning. We held a whispered consultation, and decided to have

L

a last look at the engine. I thereupon clambered up and had a look at the magneto and carburetter, hiding the light as much as possible with my leather coat, but I could not see anything wrong externally, and my observer whispered up to me that I must hurry up as he thought the Huns were approaching. I thereupon stopped my electric light display and clambered down. We had decided that it was best not to set the machine alight, as then the Huns would have spotted and caught us. So instead I took out my large Jack knife and destroyed everything as much as possible, including the tail plane and rudder, and having already destroyed all maps, we crept away. It was rather hard getting across the road, cavalry seeming to be on the alert, as though they had been looking for us. We crawled a good way on our stomachs through a small swamp, and then seemed to get away from the patrols. We walked east all that night, it being in the right direction towards Switzerland, and also increasing the distance between us and what was once a perfectly good F.E.2B. On occasions we narrowly missed batteries of small guns, but were saved more than once by the ominous red gleam of a cigar tip. So we plodded on for many a weary mile, in our sheep-skin boots, and all too heavy and cumbersome flying clothes. Village after village we passed and the striking of the church bells sounded awe inspiring in the darkness. Towards morning we came to a fairly thick hedge away from the road, but quite near a village. Here we decided to lie up for the next day. We accordingly made ourselves as snug as possible in the middle of the hedge in a muddy hollow, after having camouflaged the hollow in front and rear with dry branches. We thereupon lay down in the mud and tried to forget our troubles in sleep. It was so perishing cold, however, that sleep was next to impossible. Just about daybreak I heard the bleat of a lamb, and was half-decided to go in the direction of the sound, in order to procure something to supply us with food, which we were in great need of, when from the same direction I saw a cart approaching, and two Huns walking behind. This was the first alarm. The second was not long in coming either, and this time in the shape of dozens of Huns proceeding in batches of about twelve each from the village towards the trenches. We were in a frightful stew, as they passed our hedge only at a distance of about thirty yards. Later on, however, we plucked up courage and watched their every movement. They were fully equipped for the trenches, and seemed to be entering a communication trench just behind the brow of a hill, immediately in front of us. About midday we heard the drone of an aeroplane, but could see nothing of it at all, as the day was too misty. Presently, however, the sound came towards us, and just as it was more or less over us, a lot of pamphlets came floating down from the low clouds above. One of these pamphlets came down within twenty yards of us, at the same time as a party of Huns were coming from the village to the trenches, with a big burly sergeant in charge, who had a dog with him. He, of course, must turn back from the rest, accompanied by his faithful hound. I determined he would spot us and then for a merry time. But no, neither he nor his dog saw the two scared beings flattened down in the hollow of the hedge. He picked up the pamphlet, and was too busy reading it to notice us on his way back past the hedge, even though he passed us at ten yards distance. Oh, what sighs of relief we heaved after this party was clear again. The pity of everything was that had we had pigeons on our machine we could have sent the pin point of the place, and the French batteries could have killed quite a number of Boches on their way to the line, as I carried a map which even had the enemy captured would have shown them nothing. Also we could have chosen a suitable field for landing and taking off on and arranged for a machine to pick us up that evening. We held counsel as to what was best as regards our plans for that night. Although we knew nothing much about trench warfare we decided to make a shot at getting across the line that night. We waited impatiently for darkness to come. When it came, however, the French 75's became busy, trying to cut off a Bosche working party, I suppose, with barrage fire. The Huns replied likewise, and before long a fine noise was being made, and the night was lit up with a red glare from the flashes of the guns. This didn't seem the spot to try and get through, so we decided to go further East towards Switzerland. I knew of a tributary of the Moselle river which flowed towards our side of the line, and this seemed to be the one chance of getting across, even should there be barbed wire in it. Then if the Hun didn't guard his Aerodrome, well there was a chance of pinching one of his machines; then again, if food were obtainable we could always strike for Switzerland as a last resource. Anyway, we decided that food had to be obtained at all costs that night, for we were perishingly cold and stiff, and ravenous with hunger. Hardly had we left our refuge of that day when we were forced to hide behind some bushes, as a Hun with full kit came towards the village. I was very tempted to hit him on the head and obtain both food and equipment, but some people were working in a field quite near, and might have heard him cry out for help, so we let him pass unmolested. We walked in an easterly direction, and slightly away from the line in order to see if there were more live stock further behind the line. There was absolutely nothing to be had on the land, for in February all the fields are ploughed up, and also very heavy to walk over. We prowled through the outskirts of some villages, but could not get anything in the food line. About midnight we came to a dam, and on the dam wall we saw Army waggons lined up. We crept along and began to search them, but could not find a morsel of food. We then noticed a small room on raised foundations on the opposite side of the dam wall to the water. We crept along to investigate, and came to a plank reaching from the road on the dam wall to the door of the room. I tip-toed along the plank, followed by my observer, and saw the gleam of a light shining through the crack in the door. I put my eye to the crack and saw a Hun sitting at a table, and on his right hand side stood a pot of honey. Well, where there is honey there is generally other food too, so I whispered to my observer that this was our chance, the hut being absolutely isolated from any other houses. "I'm going to jump in and deal with that Bosche," I said, "and if there should be anyone else, you look after him." I did not give him much time to think, I just swung open the door and made a bound towards the Hun at the table. He sprang up from his chair with a frenzied cry, and I dealt a blow at his head with the stick which I had cut that day from the hedge, he dodged the blow and it fell on his shoulder. This staggered him for a moment, and I didn't give him a chance to recover, but rushed him backwards until he tripped over a bed, and then I had him by the throat; and lay on top of him on the bed. Meanwhile my observer, who had been balancing on the plank behind me, followed in the rush, but had hardly put his foot on the doorstep when a Hun from a corner bed sprang up and dealt a blow at his chest. The blow staggered my observer, and he lost his balance. To regain it he put his leg out behind him, only to step into space and he fell a good nine feet on to terra firma outside. This second Hun who had appeared from nowhere, immediately slammed the door, and shot the bolt too. He also seemed highly perturbed, as he kept making child-like noises, and every now and then a frenzied guttural grunt. On locking the door he rushed towards me, and I realised the game was up, even though my one Hun was pretty near unconscious, but instead of hitting me on the head with a good punch the second Hun tried to pull me off his comrade, only the combined weight of the man under me and myself and my hold on the bed with my free hand was too much for him, so he gave it up and rushed away, making awful noises, to a gun rack, and seizing a Mauser, he rammed two or three cartridges in, and presented the weapon at my back. This was becoming a bit too cold-blooded, so I decided it was time to give myself up. Accordingly I relinquished my hold of my enemy's throat, and sat facing my new opponent, alongside my late victim. The brute I had been strangling sat up in a dazed fashion, and after gazing at me for a few seconds he went mad. His eyes were blazing and seeing his comrade covering me with the rifle, he thought he would have his revenge, so he sprang up and rushed at me like a wild bull. I put up my hands to guard myself, and then noticed the man with the rifle shift round to the right to get a better aim at me. Things were decidedly nasty, and it only took me a very few seconds to see that the best thing to do was not to hit back at my mad *friend*, but to let him hit me a good blow in the face and pretend to have fainted. This I did, and received a nasty blow on the chin; immediately I toppled over backwards on the bed and lay there as if unconscious. The madman, however, thought this was the chance of his life, and rained blow after blow at my unguarded face, until the one side looked more like a pudding than anything else. Oh, how I swore vengeance under my breath. After he had tired himself hitting my face, he stood still and asked the second Hun for his rifle to shoot me with. I understood what he said, and decided

to make a bid for my life at the very least, and if this failed I decided
to damage them as much as possible before my turn came.   I therefore sat up and asked them for water.   "Water," shouted the
brute, "Do you think I'll give you water?"   Then he cursed me
for an Englishman, and told me he was going to shoot me for daring
to attack him, and he was just working himself up to do the deed,
despite my attempts to make myself heard, which was impossible
against his tirade, when we all heard a shout from the outside.   God
knows that if this interruption had not come he would have been as
good as his word.   My observer, when he picked himself up from
the fall, hearing the awful cries of the Huns inside the room rushed
towards the lights of a village in the distance in order to stop the
Huns from murdering me as he thought, and pretty near true too, by
getting help from other Bosches.   He came to a ditch, however,
which he could not cross, and so rushed back to the hut with the idea
of setting light to the grass round the foundations.   This also failed
for he found he had no matches, so in desperation he called out to
me, and honestly saved my life by doing so.

This cry from outside put fear into the two brutes in the hut,
and they held a flurried whispering consultation together.   I seized
the golden opportunity of telling them that I had only attacked them
for food, as we had been without food for three days (I could not
give them correct information).   This appeased them slightly, and
I shouted to my observer to boot it before they plucked up courage
to look for him too, but he, poor fellow, was too done in (his con-
stitution was not strong, having had an attack of Spotted Fever a
short time before), and said he preferred to hand himself up with
me.   I therefore told the Huns that my friend would hand himself
up too, provided they took us to a German officer.   I also told him
he would be sure to get an "Iron Cross" if he did so, and this
rather took his fancy.   They accordingly got some stout wire,
bound my hands and tied me to the bed like a turkey ready for
Christmas.   They didn't seem to trust me at all.   They then questioned me repeatedly as to whether I was sure there were only two
of us.   More "wind up."   I reassured them on this, so both armed
with rifles, they swung the door open and fired a volley straight out
of the door.   My observer was just in front of the door as it hap-

pened, only fortunately for him was lying on the ground, being tired after our long tramp; so the bullets all whistled over his head. I told them they would never get him to give himself up if they did such foolish things. They then had another little council of war together, and said to me that I must tell my friend to be sure to come with his hands above his head. My observer complied with these regulations, and came waddling across the plank, and into the room, whereupon he was bound up with rifle cords and fastened to me. When reinforcements had arrived we were marched to a small trench railway and dumped down nearer their headquarters, to which we were taken in a motor-car (our only motor trip in Germany) to be photographed by flashlight, and also questioned by a General who tried the usual stunt of trying to get us to take drink, but failed. This was at Dusse, and we had been captured near the village of Ommereich. We were sent to St. Avold to their Intelligence Department, where they said I did not treat them like *gentlemen*, because I turned their questioning into a farce. We were then put in Fort Kameke, near Metz, and had an awful time there; then to Karlsrhue, Landshut, and Holzminden, and finally to dear old Blighty.

AIR MECHANIC W. HAWKINS WRITES AS FOLLOWS:—

" On the night of the 9-10th August, 1917, Lieut. Fulton, accompanied by myself, set out on a bombing raid. After crossing the lines we encountered bad weather, which caused us to lose our direction. We dropped our bombs on a station, and after flying west for some time without learning anything from the ground, we fired lights, hoping to find an aerodrome on our side, but without result. Eventually we determined to make a landing. We selected a good spot, and landed safely. We were then immediately surrounded by Belgians. I spoke to them in French, and found that we were in enemy territory, and also that the Huns were coming for us. Being close by Audenarde, and being unable to make for our lines (as we had been hit by Archie and machine gun bullets in a number of places, including one of the petrol tanks), we resolved to try and reach Holland. Owing to the engine running badly we took off with great difficulty, and after flying a short while our engine failed, and we were forced to descend.   On landing I immediately took my guns to pieces, threw the parts in the wood close by, and set to work to help the pilot burn the machine, which I am glad to say we did thoroughly.   Just as we had got it burning well, German soldiers arrived on the scene and escorted us to a billet. Lieut. Fulton was then questioned by a civilian official, but he absolutely refused to tell them anything.   We were then separated, and I was taken to what was left of the machine, which was totally burnt, and parts such as navigation lamps had already been taken by Belgians. I, however, was not questioned, but taken to Audenarde, where food was given me.   Again I joined my Pilot, and we were both taken to Courtrai.   On entering Courtrai, a formation of British machines dropped some bombs in the neighbourhood, which put the wind up the Huns, but whether they did any damage I could not ascertain.   Entering what I supposed to be Officers' Quarters, we were met by a Hun airman, Lieut. Muller, who questioned me, alone. At first he was very friendly, but when I refused to tell him anything he dismissed me.   A man was sent for, who gave me food (black bread, sausage, and weak coffee).   Whilst having tea some more British machines dropped bombs, but I was not allowed to see the results.   Soon after, an officer with his head bandaged drove up in a car (who I was told was Richtnofen).   As it became dark my Pilot joined me, and we were taken to Inglemunster, to a billet occupied by British airmen and some infantry.   We stayed there the night and slept on the floor.   Next morning, we were told British machines had been over during the night.   Here I was separated from my Pilot and sent on with some infantry to Ghent.

Arriving at Ghent in the evening, our party (80 men) was put in what was no more than a dungeon, with five filthy beds.   A slice of black bread, and a cup of weak coffee (the first meal of that day) made from either burnt acorns or barley, was given to each of us. Turning us out at 5 a.m. next morning, they gave us a similar meal and put us in a train in which we travelled until the following night. Next morning, without food, we continued our journey, and arrived at Haltern (4 miles from the Camp).   Walking up a long hill we reached the Camp, which appeared filthy and black. We had to state our rank, and in order to evade working for the Huns (*i.e.*, making munitions, working in coal and salt mines), I put down my rank as *Corporal*. We were then taken to the Disinfection House. Our hair was shaven to the scalp, and we were sent underneath some sort of shower bath, with no soap. Then we passed into a large room, where we saw some awful sights, in the shape of Russians who had been working in France. They were simply human skeletons, with their ankles swollen to a huge size, several dying there, and others, through weakness, had to be carried out. After having obtained our clothes we were taken to Group 111, Dulman Lager. I was there several weeks, and all the time I was raving hungry. In the morning we received the weak coffee, " noon pig wash," in the form of black fish, which we termed "sea-lion," and some yellow matter which we termed " sandstorm," horse beans and a drop of the water in which they were boiled, and last, but not least, their terrible " sauerkraut." At 6 p.m. the same soup and a slice of black bread. During the time we were there I was inoculated five or six times and vaccinated. Then I was sent to Group 1, where I met A. M. Robb, 100 Squadron.

At the end of four months I received my parcel, and I determined to escape, but I had neither compass nor map. About June, 1918, Corpl. Davidson, D.L.I. and myself attempted to escape, but were caught. Again in August we tried, this time with map and compass and with forged identity cards, and by means of a little disguise we managed to get out of the camp with a working party. It must be remembered that I wore two stripes in Germany, and that N.C.O.'s were not allowed out of the camp, so that in order to get out we had to change places with two privates. During the dinner time we made a dash for it, and by the time the German sentries realised it, we were out of range. Running through a wood we hid ourselves in a cornfield. Lying low until dark, we commenced our journey, but only travelled during the night, and were caught in the morning. Back we were taken to the cells, and the Commandant gave us 14 days. Our map and compass were so well concealed that they could not find them, although they ripped our linings open.

On being let out, my friend was sent to Sennelager, and I was watched very closely. Now I had no one to come with me, but hope came again. A French Officer who had been sent to Dalmen by mistake was to be sent to an Officers' Camp, but he was anxious to escape, so arranging everything we started early in October. Getting into the parcel office, just outside the wire, we concealed ourselves and waited until dark. We were now practically surrounded by sentries, the doors were locked and the windows wired, but working from 7 until 1 a.m. next morning, we managed to take the window clean out, and crawling on hands and feet into a ditch we continued about 100 yards, and by creeping along we got clear. Travelling three nights in continual drizzle we reached the Dutch frontier at Burlo, crossed over and reached Winterswyck (Holland). From there I was sent to a Quarantine Camp at Didam, where I stayed about three weeks, eventually reaching Rotterdam, from which Port I proceeded to Gravesend, arriving the day after the signing of the Armistice.

MY EXPERIENCES AS A PRISONER OF WAR

L. A. COLBERT, Lieut., R.A.F.

In the following short article, I do not include the minor brutalities of the Commandant and his staff; these were so numerous that I am forced to omit them. From time to time various articles have appeared in the leading daily papers dealing with the Tenth Army Corps Command and the Commandant we were under, so the name of Capt. Chas. Niemyer will not be new to the majority of readers. I would also like to say that the better treatment, visits to Squadrons, etc., supposed to have been given to all R.F.C. prisoners by the German Flying Corps were non-existent.

On the night of the 30th September, 1917, Lieut. Bushe and myself with several other machines, were detailed to bomb the "Zep. Shed" at Ghentrode. We left the ground soon after 8.30 p.m. and headed for the lines, which we crossed near Ypres at a height nearing on 4,000 feet. The Lys river was easily picked up and followed to a point a couple of kilometres South of Ghent. Here we changed our course for the Zep. Shed, which we easily located. We glided on to our objective with sights set for 1,000 feet and in spite of the warm reception we had, we were lucky enough to hit the shed about three-quarters length up with our big bomb, the 230 lb., at the same time I released two phosphor bombs, both bursting about 50 feet off the ground. We then made about six trips up and down the aerodrome and emptied lead into what looked like aircraft on the ground. With one drum left, we made for home, climbing to a height of about 5,000 feet. Over Thielt one solitary round from Archie burst unpleasantly near, and a few seconds later there was much vibration and some cylinders commenced miss-firing. Bushe thought we might make the lines as we had not lost height, but luck was against us and soon we lost the remaining good cylinders. I then threw the machine gun and drums overboard, and we looked round for a field to land in. We were unlucky in our choice, as we chose a ploughed field and finished upside down. After much difficulty we got a fire started from the petrol tank, which was now on the bottom, then left the machine to burn. So started our captivity. The Commandant of the village of Meulebeke, in whose outskirts we landed, wasted no time in marching us to Thielt, where we spent the few remaining morning hours in the town prison. At 10 a.m. a motor car awaited us and we were rushed off to Inglemunster, where we were interviewed by a German Officer of the Flying Corps. We remained in Inglemunster two or three days and were relieved of our boots and flying kit by a German Corporal.

The journey to Germany was made in two stages, the first ending at Ghent, which we reached via Courtrai, and the second at Karlsruhe, via Liege and Cologne. Thanks to the aid given by Belgian women as far as Liege, we entered Germany in a good condition. Cologne was the first town in which hatred was shown openly by all, and it was in this town that we arrived at night and jolly hungry. On application to our guard we were taken to the canteen on the station platform. Here we were refused food by the German Red Cross and the door shut in our faces. Crowds gathered round us and were indeed objectionable, both by deed and word. We were then taken to the station police quarters and there spent two or three hours of waiting for the train. The rest of that night and the following day were spent in travelling. No effort was made to get us any food and on our arrival at Karlruhe we were famished.

Before entering the camp at Karlsruhe, we were kept in quarantine for a period of 10 or 14 days and we lived on two bowls of soup, 5 English biscuits, and a small piece of bread per day. Here also we were questioned. I remained two days in the camp here, the food being the same as in quarantine, and as I saw later, this was the usual fare in all Prison Camps with a variation of Sundays only of a little meat in the soup. Karlsruhe at this time was being used as a collecting depot and inoculations, etc., were carried out there. It was there that I was separated from Lieut. Bushe, my pilot, and unfortunately up to the time of writing I have not seen or heard of him.

The journey to Clausthal spread over thirty hours, and once again the same old thing, no arrangements had been made for food. At the camp we were met by the Commandant, who informed us in his brutal way, that he alone was Commandant. He then had us searched and admitted us to the camp. The inmates here were all British and numbered some 250. The camp was made up in the following way :—One main building and three huts, the huts holding 40 to 48 each, and the remainder in the main building, an old hotel. Soon after being settled in a hut, I was given all the confidential news of the camp, re escape ways and means. Two tunnels had been started, one from the hut I was in, the other from the hut opposite. Unfortunately the one starting from my hut could not be cleared of water, so was abandoned, but the other was very nearly completed and the intention was to break it during the week. It was arranged to let out as many as possible, but owing to treachery the Huns started digging for the tunnel a couple of days before it was ready and the whole show was discovered. Early in November snow fell heavily and continued to do so till after Christmas, most of my time was spent in tracing maps and making escape kit, which, when finished, were hidden in secret cupboards in the walls. Towards the New Year, we had a depth of 4 to 5 feet of snow and the only means of keeping warm was to go and shovel snow. We had no fuel to burn and at night just five minutes of light to get in bed with. After the New Year we started work on an ice rink and after two or three days' work, managed to get some skating. Toboggan runs were built, and various winter sports indulged in.   As to indoor amusements, concerts, sketches, etc., were arranged and one performance per week was given.

In March, escape fever ran high once again, very many taking their chance, but I'm sorry to say not one managed to cross the frontier.   Excitement in the camp was at its height, as we were given wonderful accounts of the German break-through on the West Front.   Towards the end of May a new tunnel was started from under the Music Room in the Main Building.   The work on this was greatly retarded by a strafe which lasted just one month.   During the strafe we were not allowed any kind of outdoor sport, no music, no singing, no whistling, no newspapers, and given two extra roll calls, making it four in all per day.   Soon after this, I think about the last week in July or the first in August, the Commandant stalked into the dining hall raving like a madman.   A few minutes later numerous sentries armed with rifles, axes and spades started a search under the main building and huts, and so was our last tunnel discovered.   The reason of this sudden entry was explained later. The Commandant's brother, who had the camp at Holzminden, lost 27 officers during the night by a tunnel, and he had 'phoned his brother warning him that the chances were 100 to 1 that we were making one.   Towards the end of August conditions changed as things changed on the West Front.   It was about this time that a large batch of officers came in from Heidelberg, and strange to say I met one from 100 Squadron, who was in the Squadron with me; he did not recognise me till I mentioned my name.   His was Lieut. Goddard, and he was the first officer of 100 Squadron that I met in Germany.   September and October passed very quickly, and maps of the various fronts could be seen everywhere in the camp.

The day the Armistice was signed, all officers in arrest were liberated, our food parcels being given us uncensored. We were permitted to walk outside the camp without guards, and at this time had plenty of skating on the lakes round the camp.   Concerts, dancing and various celebrations took place almost every night without the aid of a German guard.

We left Clausthal on the 11th December for the German Baltic port of Warnemunde, where we embarked for Copenhagen.   Here we gained our freedom at last!

DIARY OF SEC-LIEUT. F. CHAINEY
(From 16th September to 23rd December, 1918).

On Monday, September 16th, Johnson, Pitman and I started off on a Night Bombing Raid for Frankfort. We had quite a good journey there, following up the Vosges the whole way without being troubled by "Archie" or searchlights. Just before we got to Frankfort I went into the front of the machine to guide Johnson over the target and pull the bombs. I spotted a place well lit up, took sight, and pulled the bombs. Turning back into the engine room to see if all the bombs had dropped, Johnson tapped me on the shoulder and pointed to one of the propellers, which was stationary. We turned back immediately South, and I at once attempted to start the engine, but all my efforts failed, so we were forced to land near Darmstadt. We made a splendid landing on a ploughed field, and set fire to our machine. Lights were seen approaching, so we made off for a forest close by to make up our plans of escape. Throwing off our flying kit, we decided to go south towards the Swiss frontier. That night we covered about 14 kilos, passing through a Hun village which was absolutely deserted, and settled down in a wood for the next day. As it happened we had some biscuits, a tin of beef and a box of chocolates with us, so we had a little food to go on with. Water was very short, as all the small rivers seemed to be dried up. The next night we left our hiding place about 10.30 and carried on south to strike a stream, where we hoped to get water. After walking a couple of hours, we came across a pump by the roadside, which was quite a godsend to us, as we were parched. We then carried on through another village to a wood, where we decided to settle the next day. We were unable to get much sleep during the day, owing to gnats irritating us and women and children moving about in the wood. After nearly being spotted, we decided to move our position about midday and found a small shrubbery where we stayed until dark. Our food was now running pretty low and we had to eat anything we could lay hands on, in the way of turnips, beans, etc. We left the shrubbery about 9.30, making for another stream where we hoped to get water, but found it was dry, so carried on and fortunately found another pump where we had a good drink. We then made towards a railway, where we were hoping we would be able to get on a truck going south. Following the railway line we came to a crossing. Just as we reached it a gateman came out and challenged us, but we took no notice and went on striking across country. We decided it was impossible to reach our objective that night, which was a small wood south of the railway junction near Mannheim, so we looked for a hiding place and came across a small shrubbery where we stayed the next day. We were troubled quite a lot during the day by boys who were picking berries, and very nearly spotted again. The weather was now turning very bad and we were getting wet through. However, we started off again that night towards our previous night's objective. The weather was getting worse and we had no food whatever, so we decided the next best thing we could do was to give ourselves up. Making for a small village, we met a civilian and told him to take us to the nearest police station. He brought us some bread and then took us to the police station where we were locked up in a cell for the night. We were nearly ravenous and chilled to the bone, but could not get anything hot to drink or food to eat. An English Tommy, who was working in a factory close by, was brought to us in the morning and he fetched us some biscuits, tinned meat and fish. The latter was afterwards stolen by the guard. Under escort we were then taken to the station and proceeded by train to Mannheim. Arriving at Mannheim we were taken through the town to a Prisoners' Camp, where we stayed all the morning while enquiries were being made. We had several promises of food and drink and were just going to have lunch (so they said) when we were taken away again to the station, and proceeded to Karlsruhe. The guard promised us we should get something hot to drink at Karlsruhe Station, but on applying to the Red Cross we were refused, and so were taken on to an old hotel, where they received prisoners and examined them before sending them to a camp. Johnson and Pitman were put in one room, and I in another with a Frenchman and an American. We were brought some hot soup, which, though it was filthy looking stuff, we were very thankful for. Our clothes were afterwards taken away and fumigated. We were then examined by a civilian, who tried to obtain information as to our Squadron, etc., but I am afraid he was very unsuccessful. Afterwards the three of us were put in one room together and locked in. That night the town was bombed by our aeroplanes, which in a way gave us a certain amount of comfort to know that our fellows were not far off. The food in this hotel was pretty bad. We had two meals a day with a cup of coffee as substitute for breakfast. The meals consisted of stewed cabbage, soup and potatoes. We were allowed out in the courtyard for about an hour in the afternoon and there met quite a lot of fellows we knew. Every day we were being told that we should move to the camp to-morrow, which afterwards we found out was a favourite expression of the Huns "to-morrow perhaps." The days were very monotonous, as we had no books or anything to read, and we were very thankful when, after being shut up for six days, we were moved to a camp about twenty minutes walk away. The camp was quite an improvement. We were issued with Red Cross parcels and with that and the food the Huns gave us we lived fairly well. However, we were not to stay at this camp long, as it was only a distributing camp and we were to be sent to another, specially for Flying Officers. After being a week at Karlsruhe camp, we were sent to a place called Landshut. The journey took about two days and was very tiring as we were only in 4th class compartments and were not allowed any windows open. We were issued with food on the journey, consisting of sausage and black bread, and were very thankful when we arrived at Landshut to get a little exercise. When we arrived at this new camp, we were told by the Sergeant-Major that he did not expect us and so had no food for us. The camp, he said, was a Sanitation Camp, where, to quote his words, "We should all be insulated," meaning, of course, innoculated. He gave us quite a long speech in broken English, much to our amusement, especially when he told us "I will do you for all I can," and was full of apologies for not having food for us. We were given mattresses on the floor and our boots were taken from us, as the Commandant, who the Sergeant-Major said was a strong man, was rather afraid of anyone escaping. The next morning Italian orderlies brought us some more coffee substitute and a loaf of black bread, which was to last us five days. That morning we had our first innoculation.   All our clothes were taken from us again and examined, and we were given some Prisoner of War clothes and taken to the room where we were to live.   The beds here were quite good, but not altogether clean.   Our food came from a restaurant in the town, which we had to pay four marks a day for; pretty good food but very small quantities.   Every night our boots were taken away and a guard came round every two hours or so to see that we were all there.   Fortunately, with our party we had a Captain who spoke German very well, and he was able to argue with the Commandant and the Sergeant-Major about our treatment.   The Italian orderlies were quite decent to us, but of course it was difficult to make them understand what we wanted.   One morning I gave the orderly my tea-pot with tea in and asked him, as I thought, to fill it with boiling water.   Five minutes later he brought it back and seemed quite pleased with himself; showed me the tea-pot and there it was perfectly clean; he had cleaned it out instead of filling it up. The war news now was very cheerful and so kept our spirits up. Germany had offered her peace proposals, and the Truce with Bulgaria had been signed.   After spending a week in this Barrack, we were moved to another part of the camp, which was much better for us, as we had more ground to walk about on and were issued with Red Cross parcels.   The food here was not so good, but by saving our potatoes over night and a little meat, we were able to make a dish for our breakfast.   Tobacco too was very short and one could see officers walking round the ground looking for cigarette ends to smoke.   Every few days we had an innoculation or something or other, and one vaccination.   The doctor was quite a good chap and did a lot towards our comfort. Red Cross parcels stopped coming in and we had no bread or biscuits, so things were looking very black. After a few days we were always hungry as the issue of food we had was insufficient.   However, on Saturday, 19th October, we heard that we were to be moved to a permanent camp somewhere in Bavaria.   We left Landshut on the following Tuesday and went by train to Ingolstadt.   The guard was very strict on the train, we had to take our boots off and place them in the parcel racks, and, as before, no windows were allowed open.   Arriving at Ingolstadt we had a walk of about 8 kilos.   Some of our party were

M

wounded and it was as much as they could do to get there.   As before, when we arrived at our destination we were told they were not
expecting us.   It was a Fort that we went to, which was very
strongly guarded with a moat round it.   Everything seemed very
cold and miserable.   The Commandant, who was only there temporarily, knew nothing, and so we thought we were in for a very
rough time.   We had French orderlies to wait on us, who were very
good, putting us up to all sorts of dodges as to how to get food stuff
out of the Bosche.   The next day we had a good look round the
Fort, and things seemed much brighter, as there was a good space
for plenty of exercise and a tennis court.   Unfortunately we had no
racquets, etc.   The meals here seemed to be worse than they were
at previous camps, our lunch consisting of a small portion of potatoes, cabbage and soup, and some very doubtful tinned meat for
supper at night.   Luckily, after we had been there about three or
four days some Red Cross emergency parcels arrived, so things
improved.   There had been a number of English officers at
the camp before, but all their cooking and eating utensils that had
been left behind were locked up by the Bosche.   However, by the
aid of the French orderlies we managed to break into the room
where the potatoes were stored and to these we helped ourselves.
We had come to the conclusion that the only way to live was by
helping ourselves to all we could from the Bosche.   There was
absolutely nothing there in the way of amusements, so I organised a
concert party.   We found a room which was fixed up as a theatre
with a piano in it, and so were able to give quite a number of
concerts to the other officers, which made a good break in the week,
and also helped to pass the time away in rehearsal and arranging
these concerts.   It was during the interval of one of our concerts
that we heard the news that the Armistice had been signed.   One can
imagine the excitement of the fellows, especially when later we
heard that all prisoners of war were to be exchanged immediately.
The Commandant gave the news out at the morning roll call, and
told us we should be in England in a short time.   A few days after
the Armistice was signed we were told we were going to another
fort the other side of Ingoldstadt, which was a concentration camp
for prisoners before being returned.   We left this fort on

Wednesday, 20th November, and marched to the town, where we took a train to a small place about 7 miles the other side of the town. We were met here by a French officer, who had come from the fort we were going to. He told us that 300 French officers were there, and that we were invited to lunch with them. All arrangements had been made for us, and we were distributed round the various rooms. Everybody was now in quite good spirits, as we only expected to be there for a few days. By signing our parole, we were allowed out every afternoon from 1 p.m. to 5 p.m., absolutely free, so were able to go round to the various villages to try and buy food. Afterwards we found out the best way to obtain food was by exchanging rice and tea, etc. The civilian population seemed to be in a very bad way as regards clothing and food, and we were easily able to exchange any old clothes for butter and eggs. As was usual, the Bosche seemed to know nothing about when we were going away. Eight days was always the time with him. However, with fairly good food and our freedom every day, the time seemed to go fairly quickly. After being there a month we began to wonder if we had been forgotten, as there was no news as to our going. Everyone was talking of escaping, but the difficulty was in getting on the railways without a pass, as the Soldiers and Workmen's Council which had been formed was very strict, and had a guard at all railway stations. However, on the 12th December, four days before the Armistice was supposed to have ended, seven of us, who were together in one room, decided we would go off on our own. The Captain in our room, who had previously obtained a pass to go off on business about our parcels, still had the old pass with him, so we had a new one typed out, forged the signature and stamp, and so were able to get away from Ingoldstadt Station to Munich. The Captain then went to the Bavarian Minister and asked him if he could do something about getting the fellows away from the fort. He was very amiable and wired off immediately to the Swiss Consul, giving us another pass to stay on in Munich until the Sunday, when news was expected through. We had very little money between us, and so it was decided that someone should go back to the fort, where we could obtain some. Another fellow and I went back, and on seeing the

Commandant were told that official news had come through that everybody would be leaving on the following Tuesday, so I immediately wired back to my friends at Munich, telling them to return. The news proved correct, and on Tuesday, the 17th December, we left the Fort in company with the French to Ingoldstadt Station. It was teeming with rain, and everybody was wringing wet through by the time we arrived at the station. We were given 1st and 2nd class compartments, and with great cheering we left Ingoldstadt at 10.30 that morning, arriving Constance which is just on the border of Switzerland at 1 o'clock next day. The weather was fine and we had a splendid view of Lake Constance as the train ran alongside. Leaving Constance at 2.30 we crossed the border 10 minutes later. The Swiss people were very good to us, giving us coffee and cigarettes, etc., at every place we stopped at. We arrived at the first French town about 11 o'clock that night and were there met by the Mayor, who presented the English and French Presidents of the Help Committee with a bouquet each. We then proceeded to a small town near Lyon where we stayed the night at a rest camp, and the next day entrained on a hospital train for Calais, arriving there two days later. We stayed there for the night and left the next morning by special boat for Dover.

HONOURS
& AWARDS

2/Lieut. H. E. K. Eccles ...	Military Cross	17th May, 1917.
2/A.M. J. G. Guyatt ...	Promoted Corporal	11th May, 1917.
Capt. W. A. McClaughry ...	Military Cross	5th June, 1917.
2/Lieut. C. E. Blayney ...	Military Cross	5th June, 1917.
Capt. W. J. Tempest, D.S.O.	Military Cross	15th September, 1917.
Lieut. H. D. Harman ...	Military Cross	15th September, 1917.
2/Lieut. J. A. Boret ...	Military Cross	15th September, 1917.
2/Lieut. A. Wald	Military Cross	21st January, 1918.
Capt. H. T. O. Windsor ...	Military Cross	2nd February, 1918.
Sergt. G. Avery	Medaille Militaire	25th April, 1918.
Sergt. F. J. Appleton ...	Croix de Guerre	25th April, 1918.
1/A.M. E. Davidson ...	Croix de Guerre	25th April, 1918.
Flight Sergt. T. Nicoll ...	Albert Medal	25th April, 1918.
Sergt.-Major S. H. May ...	Meritorious Service Medal ...	3rd June, 1918.
Capt. F. H. Bright ...	Distinguished Flying Cross	7th July, 1918.
Capt. R. C. Savery ...	Distinguished Flying Cross	11th July, 1918.
Lieut. D. Darby	Distinguished Flying Cross	28th July, 1918.
Lieut. G. H. Box	Distinguished Flying Cross	28th July, 1918.
Capt. H. B. Wilson ...	Distinguished Flying Cross	28th July, 1918.
Lieut. R. K. Inches ...	Distinguished Flying Cross	24th August, 1918.
Capt. H. J. Miles	Croix de Guerre	8th October, 1918.
Sergt. P. J. Adkins, D.S.M., D.F.M.	Medaille Militaire	8th October, 1918.
Chief Mech. C. M. Hayden	La Medaille d'Honneur en Argent	8th October, 1918.
2/A.M. C. Dickinson ...	La Medaille Militaire en Bronze	8th October, 1918.
Capt. G. M. Turnbull ...	Belgique Legion d'Honneur	
Lieut. W. A. Barnes ...	Croix de Guerre	
Major C. G. Burge ...	Order of the British Empire	1st January, 1919.
Capt. M. G. Coombs ...	Distinguished Flying Cross	1st January, 1919.
Lieut. I. R. L. Ross ...	Distinguished Flying Cross	1st January, 1919.
Lieut. L. D. Kirk	Mentioned In Despatches ...	8th November, 1918.
Lieut. W. Richards ...	Mentioned In Despatches ...	8th November, 1918.
Lieut. F. R. Johnson ...	Mentioned In Despatches ...	3rd January, 1919.
Corpl. Mech. S. E. Fiford	Meritorious Service Medal ...	3rd January, 1919.
Sergt. Mech. A. A. Taylor...	Meritorious Service Medal ...	3rd January, 1919.
Sergt. Mech. L. Leicester ...	Mentioned In Despatches ...	3rd January, 1919.

ROLL OF HONOUR

OFFICERS

KILLED

Name.	Rank.	Particulars.
Boyd, Harry	Lieut.	Killed in Aeroplane Accident at Xaffevillers, on 25th August, 1918. Son of Mr. and Mrs. W. G. Boyd, 107, Malone Avenue, Belfast. Age 19.
Box, George Holyoake	Lieut.	Killed in Aeroplane Accident at Xaffevillers on 25th August, 1918. Age 23. Awarded the Distinguished Flying Cross 28/7/18, for conspicuous gallantry. Next of kin—Miss Box, 28, Rectory Road, Manor Park, London, E.
Collins, Leslie Ernest	2/Lieut.	Killed in Aeroplane Accident at Villeseneux on 5th April, 1918. Son of Mr. and Mrs. F. W. Collins, Beechwood, Stanhope Road, Sidcup, Kent. Age 19.
Evans, Arthur Frederic	Lieut.	Killed in Aeroplane Accident near Troyes, on 30th October, 1918. Son of Mr. and Mrs. A. F. Evans, Fazakerly House, Prescot, Lancashire. Age 32.

Lieut. A. F. Evans.

Capt. R. C. Scudamore, M.C.

182

100 SQUADRON

NAME.	RANK.	PARTICULARS.
Ford, Norman	2/Lieut.	Killed in Aeroplane Accident at Villeseneux on 5th April, 1918. Son of Mrs E. A. Ford, Thomburgh House, Carters Towers, North Queensland, Australia. Age 27.
Holmes, T. G.	2/Lieut.	Killed on the night of 5/6th April, 1917, while on Bombing Raid over German Lines. Son of Mr. and Mrs. Holmes, Petridge Wood, near Redhill, Surrey.
Inches, Robert Kirk	Lieut.	Killed in Aeroplane Accident at Xaffevillers on 25th August, 1918. Age 20. Awarded the Distinguished Flying Cross 17/11/19, for conspicuous gallantry. Son of General and Mrs. M. F. Inches, c/o Bank of Scotland, George Street, Edinburgh, Scotland.
Lockhart, W. E.	Lieut.	Killed in Aeroplane Accident at Trezennes on 12th June, 1918. Son of Mrs. M. Lockhart, Newcastle, Ontario, Canada.
Rattle, Louis Chaloner	2/Lieut.	Killed in Aeroplane Accident at Xaffevillers on 10th October, 1918. Age 19. Son of Mr. and Mrs. W. Rattle, Riverside, Preston, Lancashire.
Scudemore, Robert Capel	Capt.	Killed in Bomb Accident at Ochey on 26th February, 1918. Son of Mr. and Mrs. C. Scudemore, 31, Ashchurch Park Villas, Hammersmith, London, W.
Gardner, John Harrison	2/Lieut.	Killed in Aeroplane Accident near Sedan on 10th January, 1919. Son of Mr. and Mrs. R. Gardner, New Longton, near Preston, Lancs. Age 20.
Wood, James	2/Lieut.	Killed in Aeroplane Accident near Sedan on 10th Januarv, 1919. Son of Mr. and Mrs. A. Wood, 46, Castellain Mansions, Maida Vale, London, W.9. Age 19.
Hewett, Leonard Stanley	Lieut.	Killed in Aeroplane Accident near Cologne on 6th February, 1919. Son of Mrs. Hewett, " Carisbrook," Cricketpitch Road, Clapton, London, N.E. Age 22.
Carleton-Smith, Beavan	2/Lieut.	Killed in Aeroplane Accident, near Cologne, on 6th February, 1919. Son of Mrs. Carleton-Smith, Brampton, Aston-on-Clun, Salop. Age 20.
*Curry, Walter Howard	Lieut.	Killed in action whilst serving with the Canadian Forces. Son of Mrs. M. G. Curry, 10, Nassau Street, Toronto, Canada. Age 28.
*Haley, Arthur	2/Lieut.	Killed whilst serving with 55 Squadron on June 1st, 1918. Son of Mr. and Mrs. G. Haley, 110, Queen's Road, Buckhurst Hill, Essex. Age 22.
*Wald, Alexander	Capt.	Killed in Aeroplane Accident in England. Son of Mr. and Mrs. A. Wald, Large Bay, South Australia. Age 25. Awarded Military Cross 11th June, 1918.

100 SQUADRON

NAME.	RANK.	ADDRESS.
*Duncan, Stuart Macpherson	Lieut.	Killed in action whilst serving with another unit. Son of Mrs. G. Duncan, 160, Waverley Street, Ottawa, Canada. Age 22.
*Matthews, G. W.	2/Lieut.	Missing, believed killed, while serving with 55 Squadron.
*Brotherhood, F. R.	2/Lieut.	Killed in action whilst serving with 55 Squadron. Mrs. F. R. Brotherhood (wife), Park Avenue, Stirling, Scotland.
*Price, J. W.	Lieut.	Killed in Aeroplane Accident in Canada, October, 1918. Son of Mrs. C. W. Price, 163, Church Street, Moncton, New Brunswick, Canada.

* Killed whilst serving with other units.

DIED

Sawyer, Robert Henry	2/Lieut.	Died in England from pneumonia on 3/8/18. Age 28. Son of Mrs. Sawyer, 40, Woodfield Road, Ealing.
Rawlinson, Percy Ivan	2/Lieut.	Died in England. Son of Mrs. F. Rawlinson, Chelsea, Victoria, Australia. Age 29.

WOUNDED

Bean, C. O.	2/Lieut.	Wounded during raid on night of 30th Sept./1st Oct., 1917.
Chambers, J. A.	2/Lieut.	Wounded during raid on night of 26/27th June, 1918.
Castle, G. L.	2/Lieut.	Wounded during raid on night of 26/27th May, 1917.
Eccles, H. E. K. ...	2/Lieut	Wounded during raid on night of 6/7th May, 1917.
Holland, W. T. F. ...	Capt.	Wounded during raid on night of 27/28th June, 1917.
Worrall, E. A.	Lieut.	Wounded during raid on night of 29/30th May, 1917.

OTHER RANKS

KILLED

Cockburn, W. G. ...	2/A.M.	Killed in Bomb Accident at Ochey on 26th February, 1918. Next of kin—Mrs. M. E. Cockburn (wife), 36, South View, Tantobie, Co. Durham. Age 28.
Ekins, A. W.	2/A.M.	Brought down by A.A. fire and killed on 6th May, 1917. Son of Mr. and Mrs. A. Ekins, Hoxton, St. Neots, Huntingdonshire. Age 19.
Lowe, J. H.	Sergt.	Killed during hostile aircraft attack on Azelot, night of 30/31st August, 1918. Age 21. Son of Mr. and Mrs. F. A. Lowe, 82, Wandsworth Bridge Road, Fulham, London, S.W

2/LIEUT. A. HALEY.

2/LIEUT. L. E. COLLINS.

2/LIEUT. J. WOOD.

2/LIEUT. BEAVAN CARLETON-SMITH.

Evans, T.	1/A.M.		Killed by shell fire at Trezennes, 22nd July, 1917. Son of Mrs. A. Evans, 182, Fletcher Street, Bolton, Lancs. Age 25.
Green, T.	F/Sergt.		Accidentally killed by bomb explosion at Ochey, 26th February, 1918. Son of Mr. and Mrs. T. Green, Hoppole, Pershore Street, Birmingham. Age 23.
Lem, F.	1/A.M.		Accidently killed by bomb explosion at Ochey, 26th February, 1918. Son of Mr. and Mrs. T. Lem, 39, Carrington Road, Endcliffe, Sheffield. Age 25.
McLeod, A.	Corpl.		Accidently killed by bomb explosion at Ochey, 26th February, 1918. Son of Mr. and Mrs. A. McLeod, 13, Belgrave Street, Glasgow, Scotland. Age 22.
Sowerby, J.	1/A.M.		Killed by shell fire at Trezennes, 22nd July, 1917. Son of Mr. and Mrs. E. Sowerby, 14, Appleby Road, Kendal, Westmoreland. Age 22.

DIED

A. R. Waite	Corpl.	Died as result of injuries received in France. Son of Mr. and Mrs. C. T. Haley Waite, Woodford Hill Cottages, Nr. Thrapston.

WOUNDED

Marsden, J.	2'A.M.	Wounded by shell fire, 22nd April, 1917.
North, L.	F/Sergt.	Wounded by shell fire at Trezennes Aerodrome, 22nd July, 1917.
Robinson, R. J.	1/A.M.	Wounded by shell fire at Trezennes Aerodrome, 22nd July, 1917.
Stone, J.	Corpl.	Wounded by shell fire at Trezennes Aerodrome. 22nd July, 1917.
Wormald, J. L.	2/A.M.	Wounded by shell fire, 22nd April, 1917.

PRISONERS OF WAR

OFFICERS

Archibald, L. M.	2/Lieut.	... ...	24th October, 1917.
Anderson, D. S.	2/Lieut.	... ...	15th May, 1918.
Butler, L.	2/Lieut.	... ...	7th April, 1917.
Bushe, J. F.	2/Lieut.	... ...	30th September, 1917.

186

LIEUT. R. K. INCHES, D.F.C.

LIEUT. J. H. GARDNER.

LIEUT. L. S. HEWETT.

2nd/LIEUT. T. G. HOLMES.

100 SQUADRON

Brown, V. R.	Lieut.	28th May, 1918.
Colbert, L. A.	2/Lieut.	30th September, 1918.
Chainey, F. H.	2/Lieut.	16th September, 1918.
Fulton, E. P.	2/Lieut.	10th August, 1917.
Fielding-Clarke, A. ...	2/Lieut.	9th February, 1918.
Greenslade, R. S.	2/Lieut.	24th October, 1917.
Godard, J. S.	Lieut.	24th October, 1917.
Jones, W. H.	Lieut.	24th October, 1917.
Jackson, G. G.	Lieut.	19th February, 1918.
Johnson, F. R.	Lieut.	16th September, 1918.
Lefevre, F. M. C.	2/Lieut.	24th January, 1918.
Peile, A. H.	2/Lieut.	21st January, 1918.
Penruddocks, N. F. ...	Lieut.	17th May, 1918.
Pitman, R. C.	Lieut.	9th January, 1918.
Rickards, A. R. M. ...	2/Lieut.	6th March, 1917.
Reid, C. W.	Lieut.	21st January, 1918.
Swart, O. B.	Lieut.	9th February, 1918.
Taylor, L. G.	2/Lieut.	13th November, 1917.
Williamson, J. C.	Lieut.	17th May, 1918.

MEN

Barnes, E. W.	2/A.M.	6th April, 1917.
Guyatt, J. G.	2/A.M.	19th February, 1918.
Hawkins, W.	2/A.M.	10th August, 1917.
Johnson, A.	1/Pte.	28th May, 1918.
O'Connor, H.	2/A.M.	15th May, 1918.
Robb, D.	2/A.M.	7th April, 1918.

2/LIEUT. L. C. RATTLE.

2/LIEUT. F. R. BROTHERHOOD.

LIEUT. H. BOYD.

LIEUT. R. H. SAWYER.

LIST OF OFFICERS

Lieut. W. G. Albu	P.O. Box 1,242, Johannesburg, South Africa.
2/Lieut. D. S. Allen	4, Mornington Road, Liscard, Cheshire.
2 Lieut. D. Alexander	3, Clarendon Road, West, Charlton-cum-Hardy, Manchester.
2 Lieut. L. M. Archibald	87, Woodlawn Avenue, Toronto, Canada.
2/Lieut. R. A. Aryton	" Romola," 48, Woodstock Street, Waverley, N.S.W. Australia.
2/Lieut. D. S. Anderson	c/o R. W. Walden, Esq., Bella Vista, Upper Warlingham, Surrey.
Lieut. W. Allan	43, Harrow View Road, Ealing, London, W.
Major C. G. Burge, O.B.E. ...	Dent-de-Lion, Westgate-on-Sea, Kent, and Royal Aero Club.
Capt. L. E. Barry	14, The Grove, Golders Green, London, W.
Lieut. D. Brunt	Ardwyn, Nantygle, Monmouth.
Lieut. S. N. Bourne	Uppington Court, Wingham, Canterbury, Kent.
Lieut. W. A. Barnes	Home Farm, Smeeth, nr. Ashford, Kent.
Capt. F. T. Bright, D.F.C. ...	Angel Hill, Bury St. Edmonds, Suffolk.
Lieut. J. A. Boret, M.C.	25 Barrow Gate Road. Chiswick, London, W.4.
Capt. C. E. Blayney, M.C. ...	c/o Smith Caughy Ltd., Auckland, N.Z.
2/Lieut. C. O. Bean	Wyke Lodge, Ulwell, Swanage, Dorsetshire.
2/Lieut. J. F. Bushe	Marivale Road, Port-of-Spain, Trinidad, B.W.I.
2/Lieut. G. F. J. Boyle	37, Deanville Road, Clapham Park Road, London, S.W.
2/Lieut. L. A. Bushe	Port-o'-Spain, Trinidad, B.W.I.
2/Lieut. V. R. Brown	1,234 Prendergast Avenue, Jamestown, U.S.A.
Lieut. E. E. Blakemore	10, Devonshire Promenade, Lenton, Notts.
2/Lieut. A. Birch	83, Church Lane, Gorton, Manchester.
2/Lieut. J. K. Best	The Woodlands, Wigan Road, Standish, nr. Wigan, Lancs.
2/Lieut. C. A. Box	Sedgebrook, Impington, Cambridge.
Lieut-Col. M. G. Christie, C.M.G., D.S.O., M.C.	Peters Court, Barnet Green, Birmingham.
Capt. W. E. Collison	9a, Young Street, Kennington, London, S.W.
2/Lieut. D. E. P. Chaplin ...	Chelsea Court, Chelsea Embankment, London, S.W.
2/Lieut. E. T. Carpenter	58. St. Peter's Road, Handsworth, Birmingham.
2 Lieut. O. Clayton	Station Parade, West Worthing, Sussex.
Lieut. A. J. Chrystall	Angell House, Buckhurst Hill, Essex.
2/Lieut. L. A. Colbert	The Hawthorns, Llangollen, N. Wales.
Lieut. J. M. Carroll	6, Upper Columbus Road, Dublin.
Capt. P. C. Campbell, M.C. ...	Ardachuidh, Colintraire, Argyllshire, Scotland.
2/Lieut. J. R. Cudemore	Lambton House, Rothbury, Northumberland.
Lieut. M. H. Colley	Alton Villa, Walley Avenue, Sale, or Calcutta Light Horse Club, Calcutta, India.
Capt. H. C. Chambers	Mokopetto, Havelock, Hawkes Bay, N.Z.
2/Lieut. H. J. Crofts	" Brynllys," Newtown, N. Wales.

SERGT. J. H. LOWE.

AIR-MECH. J. SOWERBY.

CORPL. A. McLEOD.

AIR-MECH. F. LEM.

100 SQUADRON

2/Lieut. J. A. Chambers	655, Broadway, Winnipeg, Canada.
2/Lieut. F. H. Chainey	"Cappera," 48, Falmouth Avenue, Highams Park, Chingford.
Capt. H. M. Coombs, D.F.C. ...	Kenilworth, Cypress Road, Newport, Isle of W.
2/Lieut. A. Cooper	"Daphne," Old Waterworks Road, Eastbourne, Sussex.
2/Lieut. T. W. Cummins ...	10, Upper Berkeley Place, Clifton, Bristol.
2/Lieut. G. Crocker	Eastcote, Umberleigh, North Devon.
Lieut. J. H. Conover	Freehold, New Jersey, U.S.A.
2/Lieut. H. E. Duncan	74, Terrace Road, Upton Manor, Essex.
Capt. C. Dick-Cleland	14, Hillhead Gardens, Glasgow.
Lieut. J. L. Drummond	Spencer-Ville, Ontario, Canada.
Capt. D. Darby, D.F.C.	Holburn Grange, Lerwick, Northumberland.
2/Lieut. E. C. Dickens	Grain, nr. Rochester, Kent.
2/Lieut. W. G. P. Dyson ...	53, Lee Lane, Norwich, nr. Bolton, Lancs.
Lieut. J. W. Edwards	Cataraqui, Ontario, Canada.
2/Lieut. H. M. Edwardes-Evans, M.C.	Ringway Vicarage, Althringham, Cheshire.
Lieut. H. Ebrey	8, Seedley Road, Pendleton, Manchester.
2/Lieut. K. Evans	Tretower Vicarage, Crickhowell, S. Wales.
2/Lieut. B. Evans	Fisharris, Glamorganshire, Wales.
Lieut. G. L. Erwin, Jr.	Kalamazoo, Michigan, U.S.A.
2/Lieut. E. P. Fulton	Hargreaves Street, Bendigo, Australia.
2/Lieut. A. Fielding-Clarke ...	Ampthill, Reading.
Lieut. W. M. Foster	Claremont, Norton, Stockton-on-Tees, Durham.
2/Lieut. E. Fearnside	150, Parkview Villas, Hexthorpe, Doncaster.
Lieut. G. A. Firby	772, Logan Avenue, Toronto, Ontario, Canada.
Lieut. J. S. Godard	East Black, Ottawa, Canada.
Lieut. W. B. Gayner	Sunnyside, Calagari, Alberta, Canada.
Lieut. R. S. Greenslade	Buckland St. Mary, Chard, Somerset.
Lieut. W. J. C. Gibson	Combe House, Chard, Somerset.
Lieut. W. T. Gilson	10, Hurlington Court, Hurlington, London, S.W.
Lieut. J. H. Gower	23, East 18th Avenue, Denver, Coloroda, U.S.A.
2/Lieut. T. A. Greig	8, Maxwell Street, Edinburgh.
2/Lieut. W. H. Greaves	Wilmot Road, Leyton, Essex.
2/Lieut. A. E. Gwyther	92, Poulton, Fleetwood, Lancs.
Capt. H. D. Harman, M.C. ...	65, Sinclair Road, West Kensington, W.14.
Capt. N. L. Garstin	"Stutterheim," King Williams Town, Cape Prov. S.A.
2/Lieut. R. J. Housden	19, Conniston Road, Canonbury, London, N.
2/Lieut. H. B. D. Harrington ...	Henley House, 25, Flodden Road, 5, Wyatts Park, London, S.E.
2/Lieut. J. Harper	Kenilworth House, Clontaff, Dublin.
Capt. W. T. F. Holland	Compton Hill, Farnborough, Surrey, and Cavalry Club, London.
Lieut. E. G. Hilton	Lambourne, Berks.
Lieut. L. Harper	Chichester House, Antrim Road, Belfast.
2/Lieut. H. A. Hewitt	77, Balham Park Road, Balham, London, S.W.
Lieut. W. V. Hyde	Ravenscourt, Leyland Road, Lee, Kent.

100 SQUADRON

Lieut. E. E. Howard	20. Clifton Villas, Maida Vale, N.W.
Lieut. W. Hallitt	9, Ashfield Road, Berkley, Huddersfield.
Lieut. J. Henry	Glenburn, Hamilton, N.B.
2/Lieut. S. C. Harker	14, St. John's Avenue, Bridlington, Yorkshire.
2/Lieut. D. L. Hobson	Mount Elgin, Ontario, Canada.
2/Lieut. C. A. Hall	Carlton House, Worksop, Notts.
2/Lieut. G. R. Herrett	4, High Street, Brentwood, Essex.
Lieut. C. E. Haines	105, High Street, Stevenage, Herts.
2/Lieut. G. Harvey	128, Well Lane, Treeton, nr. Rotherham, Yorks.
Capt. C. Ingram	Bath Club, Dover Street, London, W.
Lieut. G. G. Jackson	94, Grove Park, Denmark Hill, London, S.E.5.
2/Lieut. W. H. Jones	54, St. Helen's Road, Swansea, S.W.
Lieut. F. R. Johnson	Cumner Vicarage, Oxford.
2/Lieut. T. Jamieson	Greenmowe, Lingev Scotland.
2/Lieut. H. Jackson	9, Toller Drive, Toller Lane, Bradford, Yorks.
Capt. W. E. Kemp	97, Edith Road, West Kensington, London, W.
2/Lieut. P. Kent	72, Hands Road, Sheffield, Yorks.
2/Lieut. T. W. Kerr	c/o Kerr Bros., 533, Collins Street, Melbourne, Aus.
Lieut. A. R. Kingsford	27a, Maidstone Road, New Southgate, London, N.
Capt. R. P. Keely	8, Warrington Gardens, Maida Vale, London, W.
2/Lieut. V. C. Kirtley	750, Pretorius Street, Pretoria, Transvaal, S.A.
2/Lieut. E. W. King	12, Church Street, Chipping-Norton, Oxon.
Lieut. L. D. Kirk	Uledh Tower, Dalmuir, Scotland.
Lieut. J. J. King	1,522 Astor Street, Chicago, U.S.A.

AIR-MECH. A. W. ELKINS.   AIR-MECH. W. G. COCKBURN.

193

N

100 SQUADRON

Lieut. R. S. Lewis	3, Hope Park, Bromley, Kent.
Lieut. C. A. Lunghi	36, Charleville Mansions, Kensington, London, W.
2/Lieut. H. F. Lindo	120, Westbourne Terrace, Hyde Park, London, W.
2/Lieut. L. V. Labrow	28, Harlington Gardens, Gunnersbury, London, W.
Capt. R. Lindsay	Services Club, 19, Stratford Place, London, W.
Lieut. C. E. Lucas...	267, Brook Street, Sarnia, Ontario, Canada.
2/Lieut. F. E. Le Fevre, M.C. ...	" Donfraneen," Cornwall Road, Sutton, Surrey.
2/Lieut. W. B. Lane	Coates Farm, Swyncombe, Henley-on-Thames.
2/Lieut. T. H. L. Lewis	Imperial Hotel, London, W.C.
Capt. C. G. R. Lewis	Llanbedr Rectory, Crickhowell, Breconshire.
2/Lieut. A. Lister	21, Aylesford Road, Handsworth, Birmingham.
2/Lieut. P. Loftus	Cloonduff, Glenhest, Newport, Ireland.
2/Lieut. M. B. C. Lake	11, Warminster Road, South Norwood Park, London.
2/Lieut. W. V. Leftley	Ightham Mote, Sevenoaks, Kent.
2/Lieut. J. G. Lethbridge ...	251, West 98 Street, New York, U.S.A.
Major W. A. McClaughry, D.S.O., M.C., D.F.C.	45, Melbourne Street, Adelaide, S. Australia.
2/Lieut. J. Murch	23, Fortis Green Avenue, East Finchley, London, N.
Lieut. R. J. Montgomery-Moore...	c/o J. Banks Pittman, 17 to 18, Basinghall Street, E.C.
Lieut. W. K. McNaughton ...	531, Notre Dame Street, Lachine, Quebec, Canada.
2/Lieut. H. Morley	111, Hill Lane, Southampton.
2/Lieut. C. A. McCreath	Rosath Hill, Harrow-on-Hill, London.
Lieut. R. A. Martin	Woodgate, Sanderstead, Surrey.
Capt. H. J. Miles	70, St. Leonard's Road, Hove, Sussex.
Lieut. E. C. Middleton	Northcote House, Kensington, London, W.
Lieut. A. H. Matthews	Bridge House, Harold Wood, Essex.
2/Lieut. E. Mason	131, City Road, Birmingham.
Lieut. J. V. McKenzie	421, Keele Street, Toronto, Canada.
2/Lieut. H. C. Monckton... ...	South Eastern Hotel, Ashford, Kent.
Lieut. A. R. Nock	Rivington, Holywalk, Leamington Spa.
Lieut. H. Nunn	23, Bishops Road, Highgate, London, N.6.
Lieut. L. A. Naylor	c/o Royal Bank of Canada, London.
Lieut. J. J. O'Loughlin	Toronto, Ontario, Canada.
Lieut. G. A. O'Sullivan	41, Cambridge Mansions, Battersea, London, S.W.
2/Lieut. F. Petch	South Villa, Kensington Road, Bristol.
2/Lieut. A. H. Prosser	250, Brearley Street, Birmingham.
Lieut. J. W. Price	163, Church Street, Moncton, New Brunswick, Canada.
Lieut. R. C. Pitman	426, Eight Street, Saskatoon, Canada.
Capt. I. W. Parnell	Hillmorton, Rugby.
2/Lieut. J. C. E. Price	188, New Road, Copnor, nr. Portsmouth.
2/Lieut. G. L. Pollard	20, Harrogate Road, Bradford, Yorks.
2/Lieut. A. H. Peile	39, Kensington Gardens Square, Bayswater, London, W.
Lieut. N. F. Penruddocke ...	Winchester House, Meads, Eastbourne.
2/Lieut. F. Pascoe	8, Inkerman Street, St. Thomas, Swansea, Wales.
Lieut. S. T. Proctor	44, Calyton Park Square, Newcastle-on-Tyne.

100 SQUADRON

Lieut. L. S. Potter	49, Fawnbrake Road, Herne Hill, London, S.E.
Lieut. C. H. B. Price	Station Road Chambers, Knighton, Radnorshire.
Lieut. H. V. Peberdy	Barwell House, Mountsorrel, Leicestershire.
Lieut. H. H. Peppercorn	Charmans, Westerham, Kent.
Lieut. C. R. Richardson	" Lascelles," Shortlands, Kent.
Lieut. R. H. Reece	315, Commonwealth Avenue, Boston, Mass, U.S.A
Lieut. F. S. Reed	Kimberley Club, Kimberley, S.A.
Lieut. C. W. Reid	c/o Reuters' Agency, St. George's Street, Cape Town, S.A.
Capt. P. W. Rutherford, M.C. ...	70, Gracechurch Street, London, E.C.
2/Lieut. W. Rogers	152, Stow Hill, Newport, Mons.
Lieut. H. V. Roe	10, Oakhill Road, Putney, London, S.W.
Lieut. O. R. L. Ross, D.F.C. ...	Elgin Terrace, Limestone Road, Belfast.
2/Lieut. W. Richards	4, Mostyn Crescent, Llandudno, N. Wales.
2/Lieut. J. M. Rennie	15, Havswell Road, Arbroath, N.B.
2/Lieut. H. T. Ross	40, Daresburv Street, Cheetham Hill, Manchester.
Capt. I. G. Roberts	Brynaber, Llanwnda, Carnarvonshire, N. Wales.
2/Lieut. C. H. Roy, M.M. ...	17, Sutherland Terrace, London, S.W.
Major J. Sowrey	Yeoveney, nr. Staines, Middlesex.
Lieut. J. A. Stedman	38, Alexander Road, London, S.E.
Lieut. W. Stainer	48, Osmond Road, Hove, Sussex.
Lieut. R. L. Sweeney	28, Carrill Drive, Fallowfield, Manchester.
Capt. V. E. Schweitzer	Portage la Prairie, Manitoba, Canada.
Lieut. H. A. Samson	4, Carlton Crescent, Southampton.
2/Lieut. F. C. Sawyer	57, Wellesley Avenue, Newland, Hull.
2/Lieut. O. B. Swart	Germiston, South Africa.
Lieut. K. G. Siddaway	74, Holywell Road, Handsworth, Birmingham.
Capt. R. C. Savery, D.F.C. ...	The Willows, Westcott, Dorking.
2/Lieut. B. de Salaberry	253, Wilbrod Street, Ottawa, Canada.
2/Lieut. O. Sherwood	Grove House, Selby, Yorks.
2/Lieut. R. Shillinglaw	Melcombe, Lightwood Road, Buxton.
2/Lieut. J. F. A. Segner	19, Cooper Street, Manchester.
2nd/Lieut. H. G. Shaw	84, Cameron Avenue, Windsor, Ontario, Canada.
2/Lieut. F. B. Shaw	309, North Brook Street, Sarnia, Ontario, Canada
Major W. J. Tempest, D.S.O., M.C.	Ackworth Grange, Ackworth, Yorks.
Capt. G. M. Turnbull, A.F.C. ...	Mannville, Alberta, Canada.
Lieut. A. H. Thompson	Penetanguishane, Ontario, Canada.
2/Lieut. A. G. Taylor	31, Toulsea Road, Upper Tooting, London, S.W.
Lieut. A. D. Tatham	72, Princes Street, Edinburgh.
Lieut. A. J. Taylor	48, Cambridge Street, Wolverton, Bucks.
2/Lieut. R. T. Tarrant	63, Redfern Road, Harlesdon, London, N.W.
Lieut. J. J. Van Schaack	Sycamore Road, Hutford, Conn, U.S.A.
Lieut. D. E. White	1,400 Alaska Buildings, W.E., and Co. Seattle, Washington, U.S.A.
Capt. C. C. Waddington	Ormidale, Bickley, Kent.
Capt. F. W. Wells	124 Kloof Street, Capetown, South Africa.
Lieut. K. Wallace	6, Lovaine Place, Newcastle-on-Tyne.
Capt. H. T. O. Windsor, M.C. ...	Ellersmere, New Church Road, Hove, Sussex.

Capt. H. B. Wilson, D.F.C.	...	Verona, Waldingham, Surrey.
2/Lieut. J. C. Williamson	...	Gwenalt, Oswestry, Salop.
2/Lieut. P. Wilkins, M.C.	...	41, Tenton Place, Porthcawl, E. Wales.
2/Lieut. W. B. Warneford	...	1, Baker Street, Burton Lane, York.
2/Lieut. A. Ward ...	... ...	Court Road, Lyne, nr. Chertsey, Surrey.

OTHER RANKS

Avery, G.	... ...	Sergt.	East Court, Tenterden, Kent.
Airey, C.	... ...	Corpl.	25, Chaucer Road, Fleetwood, Lancs.
Aylett, C.	... ...	A.M.2	10, Tydenham Grove, Manchester.
Appleton, F. J.	...	Sergt.	157, High Street, Stockton-on-Tees.
Atkinson, J. E.	...	A.M.2	37, Wellgate, Clitheroe, Lancs.
Anderson, J. ...	...	Corpl.	60, High Riggs, Edinburgh.
Allum, R. T.	...	Corpl.	8, Coldacutt Street, Caversham, Reading.
Adams, D.	... ...	Sergt.	50, Green Street, Hyde, Cheshire.
Andrews, F. J.	...	F/Sergt.	11, Waterloo Road, Shoeburyness.
Allinson, F. N.	...	A.M.1	37, Charles Street, New Sheldon, Durham.
Abbott, J. T.	...	A.M.3	37, Moor Pool Avenue, Harbourne Estate, Birmingham.
Appleby, A. B.	...	A.M.2	Station Road, Yale, Bristol.
Austin, E.	... ...	A.M.3	42, Albert Street, Islington, Barnsbury, N.
Andrews, A. E.	...	A.M.3	21, Haberdasher Street, Hoxton, N.E.
Adkins, P. J., D.S.M., D.F.M.		Sergt.	6, Seymour Villas, Woolacombe, N. Devon.
Adair, R.	... ...	Sergt.	87, Canehill Road, Belfast.
Adams, H.	... ...	Pt.2	Mayfield House, Wilstone Road, Penlan, Newport, Mon.
Balon, M. N.	...	A.M.3	27, Carfin Street, Glasgow.
Bell, T. W. W.	...	Corpl.	32, Cardigan Street, Kennington, London, S.E.2.
Betts, J. E.	...	S.M.	27, Walpole Terrace, Kemp Town, Brighton.
Barnes, E. W.	...	A.M.2	Beverly, Hull.
Box, G. F. W.	...	A.M.2	2, Clyde Villas, Maison du Place, Dover.
Bull, G. A.	... ...	Sergt.	121, Unett Street, Hockley, Birmingham.
Bruce, R. C.	...	F/Sergt.	162, Stapleton Road, Bristol.
Brown, A. B.	...	Sergt.	50, Union Street, Buckland, Dover.
Breeze, T.	... ...	A.M.1	Willow Bank, Winsford, Cheshire.
Blythe, B.	... ...	A.M.2	4, Rombalds Crescent, Armley, Leeds.
Blyth, W.	... ...	A.M.1	42, High Street, Johnston, Renfrewshire.
Blamire, F.	...	A.M.1	Burton, Carnforth, Westmoreland.
Brown, A. H.	...	A.M.2	Grove Lodge, Broadwater, Worthing.
Bird, J. R.	... ...	Corpl.	54, Holly Street, Dalston, London, N.E.
Bell, F. A.	... ...	A.M.2	Rock House, Doncaster Road, Mexborough.
Bell, A. L. ...	...	A.M.2	81, High Street, Marlboro, Wilts.
Barker, W.	... ...	F/Sergt.	309 Bramford Road, Ipswich, Suffolk.

100 SQUADRON

Barton, F.	A.M.3	364, Cricklewood Lane, London, N.W.
Bullock, H. W. ...	Corpl.	8a Shatton Street, Piccadilly, London, W.
Burmiston, H. M. ...	Sergt.	Old Bank, Worcester.
Baker, G.	A.M.2	211, Leahurst Road, Hithergreen, Lewisham.
Brewer, B.	A.M.2	17, Blackbull Road, Folkestone.
Burney, R. W. ...	A.M.1	Ravensdale, Douglas, Cork.
Brogden, S.	A.M.3	53, Duke Street, Rochdale, Lancs.
Brvanv. E.	A.M.3	17. Clerkenwell Green, London, E.C.
Burnfield, T. ...	Pt.2	Painswick Road, Stroud.
Bamford, H. W. ...	A.M.1	57, London Road, Brighton.
Butler, W. V. ...	A.M.2	Poverest Farm House, Poverest Road, St. Mary Gray, Kent.
Berge, J.	A.M.2	Golden Lion, Broadway, Bessley Heath, Kent.
Bliss, W. J.	A/Corpl.	Trent Valley, Kew Gardens, Southport.
Butcher, G. H. ...	A.M.2	106, Southampton Road, East Leigh, Hants.
Brown, W. G. ...	A.M.2	Lowick, Thrapston, North Hants.
Beer, H. W. ...	A.M.2	1, Leonard Road, Southall, Middlesex.
Betts, W.	A.M.3	70, Wellington Street, Keighley, Yorkshire.
Bradley, A. ...	A.M.3	45, Henrietta Street, Bulwell, Nottingham.
Barnes, W. R. ...	A.M.3	10, Belgrave Road, Ebby Road, St. John's Wood, N.W.
Baker, W. A. ...	A.M.2	Idns House, Chepstow, Newport, Mon.
Brooks, C. H. ...	A.M.2	Elmcot, Portsmouth Road, Milford, Surrey.
Bell, D. W.	Pt.2	40, Beaufoy Road, Plaistow, London.
Brown, R. T. ...	A.M.2	4,Kirk Road, Wishaw, Scotland.
Bradshaw, J. ...	A.M.3	13, Chapel Street, Redcliffe, nr. Manchester.
Bowe, J	A.M.3	30, Greendale Road, Port Sunlight, Cheshire.
Bassett, S. E. ...	Corpl.	81, High Street, Plumstead, London, S.E.
Brown, J. B. ...	Pt.2	1, Tento Place, Leith, Scotland.
Bedding, A. ...	Pt.1	54, Southmoor Road, Oxford.
Batute, W. J. ...	Pte.2	34. London Street, Kings Cross, London, N.
Baxter, J.	Pt.2	67, Dansound Lane, Hull.
Blyth, G.	Pt.1	84, James Rickett Avenue, Garden Village, Hull.
Buttle, A. J. ...	Pt.2	65, Warwick Road, Ealing, London, N.
Bannatyne, J. H. ...	Pt.2	Braeside Cottage, Pittenzie Road, Crieff, Perth.
Barnes, C.	Pt.2	5, James Street, Newport, Mon.
Beale, D. W. ...	Pt.2	Blenaven Court, Yarm, Yorks.
Brown, G.	Sergt.	83, Sider Road, Ipswich.
Brown, R.	Pt.2	3, Bywater Street, Leeds.
Burns, J.	Pt.2	20, Gretham Street, Lurgan, Co. Armagh.
Bethell, S. B. ...	Pt.1	57, Sweet Briar Walk, Silver Street, Edmonton London.
Barber, G.	Pt.1	13, Wynyatt Street, London, E.C.
Crickmore, C. B. ...	A.M.1	150, Green Walk, Barnes, Crayford, Kent.
Cuss, A. E.	A.M.2	76. Harold Terrace, Leeds.
Caplin, W. J. ...	A.M.1	68, Warlock Road, Paddington, London, W.
Cox, S. G.	Pt.1	6, Villiers Road, Stapleton Road, Bristol.
Cole, W. H. ...	A.M.3	18 Elton Street, St. Paul's, Bristol.

Clewly, W. F.	...	A.M.1	13, Theme Grove Road, Upton Park, London, E.
Crowther, F.	...	A.M.2	Rostrevor, North Drive, St. Anne's-on-Sea, Lancs.
Claque, H. F.	...	A.M.1	93, Shakespeare Street, Manchester.
Colthurst, S.	...	A.M.2	370, Mare Street, Hackney, London, E.8.
Conran, T. ...	...	A.M.3	3, West Tower Street, Stedly, Salford, Lancs.
Coleman, A.	...	A.M.1	13, St. Mary's Square, Paddington, London, W.
Clarke, J. W.	...	A.M.2	Carsley, Biscot Road, Luton.
Catton, F. ...	...	Sergt.	40, High Street, Blackfriars Road, London, S.E.
Christian, F. H.	...	A.M.2	28, Majow Road, Sydenham, London, S.E.
Clarke, J. ...	...	A.M.2	158 Percv Road, Shepherds Bush, London.
Carev. G. W. E.	...	Pt.1	28, Douglas Road, Handsworth, Birmingham.
Capon, A. E.	...	A.M.1	Langham, Bury St. Edmunds.
Chettle, A. ...	...	A.M.1	5. Wimbart Road, Upper Tulse Hill, Brixton, S.W.
Cook, M. H.	...	Corpl.	3, Elm Tree, Newtown, Carlisle.
Coles, S. ...	...	A.M.2	40, Buller Road, St. Thomas, Exeter.
Chapman, R. P.	...	A.M.2	Belmont, Sunninghill, Berks.
Carter, L. E.	...	A.M.1	170, Brecknock Road, Tufnell Park, London, N.
Cann-Lippencott	...	A.M.2	14, Nevern Place, Earls Court, London, S.W.5.
Clayton, A. ...	...	A.M.3	214, Holmes Lane, Hillsboro, Sheffield.
Clarke, E. G.	...	Pt.2	109, Clarendon Road, Notting Hill, London, W.10.
Choate, C. ...	...	Corpl.	Pumping Station, Byfleet, Surrey.
Collett, J. A.	...	A.M.3	13, Paradise Row, Stockton-on-Tees.
Coles, L. U.	...	Corpl.	51. Hagard Road, Twickenham.
Clark, A. J.	...	Pt.1	38, Pellerin Road, Stoke Newington, London, E.C.
Chewter, J. W.	:..	A.M.3	15, Prospect Place, New Cross, London, S.E.
Cromack, B.	...	Sergt.	Ghillview House, Church Lane, Shipley.
Crutchett, C.	...	Sergt.	9, Havelock Place, Green Street, Bethnal Green.
Clerico, J. ...	...	Pt.2	Newton Street, St. John's Road, Oxton, London, N.E.
Connelly, P. ...	...	Pt.2	Providence Hill, Strainland, Halifax.
Clavton, A. ...	...	A.M.3	" Shales," West End, Bitterne, Southampton.
Colebrook, A.	...	A.M.3	" Egdan," Dartford Road, Seven Oaks, Kent.
Coppock, S. D.	...	A.M.3	50. Albany Road, Victoria Park, Manchester.
Cornish, W. G.	...	Sergt.	232, Northwood Road, Thornton Heath, Surrey.
Cooper, H. ...	...	Pt.2	241, Bloxwick Road, Walsall, Staffordshire.
Cook, W. C.	...	A.M.3	38, Martin Buildings, Wellington, Somerset.
Campbell, H.	...	Pt.2	3, Mourview Street, Portadown, Co. Armagh.
Clements, G.	...	Pt.2	41, Joseph Street, Shankle Road, Belfast.
Clements, L.	...	Pt.2	10, Mount Street, Belfast.
Campbell, J.	...	Pt.2	8, York Street, Waterside, Londonderry.
Caffry, W. ...	...	Pt.2	30, Maralin Street, Belfast.
Crowther, A.	...	A.M.3	12, Cholmley Street, Allanby Road, Hull, Yorks.
Doyle, W. ...	...	Sergt.	c/o Cox & Co., Charing Cross, London, W.C.
Dyson, W. H.	...	S.M.	16, Pennyfarthing Street, Salisbury.
Deadman, H.	...	F/Sergt.	105, Leslake Road, Kensal Rise, London, N.W.
Drane, J. W.	...	A.M.2	6, Blandford Avenue, Beckenham, Kent.
Drage, H. H.	...	Coryl.	177, Powerscroft Road, Clapton, London, N.E.
Day, H. G. ...	...	A.M.1	34, Cladrew Street, Camberwell, London, S.E.

Davidson, E.	...	Corpl.	Holywell Green, near Halifax, Yorks.
Dare, F. S. ...	...	A.M.2	Kenmore, Friem Lane, Whitstone.
Daniel, J. ...	...	Corpl.	Gillibrand Walk, Chorley, Lancs.
Devon, R. P.	...	A.M.3	159, Midland Road, Masboro, Rotherham.
Dean, J. W.	...	A.M.1	West View, Marlborough Road, Gillingham, Kent.
Dickinson, C.	...	A.M.2	4a, Temple View Road, York Road, Leeds.
Dyke, W. G., D.C.M.		Sergt.	6, Avenue Road, Attleboro, Nuneaton, Warwickshire
Dodds, R. ...	...	A.M.3	85, Fearnley Street, Tong Road, Leeds, Yorks.
Dunn, J. M. R.	...	A.M.2	9, Honley Road, Lewisham, London, S.E.
Dawson, J. E.	...	Pt.2	1, New Park Road, Queensboro, Bradford.
Dibdon, W. G.	...	A.M.3	" Deepdene," Bitterne Park, Southampton.
Dowdell, J. ...	...	A.M.3	67, Mayple Road, Hordfield, Bristol.
Dixon, J. ...	...	A.M.3	26. Sorly Street, Sunderland.
Davies, A. ...	...	Pt.2	1, Kent Street, Birmingham.
Dole, G. S. ...	...	Pt.1	26, Dartmoor Street, Notting Hill Gate, London, W.
Delaney, M. ...	...	Pt.2	4, Chestnut Place, Clautrassil Street, Dublin.
Doran, P. ...	...	Pt.2	Balnamona, Avoca, Co. Wicklow, Ireland.
Eldridge, F. O.	...	A.M.1	57, Batchington Road, Hove, Sussex.
Edson, E. ...	...	Sergt.	76, Hormby Street, Bury, Lancs.
Edmondson, F. S.	...	A.M.2	Bolton-by-Bowland, near Clitheroe, Lancs.
Eastwood, A.	...	Corpl.	87. Commercial Road, Macclesfield.
Elliott, P. ...	...	A.M.2	Gilling Castle Gardens, Malton, Yorks.
Earnshaw, T. W.	...	A.M.1	Smithfield Road, Gleadless, nr. Sheffield.
Ellison, W. ...	...	Clk.2	206, Borough Road, St. Helens, Lancs.
Ely, T. R. ...	...	A.M.3	31, Buckingham Street, Liverpool.
Ellis, W. C.	...	A.M.3	15, Andrews Yard, Market Place, Mansfield, Notts.
Elliott, W. ...	...	A.M.3	17, South View Terrace, St. Nicholas, Carlisle.
Everard, T. J.	...	Pt.2	" The Bungalow," Alexander Road, Great Wakering, Essex.
Edwards, F. F.	...	Pt.2	12, Buccleuch Street, Edinburgh.
France, C. ...	...	Corpl.	128, Park Road, Tenton Park, Stoke-on-Trent.
Fiford, S. E.	...	Corpl.	38, New Road, Southampton.
Forester, J. ...	...	A.M.2	1, Little Poultry Street, London, W.
Flight, J. D.	...	Corpl.	North Street, Burrelton, Perthshire, Scotland.
Fisher, G. ...	...	A.M.2	Fernleigh, Portland Park, Hamilton, Scotland.
Field, P. W.	...	Corpl.	191, Coteford Street, Tooting, London, S.W.
Farrow, H. C.	...	A.M.3	6, Edwin Street, Houghton-le-Spring.
Francis, W. W.	...	A.M.2	13, Dresden Road, Upper Holloway, London, N.
Featherstone, F.	...	A.M.2	60, Brazil Street, Hull.
Ford, V. ...	...	A.M.1	34, Temple Grove, Golders Green, London, W.
Freestone, P. H.	...	A.M.2	Harlington, Mandeville, Yeovil, Somerset.
Freakley, W. J.	...	A.M.2	Cotes Heath, nr. Ecclesfield, Staffs.
Ford, A. H.	...	A.M.2	183, Loughbrough Road, Leicester.
Forrest, S. ...	...	A.M.3	38, Haygreen, Lye, Worcester.
Fiber, J ...	...	Pt.1	97, Stoke Newington Road, London, N.
Fenny, J. V. B.	...	A.M.3	37, Kyotto Lake Road, Sparkbrook, Birmingham.
Franks, J. C.	...	A.M.3	28, Chaucer Road, Gillingham, Kent.

100 SQUADRON

Fitzgerald, J.	...	Pt.2	3, Rockforth Lane, Bendon Road, Cork, Ireland.
Falkner, A. ...	...	Pt.2	31, Station Lane, Featherstone, Yorks.
Gowan, F. G.	...	Corpl.	99, Bulow Road, Fulham, London, S.W.
Guyat, J. G.	...	A.M.2	125, Pinner Road, Bushly, Watford, London.
Griffiths, R. ...	...	A.M.2	29, Albert Terrace, Runcorn.
Gamester, E. A.	...	A.M.1	10, Bond Street, Engerfield Green, Surrey.
Gillett, R. W.	...	A.M.2	73, Endlesham Road, Balham.
Gavin, A. ...	...	A.M.1	Felkland Palace, Felkland, Fife, Scotland.
Green, G. E.	...	Sergt.	14, Maxfield Street, Leicester.
Gray, L. V.	...	A.M.2	Edmondhurst, Dudley.
Goldwin, A. A.	...	A.M.3	743. High Road, Tottenham, London, N.
Grant, A. D.	...	A.M.3	Belle Vue, Methill, Peterhead, Aberdeenshire.
Greeve, W. C.	...	A.M.3	69. Pownall Road, Queen's Road, Walston, N.E.
Gate, D. ...	...	Pt.2	Rodwell, nr. Lewes, Sussex.
Goulding, A.	...	Pt.2	10, Regents Street, Moulton, nr. Northwich, Cheshire.
Greer, W. J.	...	Pt.2	113, Wayneford Street, Mill Hill, Glasgow.
Greenley, W.	...	Pt.2	15a, Prospect Terrace, Bishophill Junior, York.
Griffiths, G. ...	...	Pt.2	Rock Cottage, Little Sutton, nr. Chester.
Hinton, F. M.	...	Corpl.	28, Albert Road, Hansworth, Birmingham.
Hawkins, W.	...	A.M.2	Plume of Feathers, Minehead, Somerset.
Hunter, G. W.	...	Corpl.	22, Lutton Place, Edinburgh.
Hodge, A. V.	...	Corpl.	5, North Street, Tywarddreath, Cornwall.
Hemsworth, F. C.	...	A.M.1	Eastend, Alford, Lincs.
Hazledene, B.	...	A.M.2	West View, Bacup, Lancs.
Horsfield, J. W.	...	A.M.2	Castle Hotel, Pickering, Yorks.
Hopewell, A. J.	...	Corpl.	17, Harold Street, Bingley, Yorks.
Hood, R. ...	...	Corpl.	94, Chobham Road, Stratford, Essex.
Healy, D. ...	...	Corpl.	The Red House, Pennarforth, Cornwall.
Hearn, F. C.	...	A.M.3	42, Locket Road, Wealdstone, Middlesex.
Hayes, F. ...	...	A.M.2	15, Cuthbert Road, Hillsboro, Sheffield.
Harris, C. A.	...	Pt.1	Laburnum Cottages, 24, Latimer Road, Teddington.
Hutch, F. ...	...	F/Sergt.	62, Newland Terrace, Queen's Road, Battersea, S.W.
Hawkins, S.	...	A.M.1	34, Highfield Road, Seeley, Manchester.
Hastie, A. ...	...	A.M.1	Ladvwell, Motherwell, Scotland.
Hart, W. A.	...	A.M.1	58, Congrave Road, Walthall, Eltham, London, S.E.
Hart, H. L.	...	A.M.2	2, New Briggate, Leeds, Yorkshire.
Hullett, J. W.	...	A.M.1	50, Montpelier Rise, Golders Green, London, N.W.
Haigh, E. A.	...	A.M.1	8, Canada Road, Slough, Bucks.
Hall, T. ...	...	A.M.1	Penlie, Palmers Avenue, Grays, Essex.
Hentrick, T.	...	A.M.1	12, Mornington Road, Bow, London, E.
Hardwick W.	...	Ck.1	38, Kave Street, Bradford, Yorkshire.
Hayden, C. M.	...	F/Sergt.	35, Wellwood Road, Goodmayes, Essex.
Hall, J. W. ...	...	A.M.1	Ripley Lodge, Tanat Drive, Mossley Hill, Liverpool.
Homer, E. ...	...	Spr.	75, Fisher Street, Great Bridge, Tipton, Staffs.
Howard, C. ...	...	A.M.2	10, North Street, Chichester.
Honeysett, B. T.	...	Corpl.	Horsefair, Banbury.

Horsburgh, A.	...	Pt.2	108, Tipping Street, Ardwick, Manchester.
Hunter, R. ...	...	A.M.3	34, Clements Road.
Higgins, C. E.	...	Pt.1	34a, Harrogate Road, Chapel Allerton, Leeds.
Hustwick, R. J.	...	S.M.	14, John Street, Wodebottom, Shipley, Yorkshire.
Harlow, G. ...	...	Pt.2	Compton Street, Ashbourne, Derbyshire.
Heriet, F. ...	...	A.M.1	39, Providence Place, Brighton.
Hedly, W. ...	...	A.M.3	12, Tyrell Street, Bensham, Gateshead-on-Tyne.
Harvey, W. G.	...	A.M.3	30, Bulwer Road, Ipswich.
Hobbs, P. ...	...	A.M.3	27a Welsh Street, Chepstow.
Henderson, S.	...	A.M.3	9, Dawson Terrace, South Hylton, Sunderland.
Hamilton, J. M.	...	Pt.2	67. Adam Street, Belfast.
Hyndman, R. M.	...	Pt.2	65, Mossfield Street, Belfast.
Hayles, J. H.	...	A.M.3	1, Orchard Road, East Cowes, Isle of Wight.
Howe, T. W.	...	A.M.3	53, Great Brooms Road, High Brooms, Tunbridge Wells.
Herd, D. W.	...	Pt.2	5, King Street, City, Glasgow.
Isaacs, S. A.	...	Pt.2	15, Villa Road, Brixton, London, S.W.9.
Jones, W. V.	...	A/Corpl.	222 Lozelles Road, Birmingham.
Jolliffe, C. ...	...	Sergt.	1, Oxford Street, Wolverton, Bucks.
James, F. W.	...	F/Sergt.	263, Eccleshall Road, Sheffield.
Johnson, D. ...	...	Corpl.	76, Ranger Street, Accrington.
Jeffrey, T. F.	...	A.M.2	62, East Street, Farnham, Surrey.
Jones, T. L.	...	A.M.2	21, Hardinge Street, Upper Street, London.
Johnson, R. C.	...	A.M.2	48, Cherry Tree Lane, Beverley, Yorks.
Jones, E. ...	...	A.M.2	10, Darley Street, Springfield Road, Sale, Cheshire.
Jones, R. D.	...	A.M.2	42, Melody Road, Wandsworth, London, S.W.
Johnson, J. ...	...	A.M.2	35, Heather Street, Clayton.
Jamieson, R. J.	...	Pt.2	Hardwick Hall, Castle Eden, Durham.
Johnston, W.	...	Pt.2	25, Deck Street, Leith, Scotland.
Jackson, J. ...	...	A.M.1	9, Lord Street, Crewe, Cheshire.
Johnson, A. ...	...	A.M.2	240, Nicholas Street, Dublin.
Jones, A. ...	...	A.M.3	306, Park Road North, Birkenhead, Cheshire.
Jackson, W. ...	...	Pt.2	19, All Saints Road, South Acton, London, W.
Jobe, D. ...	...	Pt.2	8, Harwist Crescent, Newcastle-on-Tyne.
Jenner, P. J.	...	Ck.3	80, Water End, Woodston, Peterboro.
Jones, A. H.	...	Pt.2	40, John Street, Pentre, Rhondda Valley, S. Wales.
Joyes, C. ...	...	Pt.2	36, Portland Road, Worthing, Sussex.
Jacobs, J. ...	...	Pt.2	18, Glenhurst Road, Brentford, Middlesex.
Jenkins, E. J.	...	Pt.2	5, Wick Road, Ewenney-in-Brigend, South Wales.
Jones, W. D.	...	Pt.2	14, St. Nicholas Road, Maestog, South Wales.
Jacobs, F. C. W.	...	Pt.2	20, George Street, Worcester.
Kelly, A. H.	...	A.M.1	102, Carlton Vale, Kilburn, London, N.W.
Kirby, W. ...	...	A.M.3	6, Stocks Lane, Summer Lane, Barnsley.
King, F. H. ...	...	A.M.2	The Barn, Gordon Avenue, Camberley, Surrey.
Kapelle, L. ...	...	Pt.2	1, George Square, Biggan, Lanarkshire.
Kelly, J. ...	...	A.M.2	46, Hillside Road, Barkenend Road, Bradford.
King, C. E. ...	...	A.M.1	88, Corthorpe Road, Hampstead Heath, London, N.W.

100 SQUADRON

King, F.	... ...	Ck.2	127, Columbia Road, Hackney, London, E.
Kemp, A.	... ...	Pt.2	14, St. Michael's Road, Maestag, South Wales.
Layton, J. H.	...	Pt.1	53, Daca Street, Deptford.
Lowe, J. H.	...	Sergt.	82, Wandsworth Bridge Road, Fulham, S.W.
Love, G. A. ...	...	A.M.1	Calais House, Wanborough, Swindon, Wilts.
Lloyd, S. D. ...	...	Pt.1	7, Rodney Road, Great Yarmouth.
Lloyd, S. A. ...	...	Sergt.	Ty Llwyd, Gwaelod-y-Garth, Taff's Well, nr. Cardiff.
Lewis, T. D.	...	A.M.2	124, Thornton Road, Bootle, Liverpool.
Leek, T.	... ...	A.M.2	7, Mewfort House, Conybere, Balsall Heath, Birmingham.
Lawson, E. ...	...	A.M.2	3, George Street, Liff Road, Lochee, Dundee.
Lee, T.	... ...	A.M.2	7, Vincent Parade, Balsall Heath, Birmingham.
Ladkin, A. ...	...	A.M.3	33, Wetherly Street, High Openshaw, Manchester.
Longton, W. S.	...	A.M.2	Fairbrother Farm, Crow Lane, Newton-le-Willows.
Lorbegh, E. F.	...	A.M.2	185, Kennington Road, High Street, London, W.
Lear, J. S. ...	...	Corpl.	Hedon, Hull, Yorkshire.
Larmer, Z. L.	...	A.M.3	78, Otter Street, Derby.
Leicester, L.	...	Sergt.	The Poplars, New Street, Sutton, St. Helens, Lancs.
Lovett, W. ...	...	Pt.2	28, North Road, Hoddesdon, Herts.
McDonald, J.	...	A.M.3	Knockfin Tomich, Strathglass, Beanly, Inverness-shire.
Meredith, P. ...	...	Pt.1	43, Kingston Road, Southville, Bristol.
Minns, C. P.	...	Pt.1	90, Castle Street, Oxford.
Morton, F. W.	...	F/Sergt.	6, Boundary Road, Notting Hill, London, W.
Morris, J.	... ...	Pt.1	24, Alma Street, Luton, Beds.
Metcalfe, A. ...	...	Corpl.	Main Street, Creswell, Derbyshire.
McGuiness, J.	...	A.M.1	95, Mossblown, Annbank Station, Argyleshire.
McFall, J. L.	...	A.M.2	Rossbank, Port Glasgow, Scotland.
McBain, D. ...	...	Sergt.	2, Westburn Place, Whiteinch, Glasgow.
Marsden, J. ...	...	A.M.2	63, Wallshaw Street, Oldham, Lancs.
Manfield, R. J.	...	F/Sergt.	Schwyn, Bemerton, Salisbury, Wilts.
Moors, E. C.	...	Corpl.	87, Milkwood Road, Herne Hill, London, S.E.
Marshall, G. C.	...	Sergt.	52, Anglesea Road, Plumstead, London, S.E.
Marsh, W. ...	...	A.M.2	2, Marlborough Avenue, Fishponds, Bristol.
Mercer, G. E.	...	A.M.2	15, Rathen Road, Withington, Manchester.
Mancine, A.	...	A.M.3	43a, Myddleton Street, Clerkenwell, London, E.C.
Martin, H. R.	...	A.M.2	70, Northampton Road, Market Harboro.
May, S. H. ...	...	S.M.	51, Talma Road, Brixton, London.
Mott, A. G. ...	...	A.M.3	63, Greenside Road, Croydon.
Morrall, V. ...	...	A/Corpl.	65, King's Road, Evesham, Worcester.
McCarroll, A.	...	A.M.3	55, Man Street, Saltcoats, Scotland.
Murphy, J. ...	...	A.M.2	270, Wargrave Road, Newton-le-Willows, Lancs.
Middlehurst	...	A.M.1	111, Bryn Road South, Ashton-in-Makerfield, nr. Wigan.
Matthews	... ...	Pt.2	Mill House, 5, Church Road, Croydon.
Moy, C.	... ...	A.M.1	34, Morkton Street, Pimlico, London, S.W.
McClean, J. ...	...	Pt.1	Clive Street, Dykehead, Shotts, Scotland.

Madderson, J. ...	Pt.2	51, Bonford Street, Birmingham.
Marshall, E. W. ...	Pt.2	37, Everington Street, Palmer Road, Fulham, London, S.W.
Mitchell, J. G. ...	Pt.2	18, Victoria Street, Islington, London, N.
Melville, J.	A.M.3	Moah Rapness, Wisky, Orkney, Scotland.
McGilly, P.	Pt.2	5, Etriol Street, Enniskillen, Ireland.
Magee, R.	Pt.2	29, Lombeg Road, Lesburn, Co. Antrim, Ireland.
Moore, A.	A.M.3	26, Blackmoorfoot Road, Crossland Moor, Huddersfield.
Nash, F. E.	Sergt.	18, Hampton Park, Redlands, Bristol.
Nelson, G. McK. ...	Clk.2	105, Addison Road, King's Heath, Birmingham.
Nash, G. W. ...	A.M.2	Railway Hotel, Newbury, Berks.
Nicol, C.	A.M.1	70, High Street, Auchterander Street, Perth.
North	F/Sergt.	58, Highgate Road, Copnor, Portsmouth.
Nicoll, T.	F Sergt.	Edendale, Southland, New Zealand.
O'Doherty	A.M.1	20, Amberley Road, Paddington, London.
O'Donoghue, J. H.	Sergt.	12, Ingestre Road, Stafford.
O'Connor, H. ...	A.M.2	24, Sandhurst Place, Harehills Lane, Leeds.
Owens, W. G. ...	Sergt.	Fairfields Villas, Pogmore Vale, Glamorganshire.
Over, W.	Corpl.	Hawley, Blackwater, Hants.
Oswell, F.	Pte.2	27, Park Avenue, Madeley, Salop.
O'Brien, C. ...	Pte.2	Tanner Hill, Ballycogley, Co. Wexford, Ireland.
Pratley, R. W. ...	A.M.3	Fordwells, nr. Witney, Oxon.
Pagels, A. G. ...	A.M.2	113, Hanley Road, Stroud Green London, N.
Perry, H. H. ...	A.M.2	Glvn Cottage, Gresham Road, Edgware, Middlesex.
Pearson, G. M. ...	A.M.2	7, Whitehare Grove, Lincoln.
Payton, C. W. ...	A.M.2	Calton Vicarage, Ashburne, Derbyshire.
Pannett, H.	A.M.2	School House, Dumford Road, Holmefirth, Huddersfield.
Pearson, W. G. ...	A.M.2	Helensdale House, Victoria Street, Dumstable, Bedfords.
Perrin, A. A. ...	A.M.2	Walton House, Heath Park Road, Romford, Essex.
Podmore, W. J. ...	A.M.2	Rose Cottage, Spring Hill, Wellington, Salop.
Parish, E. J. ...	Corpl.	19, Wycliff Road, Handsworth, Birmingham.
Preston, R. B. ...	Pt.1	156, Malham Road, Forest Gate, London, S.E.
Pearson, F. C. ...	Pt.2	
Palmer, H.	Sergt.	27, Keswick Road, St. Helens, Lancs.
Park, D.	Pt.2	87, Lewisham Road, London, S.E.
Park, W.	Pt.1	3c, Devonshire Buildings, Barrow-in-Furness.
Parks, J. A.	Pt.1	5, Lewis Street, Newport, Mon.
Poustie, D.	A.M.3	17, Argyle Street, Ayr, Scotland.
Peel, A.	Pt.2	31, Canal Street, Longeaton, Derbyshire.
Riches, A. W. ...	Pt.2	3, Dock Terrace, Skirbeck, Boston, Lincs.
Runagall	Pt.2	Huslemere, Talsh Road, Upper Park Stone, Dorset.
Robb, D.	A.M.2	Salsburgh-by-Holytown, Lanarkshire, Scotland.
Richards, A. J. ...	Pt.1	6, Sycamore Terrace, Walseley Street, Birmingham.
Robinson, W. B. ...	A.M.2	5, Luck Lane, Marsh, Huddersfield.
Robinson, R. J. ...	A.M.2	24, Webbs Lane, Middlewich, Cheshire.
Roberts, A. M. ...	Sergt.	267, Walphall Street, Crewe.

100 SQUADRON

Riley, C. F.	Sergt.	4, Church Grove, Churchill Road, Handsworth, Birmingham.
Rich, J.	A.M.1	3, Handel Street, Russell Square, London, W.C.
Rivitt, C. H. ...	A.M.1	52, Gladstone Road, Sparkbrook, Birmingham.
Rands, J. E. ...	A.M.1	45, Chestnut Avenue, Hyde Park, Leeds.
Rose, H.	A.M.3	104, Parson Street, Glasgow.
Reid, T.	S.M.	39, Thornhill Gardens, Weir, Hartlepool.
Ramsden, C. H. ...	Corpl.	43, Gorsefield Street, Birkenhead.
Ringrose, W. A. ...	A.M.2	Co-operative House, Whyburn Street, Hucknall, Notts.
Reid, W. W. J. ...	Sergt.	106, St. Mark's Road, Salisbury.
Royle, A. H. ...	A.M.3	13, Parkfell Avenue, Rusholme, Manchester.
Reed, H.	Pt.2	Testaville House, Missely, nr. Southampton.
Roberts S.	Pt.2	60, Capel Street, Newport, Mon.
Rowan, E. T. ...	S.M.	12, Gladwin Road, Putney, London, S.W.
Rees, N. W.	Pt.1	Hendrewen Hotel, Treherbert, S. Wales.
Reeve, P. A. ...	Ck.3	52, Clarence Road, Gorleston-on-Sea, Gt. Yarmouth.
Shackleton, H. ...	A.M.2	10, Holderness Street, Todmorden, Lancs.
Stewart, G.	Pt.1	37, St. Leonards Place, Dumfermline, Scotland.
Sullivan, D.	Pt.1	29, Adelaide Road, Chislehurst, West Kent.
Simmons, J. W. ...	A.M.3	15, Hartlington Street, Dublin Road, Belfast.
Stott, J.	F/Sergt.	82, Cemetery Road, Southport, Lancs.
Stone, J.	Corpl.	17, Antique Street, Greenock, Scotland.
Smith, F. W. ...	Sergt.	22, Stormont Road, Clapham Common, London, S.W.
Smallman, A. ...	F/Sergt.	32, Brevitt Road, Wolverhampton.
Shaw, A. E.	Sergt.	14, Gillies Street, Kentish Town, London, N.W.
Sibley, R. A. ...	F/Sergt.	53, Aldworth Road, Stratford, London, E.
Selby, F. W. ...	A.M.2	Fiblesly House, Wellington Place, Willenhall.
Scarth, H.	A.M.1	5, Bankfield Terrace, Fartoon Top, Pudsey, Leeds.
Sams, S. E.	A.M.1	64, Kustin Street, Old Kent Road, London, S.E.
Swainson, J. ...	A.M.3	69, Anthony Street, St. George's, London, E.
Stirling, A.	A.M.2	46, Raeberry Street, Glasgow.
Staddley, H.	Corpl.	25, Cumberland Road, Sidget Green, Bradford.
Stones, D.	A.M.2	84, New Street, Wellington, Shropshire.
Samuel, S.	A.M.2	36, London Road, St. Albans.
Shambrook, G. ...	A.M.2	27, Bruce Grove, Watford, Herts.
Spear, L.	A.M.2	4, Evelyn Street, Durham, Sunderland.
Stock, G. W. ...	A.M.2	118, Ashby Road, Loughborough, Leicestershire.
Seymour, W. J. ...	A.M.2	Greenfield Villas, Port Reath, Cornwall.
Sidgwick, F. C. ...	A.M.2	29, Newby Terrace, Port Clarence, Durham.
Slater, E. V. ...	A.M.3	7, Dongala Road, Philip Lane, Tottenham, London.
Slater, H.	A.M.3	8, Morfield Grove, Tongem Moor, Bolton, Lancs.
Smith, E. T. ...	A.M.3	58, South Oak Street, Burton-on-Trent.
Skinner, G. C. ...	A.M.3	11, Westbury Hill, Westbury-on-Trym, Bristol.
Smith, O.	A.M.3	Scape View, Leymoor Road, Golcar, Huddersfield.
Shepperd, F. W. ...	A/Corpl.	90, Wakeman Road, Kensal Rise, London, N.W.
Sacks, M.	A.M.2	13 Ramsden Terrace, North Street, Leeds.

Strangeward, E.	...	A.M.3	2, Woolland Terrace, Oldchurch, Pontefract.
Stokesly, J.	... ...	Pt.2	10, Solway Street, Bridgetown, Glasgow.
Small, J. A.	... ...	Pt.1	28a, Charter Street, Accrington, Lancs.
Smith, A.	... ...	Pt.2	20, Harwell Road, Sheffield.
Squire, L. H.	...	Pt.1	18, Bolckon Street, Middlesbrough.
Seddons, R.	...	Pt.2	140, Lodge Terrace, Burnlev Road, Padeham, Lancs.
South, E. G.	...	Pt.2	Stanley Cottage, North Road, Tollesbury, Essex.
Sampson, A.	...	A.M.3	Windsor House Farm, Barrowgurney, nr. Bristol.
Simpson, J. A.	...	Ck.3	188, Bolton Street, Bury, Lancs.
Spriggs, H.	... ...	A.M.3	21, Church Street, Isleworth, Middlesex.
Turner, J.	... ...	Sergt.	56, Garnston Mount, Woodhouse, Leeds.
Tilbury, H. R.	...	A.M.1	28, Nailour Street, Caledonian Road, London, N.
Thomas, C. W.	...	A.M.1	Palace View Terrace, Douglas, Isle of Man.
Thom, J. H.	...	Corpl.	Cogham House, Fore Street, Heavitree, Exeter.
Templeton, M.	...	A.M.1	22, Cressilles Road, Meybole, Scotland.
Taylor, A. A.	...	Sergt.	173, Lancaster Road, Notting Hill, London, W
Tape, P. G.	...	A.M.1	4, Fore Street, Holsworthy, Devon.
Turvey, H. W.	...	A.M.2	26, Mayfield Road, Oldfield Park, Bath.
Titmuss, F.	...	A.M.2	Limbury Road, Seagrave, Luton.
Thompson, F.	...	A.M.2	New Barn Farm, Duxbury, nr. Coppull, Lancs.
Thomson, A. C.	...	A.M.2	41, Park Road, Peterborough.
Turner, A. H.	...	Pt.1	19, Prince's Place, Holland Park Avenue, London.
Tofield, A. J.	...	Pt.1	Solesbridge Lane, Chorley Woods, Herts.
Tolley, F. C.	...	Ck.3	36, Kendal Street, Preston, Lancs.
Tribe, E. A.	...	A.M.1	35, Brunswick Street, Hove, Sussex.
Taylor, E.	... ...	Pt.2	9, Howley Place, Paddington, London, W.
Tranter, G. H.	...	Pt.2	11, Wolseley Street, Kempson Lane, Birmingham.
Taylor, F.	... ...	Pt.1	4, South View, Nelson, Lancs.
Tremble, J.	... ...	Pt.2	3, Wards Lane, Dublin.
Vickers, R.	... ...	A.M.1	10, Alfred Street, Merton Colliery, Durham.
Vickers, P. A.	...	Corpl.	Strathmore Carberry, Musselburgh, Scotland.
Uphill, V. C.	...	A.M.3	Michaelstow Hall, Dovercourt, Essex.
Underhill, W.	...	Pt.2	Kingston, Thornbury, Gloucestershire.
Ure, W.	... ...	A.M.2	83, Wallace Street, Falkirk, Scotland.
Whatley, J.	... ...	Corpl.	52, Beresford Street, Camberwell, London, S.E.
Waite, D.	... ...	A.M.3	66, Bessborough Place, Westminster, London, S.W.
Waite, A. R.	...	A/Corpl.	Woodford Hill, Thrapstone, Northamptonshire.
Wise, S.	... ...	A.M.2	15, Highfield Road, Isleworth.
Woodbridge, R. W.		Corpl.	58, Erskine Road, Walthamstow.
Watkins, R.	...	A.M.2	111, Kensal Road, North Kensington, London, W.
Watson, J. A.	...	A.M.1	17, Cross Street, St. Annes.
Watts, J. W.	...	A.M.1	53, St. Stephen's Road, Sneiton, Notts.
White, E. C.	...	A.M.2	24, Holford Square, London, W.C.
Weston, G.	...	A.M.2	102, Ritson Street, Liverpool.
Wermald, J.	...	A.M.1	16, Carrington Street, Barnesley, Yorks.
Wigley, A. R.	...	A.M.1	" Chandos," Arthur Road, Bexhill-on-Sea.
Willis, E. W.	...	Sergt.	" Gardener's Arms," Coxwell Street, Farringdon, Berks.

Wilks, A. O. G.	...	A.M.1	11, Reading Street, Swindon, Wilts.
Woolnough, E.	...	Sergt.	25, Paradise Place, Leistone, Suffolk.
Walmer, L. H.	...	A.M.3	379, High Street, North, Manor Park, Essex.
Wickham, H.	...	A.M.1	94, Albion Road, Queen's Road, Dalston, London, N.E.
Waelend, R.	...	A.M.2	14, London Road, Plaistow, London.
Wills, J. A. C.	...	Corpl.	25, Parsons Green, Fulham, London.
Weideman, E.	...	A.M.1	154, Birchanger Road, South Norwood, London, S.E.
Wallwork, E.	...	A.M.2	6, Old Pole, Walden, nr. Manchester.
Watson, R. H.	...	A.M.3	"Gleyness," Ferry Road, Rye, Sussex.
Wise, H.	...	A.M.2	Appleton, Wisk, Yorkshire.
Wiggett, F.	...	A.M.2	Cool Lane, Hathersage, Derbyshire.
Warrior, R. N.	...	A.M.1	Argyle Grange, Leeming, Redale, Yorks.
Wright, F. T.	...	Pt.1	29, Hide Abbey Road, Winchester, Hants.
Wells, J.	...	Sergt.	Windmill Lane, Belper, Derbyshire.
Warrilow, G.	...	A.M.1	Fox Lane, Alrewas, Burton-on-Trent.
Winsborough, H.	...	Pt.1	1, Torbay Villas, Chelston, Torquay, Devon.
Wellburn, J. R.	...	Pt.2	40, Kirkgate, Bridlington, Yorks.
Wrigley, H.	...	Pt.2	Woodbank, Grange Road, Delphy, nr. Oldham, Lancs.
Walls, T.	...	Pt.2	84, Corporation Street, Newcastle-on-Tyne.
White, W. S.	...	Pt.2	50, Baker's Lane, Ealing, London, W.
Wacey, G. H.	...	Pt.2	The Heath, Blowfield, Norwich.
Watson, W.	...	Pt.1	28, McLellan Street, Paisley Road, Glasgow.
Whitehouse, W.	...	Pt.2	22, Old Mill Lane, Leicester.
Wilkins, W.	...	Pt.2	8, Prince's Street, Treforest, South Wales.
Walsh, J.	...	Pt.2	57, Devon Street, Saltley, Birmingham.
Williams, W. G.	...	Pt.2	3, Mountain Road, Aberavon, Port Talbot, S. Wales.
Watts, J.	..	Pt.2	14, Bray Street, Crumlin Road, Belfast.
Young, G. C.	...	A.M.1	21, Spring Gardens, East Molesey, Surrey.
Yates, W.	...	A.M.3	34, Evesham Road, Portway, West Ham, London, E.

Major C. G. Burge, O.B.E..

COMMANDED THE SQUADRON FROM 13TH JUNE, 1918, TO END OF HOSTILITIES.

CHAPTER X

CONCLUSION

NOW that my work is completed I would like to thank again all those who have either so kindly contributed or given me valuable suggestions. I regret that many suggestions put forward could not be put into effect. Owing to the impossibility of collecting much information of value and interest, the work must remain in certain details incomplete. I have, however, been able to supplement this work considerably with photographs and detailed information of the bombing done by the Squadron during the period October, 1917, to November, 1918, in its prolonged attack upon Germany. I trust that my readers will otherwise find the book of interest and of the kind which they will appreciate.

I would like to take this opportunity of thanking all ranks for the admirable manner in which they have one and all carried out their duties whilst serving under my command. It has been a great honour and pleasure for me to have commanded such a Squadron as No. 100; I need hardly say that some of the happiest days of my life were spent during that time, days which I shall always look back upon with great pride. My task as C.O. was considerably lightened by the energetic and whole-hearted support which I at all times received from one and all serving under me. Pilots and Observers, always full of determination and keenness, unselfish and cheerful at all times, won for themselves and the Squadron the greatest admiration. Like gentlemen and sportsmen, they played the game throughout. The every day order of our much respected Chief—General Trenchard—to " keep it going " was carried out to the letter.

No less can be written concerning the Ground Personnel. Their task was no light one, and their devotion to duty greatly contributed towards the success of the Pilots and Observers. Although the work of Ground Personnel was less romantic and conspicuous, their task was one entailing great hardships and hard work. The excellent manner in which they supported and co-operated with the Pilots and Observers ensured success. They experienced frequent and at times severe aerial bombardments, but with a full sense of duty their courage was not undermined in the least. They too "kept it going." Lastly, I cannot speak too highly of the "Esprit de Corps" whicn so strongly existed.

I mentioned in the Introduction, that it was to be hoped that the Squadron would not be disbanded. I regret to relate that the Squadron is now practically non-existent. I would, however, point out to all ranks that our traditions must not leave us; to quote Major-General Trenchard's words to me, " It's traditions which count and which make people keep straight, and although the Squadron has been disbanded, those who belbnged to No. 100 Squadron should remember in the future *what a Squadron* they belonged to." Apart from it being our duty to see that traditions are kept, these words, coming as they do from one whom we have learnt to look up to and respect, must strongly appeal to us. I hope to see members of the old Squadron availing themselves of the opportunity afforded them yearly of attending the annual Squadron Dinners, a notification of which appears in this work. I have found it difficult to get into touch with a number of members owing to the unsettled state of affairs existing, but should, as I hope, the notification of this work finally reach them, I would particularly request that any errors in addresses published in this work be notified me without delay. I will now wish one and all the best of good luck and every success in the years which lie ahead.

C. G. Burge.

14/2/19.

NOTE.—Since writing the above I have heard indirectly that the old Squadron is to take its place among the Regular Squadrons to be formed on the conclusion of Peace, no matter how few Squadrons there are ultimately to be. This is indeed news which will be received with great enthusiasm by all Ranks who have served with the Squadron.   I am sure one and all will wish " 100 " success in its peace-time rôle. To all those who serve in the Squadron, we offer our best wishes.   Our message to them is this :—" Keep up the good name of ' 100,' carry through its traditions, ' KEEP IT GOING,' and play the game ! "

C. G. BURGE.

June, 1919.

Printed and bound by Antony Rowe Ltd, Eastbourne

www.ingramcontent.com/pod-product-compliance
Lightning Source LLC
Chambersburg PA
CBHW060422100426

42812CB00030B/3272/J